HOME ★ FIRES
BURNING

HOME ★ FIRES BURNING

Married to the Military—
for Better or Worse

KAREN HOUPPERT

BALLANTINE BOOKS · NEW YORK

Published in the United States by Ballantine Books, an imprint of The Random House
Publishing Group, a division of Random House, Inc., New York.

Ballantine and colophon are registered trademarks of Random House, Inc.

Library of Congress Cataloging-in-Publication Data

Houppert, Karen, 1956–
Home fires burning : married to the military, for better or worse / Karen Houppert.
p. cm.
ISBN 0-345-46169-X (hardcover : alk. paper)—ISBN 0-345-46170-3 (pbk. : alk. paper)
1. Military spouses—United States. 2. Families of military personnel—United States.
I. Title.

UB403.H68 2005
355'.0092'273—dc22
2004062001

Printed in the United States of America

Ballantine Books website address: www.ballantinebooks.com

1   3   5   7   9   8   6   4   2

First Edition

Book design by Susan Turner

For my mother
Patricia Houppert

CONTENTS

INTRODUCTION

IN 1969 MY DAD, A U.S. AIR FORCE PILOT, WENT TO VIETNAM.

While he was gone I attended Mrs. Hix's first-grade class at an elementary school in the Detroit suburbs; I learned to read.

When my dad came back in 1970, instead of listening to Glen Campbell and the Beatles he listened to Motown, Led Zeppelin, and Iron Butterfly. He brought back a new hi-fi system with a reel-to-reel—the center of the living room for years to come—and some dolls and silk pajamas for my sisters and me.

That is everything that I remember of the year my dad spent in Danang.

Except for this: My mom belonged to a club. Occasionally, Grandma would come over to baby-sit and Mom would go out with the "ladies," as they were then called. These were her waiting wives' club nights.

They were enveloped in mystery. Just what *is* a waiting wives' club? What do they do? What are they waiting for?

AT THE AGE OF SIX I found the idea of this club intriguing. Clubs meant there were insiders and outsiders. Everyone knew, as even I knew, that it was generally better to be an insider than an outsider—though being a member of this particular club was a dubious honor. While I didn't know that my mother's waiting wives' club was a group of seventy-five women whose husbands were serving in Vietnam—and that some of those husbands probably wouldn't come home—I was learning, as all military families do, that we have an uneasy relationship with clubs and the insider-outsider dichotomy they represent.

And that is peculiar because the military is big on clubs. Not only are there waiting wives' clubs, still called that by some air force wives, but there are equivalents in the navy, the marines, and the army where they are now called family readiness groups. In addition to these "clubs" for wives whose husbands are deployed, there are coffee groups, officers' clubs, officers' spouses' clubs, enlisted clubs, enlisted spouses' clubs, and clubs for single soldiers. Then there is the air force base, or army post, or marine camp, each a great big fenced-in club that separates military families from civilians. It becomes a way of looking at the world: us and them, insiders and outsiders.

As a child, you are very aware of your membership in this military club with its language and rituals and rules. As a preschooler, I could have told you which base pool was *ours*—the officers' club pool—and which one belonged to the "nancy-Os" as we called the NCOs or noncommissioned officers. I could've told you that SHAPE stands for Supreme Headquarters Allied Powers Europe before I could have told you how to turn a fraction into a percent. And always, I could summon the last four digits of my father's Social Security number more easily than I could my own ever-changing phone number; this was a military dependent's ticket to ride, everywhere from the dentist's office to the school physical to the sign-in sheet for a ski trip. As a second-grader, I could tell at a glance the difference between a T-37 and a T-38, though I'd struggle to distinguish a Ford from a Chrysler—even after a year in the Detroit suburbs.

Like any extended family, or close-knit community, there is a world of traditions and inside jokes. In one joint letter my parents sent to me at camp when I was eight, they keep up the running gag—because I liked to go to work with my dad whenever he'd let me tag along—that *I* was actually the instructor pilot instead of him. "The guys in L-flight said to tell you to enjoy your leave," they write. "One of your students is almost ready to solo so he should buy you a bottle of whiskey when you get home—or should we send it to camp?" They go on to congratulate me for passing *my* solo flight, a.k.a. the boating test, saying that now I get to spend a lot more time in the water than the campers who just get to swim: "In air force jargon that's called a 'fringe benefit.' " My dad concludes by writing that my mom was out in the Alabama heat on the "flight line tour" today, "looking at mobile, the tower, and the links" and is glad he didn't go. It is too hot and he's pooped. Worse, "I've been real busy all week and have mobile 'til after midnight tonight," he says, ending the letter.

Apparently, at the age of eight, all of this made perfect sense to me.

This was my world and I was an insider in this club. But even at eight, there were moments when I was deeply ambivalent about membership in this mobile clan and wished, instead, to "pass"—in my case, as an ordinary, rooted, civilian child.

When I was in second grade we were stationed in Selma, Alabama, where my parents bought their first home—off-base—and we went to a nearby school. On the playground the first day, my younger sister and I were surrounded by two packs of persistent kids who wanted to know, were we "fer Auburn or 'Bama?" My first-grade sister had a defiant, what-the-fuck-are-you-talkin'-about look in her eye but before she could pipe up, Kamikaze girl, and permanently destroy our chances of ever "passing,"

I grabbed her hand. I squeezed hard, a fierce "shut up." I took a stab. "Auburn," I said for us. Half the playground gave a whoop. True, the other half hissed. But those who cheered joyfully welcomed us to the clan; we had established our social network for the next three years.

I think of this as my first moment of social savoir-faire. Instinctively I knew my familiar "clubs" didn't matter. Whether we were L-flight or K-flight was irrelevant on this playground. I didn't know that Auburn and Alabama were football teams but I knew very well that I *should* know—that I oughtta-better-know-on-the-double if we were going to be insiders. (We also learned to say "fer," begged our mom till she let us go barefoot to school like the other kids, and soon drawled our "ma'ams and sirs" as religiously as the cracker kid next to us; just as quickly we dropped the "fer" for some flat, Midwestern vowels, donned shoes, and mister-and-missus'd our way past the grown-ups when we were stationed in Ohio a few years later.)

We discovered that insider-outsider boundaries were fluid—and I learned to assume and shed identities as circumstances dictated. The way I saw it, the military family functioned best as a kind of chameleon. The military family—unlike the pilot or soldier or sailor who stood firmly rooted with both feet inside the military establishment—straddled two separate worlds. We were both *of* the military culture and outside it—shifting uneasily in our many different skins.

THE MILITARY HAS NEVER BEEN quite sure what to do with these families, both of the institution and outside it. And the issue has become more pressing in recent years, as the numbers of family members have increased and the numbers of deployments have increased.

In the past thirty years, military family life has undergone a radical transformation. The changes began in 1973, on the heels of the Vietnam War, when the draft was eliminated and the military became an all-volunteer force. The total number of soldiers decreased, but those who remained were likely to make a long-term career of the armed forces. Consequently, members of today's all-volunteer force are older than the draftees of earlier times, more than half of them are married, and often spouses work outside the home. Families—or "dependents," as they were then called—are a new consideration for the military, especially since unhappy wives in this all-volunteer force could urge their husbands to get out. Add to this shifts in U.S. foreign policy in the past fifteen years that have more soldiers deployed as peacekeepers, monitors of demilitarized zones, overseeing drug wars, and guarding "no-fly" zones which leave soldiers increasingly separated from their families. Indeed, there has been a 300 percent increase in overseas deployments for a force that has been cut by more than one-third over the past decade. Many soldiers are gone as much as they're home these days; one year in Iraq, one year stateside; one year in Afghanistan, one year stateside; one year in Korea, one year stateside.

Meanwhile, the wives of soldiers today—whether they call themselves feminists or not—have a different attitude toward their own careers and different expectations regarding the role fathers are expected to play in the home (like sharing the job of raising kids) than did their counterparts thirty or even twenty years earlier. Frequent moves and deployments send these two notions knocking against each other in ways that have created a myriad of problems for the military. According to multiple studies, personnel retention is a battle, recruitment goals have gone unmet, morale is low, and stress is high among soldiers and their families. Indeed one 2004 survey by the Kaiser Family Foundation, *The Washington Post,* and Harvard University found that 79 percent of military spouses say frustration with being in the army is common among families in their soldier's unit and only 36 percent say they will encourage their husbands to reenlist.

For its part, military brass insists that family stability and support are top priorities. New studies, new offices, new departments, and new acronyms are constantly being generated to help the military grapple with what it euphemistically calls "the challenges of the deployment cycle." But it's a transition fraught with problems and inconsistencies. On one hand, recruiting officers tout the armed forces as a "family-friendly" career choice. Yet, the *Army Officer's Guide,* a 1999 "dos-and-don'ts" of military life, still warns the single man who is considering a career woman as a wife that he must carefully select a "mature woman" who is willing to acknowledge the importance of sacrificing her career for her husband's. "Don't fool yourself; in modern American culture, most single American adults have strong vocational or professional ambitions, and few of them are compatible with being an Army spouse," the book says. Further, it warns that it can be "distracting and difficult to manage a good marriage with an ambitious partner in pursuit of his or her own divergent professional goals." No matter who you marry, the unofficial *Guide* goes on, explain "the facts of life" to them: "The Army's needs will always take precedence over those of your family."

Officially the rhetoric is less direct.

The government prefers the image of a "team." It suggests the Department of Defense, the soldier, and the soldier's wife are all pulling together in the same direction. And usually they are—but sometimes there are discrepancies about how to get to that goal. (And these questions can range from minor ones like why in addition to frequent deployments do husbands have to leave home for extended training so often, to major ones like, if we all agree the goal is world peace, what are we doing in Iraq?) Wives, in other words, are slightly less institutionally loyal than their husbands and therefore slightly more likely to make waves. Occasionally there are efforts to appease them.

Shortly after President George W. Bush took office in 2001 he ordered the secretary of defense to investigate "quality of life" issues for military families. A "New Social Compact" was drawn up, outlining a "reciprocal partnership between the Department of Defense, service members and families." Here's why:

> *The partnership between the American people and the noble warfighters and their families is built on a tacit agreement that families as well as the service member contribute immeasurably to the readiness and strength of the American military. Efforts toward improved quality of life, while made out of genuine respect and concern for service members' and families' needs, also have a pragmatic goal: a United States that is militarily strong.*

But what happens when the needs of this "reciprocal partnership" diverge? Or are in direct conflict? What happens when the army's traditions and needs and ideologies butt up against the reality of women's lives in 2005, as they inevitably do? Standing with one foot inside the military camp and one foot outside it, wives wonder about the alternatives.

These families that are both a part of the military club but separate from it, may be one of the biggest challenges the U.S. military faces today. The army would like to bring these families completely inside the institution, to encircle them in a great, big camouflage cloak, settle some government-issue shades on their noses, have them look out at the world through olive-tinted glasses. The Army's mission would be their mission, their loyalty to cause, khaki, and country complete. But the military cannot figure out how to do this. For hundreds of years the military has adeptly trained soldiers to accomplish their missions, but when it comes to "training" their families the military stumbles. The boot camp methods that wring compliance from soldiers—break 'em down then build 'em up as a team—alienate wives. Mandating a sense of "bonding" too often fails. Efforts to win hearts and minds are transparent—and frequently resented. Occasionally, the drive for institutional loyalty works, sometimes this sense of being united for a larger purpose invigorates families, but just as often it seems to oppress them. Wives have a sneaking suspicion that what is in the best interest of the army is not always in their best interest.

This makes army brass nervous. These wives who straddle the insider-outsider divide, with their tacit resistance and subtle complexities, throw them. They've got a big problem on their hands.

It is this nexus of tension that the book explores.

THE MILITARY IS A COMPANY town in a time when such places are almost anachronistic. And it's a *big* company town. In fact, the Department of Defense is the largest "company" in the United States with its budget of $371 billion (in contrast to Wal-Mart's $227 billion or ExxonMobil's $200 billion). With more than 2 million employees (compared with Wal-Mart's

1.4 million or ExxonMobil's 97,000) it is the nation's largest employer. Toss 2 million military family members into the mix and you've got 170 military bases and posts forming 170 mini company towns scattered across our nation.

What makes the military "corporation" different is what also makes it compelling territory for investigation: its "product" is war; its "stockholders" are the American people. What goes on inside the gates of this particular company town has repercussions that reverberate around the world. (Consider the ripple caused inside less metaphorical gates, when military protocol, training, and command structure caught our attention with the 2004 Abu Ghraib prison abuses in Iraq.) The military corporate culture, therefore, is a curious one in which Americans—Democrats and Republicans, liberals and conservatives—not only have an interest but have a voice in the decision-making process, since we directly fund this "corporation," the U.S. Armed Forces.

We not only have a right to question the workings of this company but an obligation. As the military itself is so quick to remind service members, they are the "face of democracy" abroad. Americans need to understand what face we're putting out there. We need to see how the military handles notions of democracy, in its ranks and among its family members, in order to anticipate some of the pitfalls in our foreign policy, to weigh whether our most rigidly hierarchical institution *can* represent democracy—especially as it moves in as occupier in a foreign land. If we're in the business of exporting American values via the military, we need a proper reading of the values the military is exporting. A close examination of the military family is a revealing foray into that corporate culture.

I BEGAN MY INVESTIGATION at Fort Drum, an army post in upstate New York, that touts its 10th Mountain Division as the most deployed division in the army. For the past two years, as the war in Afghanistan and then the war in Iraq unfolded I followed a group of wives there, as well as a smattering of wives at different posts and bases. I talked to army, air force, navy, and marine wives. I talked to officers' wives, enlisted men's wives, warrant officers' wives, wives whose husbands were career officers, wives whose husbands were just biding their time, white wives, African-American wives, Latina wives, wives with master's degrees as well as wives who didn't graduate from high school. I also spoke to husbands and kids. I interviewed military brass, civilians who work for the military, civilians who live near military posts, historians, and anthropologists. In the end I found that rather than interviewing broadly, I learned more by digging deep. I narrowed my investigation to a few women who offered personal, compelling stories, checking in with them regularly over the course of two years to learn what this time as a "waiting wife" was like.

When it came to selecting a few women to profile in detail, I tried to provide a range—across income, class, and education levels and also attitude. I selected women who matched the common military archetypes, only to discover they ran counter to type in interesting ways. Some of the wives profiled here had very positive experiences with the military, some did not, and many had both good *and* bad things to say. But mostly I chose women who had given some thought to their experiences and who offered interesting perspectives.

While the military has moved to gender-neutral language in all its official descriptions of the "spouses" who keep the home fires burning during deployments, I hew to the more accurate term "wives" in my book, because 94 percent of them still *are* wives. And while each branch of the service is unique—and the National Guard and Reserves have their own set of circumstances—I chose to avoid digging into the minutiae of cross-service comparisons so I didn't lose civilian readers. (For readers interested in detailed sourcing information, blind notes are cued to complete citations in the back of the book.)

Finally, I've chosen women who are scattered along the spectrum from "insider" (loyal institutional supporter) to "outsider" (those who consciously situate themselves outside the military world) because seen together they best exemplify the range of responses to this corporate culture—symbolically and practically—as well as the complexities of this existence, the uneasy relationship military families have as they straddle two worlds.

So once again, some thirty-five years after I first yearned to tag along to a waiting wives' club meeting with my mom to find out just *what* those ladies were talking about, I find our nation back at war, such clubs reactivated, my questions revived. And once again I, too, was straddling two worlds, revisiting my "hometown" as a journalist and a feminist. So I approach the book this way, as an insider with an outsider's perspective.

HOME ✷ FIRES
BURNING

Lauren

WIDOWMAKERS:
When Casualty Affairs Comes Calling

Being there at Ground Zero for the first time yesterday was very emo-
tional for me. I brought a picture of my husband and posted it there at the
memorial. He would have been very, very proud to have his picture there
with the NYPD and the fire department.

—Lauren Fidell

I WENT THROUGH A WHOLE DAY NOT KNOWING MY HUSBAND HAD been shot," 26-year-old Lauren Fidell* says. She is amazed and somewhat appalled that her best friend and the love of her life whom she'd been with since she was 16 had been lying in Afghanistan with a bullet from an AK-47 through his head while she had been shampooing the carpet. "I thought my body would know, that I would feel if something happened to him. So I was surprised when they knocked on the door that night and told me

*To keep her identity private Lauren chose to use pseudonyms for herself and her husband.

what had happened. I did not believe that he was dying. But they told me it was imminent."

"They" were of course the men in uniform.

And five months ago *they* brought Lauren the worst news of her life. While she acknowledges collapsing then, today she is unflinching. Which is not to say she doesn't cry—she does—but rather that she is undaunted by her tears, and figures I ought to be as well.

When we speak for the first time, we sit in a very public place, a huge hall at New York City's Jacob Javits Center in the midst of a Maritime Security Expo Exhibit. She is there helping to raise funds for the Naval Special Warfare Foundation, a nonprofit that gives scholarships to U.S. Navy SEAL families. We sit at a large, round table in the exhibitors' lounge; two men in suits sit on the other side of the table negotiating a contract. In the course of our conversation, Lauren tears up a couple of times; I tear up a couple of times. When people notice, they politely avert their gaze.

Lauren plows ahead. She remembers every detail of that night, June 24, 2003, she tells me, as if she were watching a movie—somebody else's tragic tale.

It was 10:30 P.M. on a warm June evening. Her children, two- and five-year-old boys, were in bed. Her younger sister was visiting from out of state. "I was getting ready for bed and I had just laid down on the couch to watch TV when there was a knock on the door," Lauren says. "I was halfway across the living room when I realized that it was too late to be a neighbor knocking. I stopped. I had a bad feeling." Lauren stood there, in the middle of the living room, stuck. They knocked again. "My sister came to the top of the stairs and said, 'Open the door. It's just a neighbor.' "

But six men stood in their dress uniforms on Lauren's porch. "They were very stern looking. One of them was the commander of my husband's group. One was a CACO officer," she says, referring to the navy's casualty assistance calls officer. "The CACO officer said my name, then he said who he was and where he was from."

Lauren looked straight at him. "I know who you are," she said.

He spoke: "Your husband was in a convoy that was attacked and he was very seriously injured and is not expected to live."

Lauren began to scream, "I'm not ready yet. I'm not ready yet." Despite the fact that her husband was a navy SEAL, one of the elite units specially trained in dangerous maritime and amphibious operations, that he'd already been called away several times to undisclosed locations in the fight against terrorists, that she was pretty sure he had been in Afghanistan these past eight weeks, she says she hadn't thought about him dying. "I'm not ready yet," she wailed.

"I wanted to talk to him," Lauren recalls. "But they kept saying, 'He's not conscious.' " He had been shot many hours earlier in a clash south of Kabul and had been transported to a hospital in Bagram. "What are his chances?" she asked. "He's dying. It's imminent," they told her. Hoping for a different answer, Lauren asked them again. And again. "It's imminent," they repeated.

"I want to talk to him," she said.

"He's unconscious."

Lauren kept insisting that she wanted to talk to him. But they kept explaining, as if she were not comprehending. "He's unconscious." Finally, they understood that Lauren didn't care whether or not he was conscious, that she thought maybe he could hear her, that she needed to try to talk to him. Eventually they got through to the hospital. "One of his buddies there beside him said, 'Lauren, I'm going to put the phone up to his ear,' " Lauren recalls.

She spoke to him. She reminded him that she was an occupational therapist and it didn't matter what his injuries were, she just didn't want him to die. "I went to school for this," she said. "You're going to come home and I'm going to take care of you. It's going to be okay." She told him what their boys had done that day. She told him that she loved him. "Everything happens for a reason," she said. And then she told him that if he had to go, "It was okay."

Recalling the incident five months later, she wonders why she said that. "I didn't mean it," she admits.

At some point, after several hours, the men in uniform left. And friends began to arrive. The SEALs are a small and tight-knit group, with 1,200 stationed in Virginia Beach, Virginia. Most of the 5,000 active SEALs have spent their entire careers together, back and forth between SEAL postings in San Diego and Virginia Beach. They have trained together, worked together, fought together, ate and slept together for weeks at a time. Their wives, often home alone, have baby-sat each other's children, gone to the movies together, shared Thanksgiving dinners, formed deep friendships. And in the dark hours of the night on June 24, they mourned together. A cluster of women sat on Lauren's bed talking, crying, and listening as Lauren tried to face death. At 3:30 in the morning, Lauren realized the time and felt some relief. "It's morning there now—and he lived," she said. Then she worried. "I thought, 'Oh my God, what if he has to retire from the navy? He's going to be crushed.' Meanwhile everyone around me knew he wasn't coming home."

"I fell asleep then. And when I woke up my sister and my best friend, Teresa, were sitting on my bed. My eyes were still closed when they asked, 'You awake?' " Lauren was, but she didn't want to be. "They said, 'Lauren, we just got word that he passed during the night.' "

"It took a second to register, like I was in a time warp. I was really mad at him. He promised me he'd come home."

LAUREN'S STORY, like all these stories of soldiers' families, begins with the knock on the door. Eleven thousand, one-hundred thirty-four knocks on the door by the fall of 2004. Eleven thousand, one-hundred thirty-four families who learn that their husband or son is dead, dying, or injured. Eleven thousand, one-hundred thirty-four encounters—often by strangers who announce a "mishap" (in air force parlance) to a primary next of kin (PNOK) and stand by helplessly as the PNOK crumbles. They meet on doorsteps, in living rooms, in kitchens, in offices. And because the military has been doing this for hundreds of years—and because there's nothing the military likes better than acronyms and uniformity and reports—a whole literature of death and dying has sprung up in the form of policy manuals, pamphlets, PowerPoint presentations, and protocols. And, as the war against terrorism drags on, a new slew of specialists has been activated, soldiers every bit as pivotal to the smooth functioning of the armed forces machine as its maintenance mechanics. Teasingly called "diggers" by their buddies, these soldiers "go where others fear to go," as the director of Mortuary Affairs at Fort Lee, Virginia, put it in his *Ode to the Mortuary Affairs Specialist:*

> *They do things that others will not do.*
> *The sights, sounds and smells of what they do,*
> *others avoid.*

On the battlefield and on the home front, soldiers are being called on to recover, identify, and refrigerate remains, to "cosmetize" them, to transport them, to notify families, to bury them, and to assist families in the weeks following a soldier's death. And every possible element that can be controlled by the Department of Defense (DOD) is orchestrated—even micromanaged and scripted—from spelling out who gets a live bugler (active duty) and who gets a boom-box version of "Taps" (vets) to specifying what rank the "notifier" must be (equal to or higher than the person who died). Perhaps because a little order helps alleviate the awful randomness of these events, the Department of Defense wants its soldiers spit-shined and on the mark here.

When it comes to death and dying, the military are Masters of Ceremony.

A soldier's death calls for a brilliant display of patriotism, a nod to the notion of *cause* as a way of affirming that this death was not in vain. While its commander in chief may occasionally stumble (the fact that President George W. Bush had not made a single condolence visit or phone call to a dead soldier's family sent a ripple of shock through the military community in November 2003), military brass understands that death matters— and may indeed be its most critical public relations campaign. Compassion and spectacle are essential to winning the hearts and minds of the American public, and the military firmly believes that these elements can—with proper attention to detail—be manufactured.

TRAINING FOR DEATH DETAIL is thorough.

"We're in a zero-defect environment," says Frederick Calladine, chief of Casualty and Mortuary Affairs at Fort Drum near Watertown, New York. "We like to make sure everything is done correctly. If we *do* make a mistake, the whole army pays the price. And that price is public ridicule, mistrust, and distrust. Then we've created an enemy of the army by the families, and we don't want to do that."

Calladine addresses his remarks to a group of forty soldiers on March 20, 2003, the evening the war with Iraq began. These men and women at Fort Drum have the dubious distinction of being the newly appointed casualty notification officers for their units. Hand-picked by their supervisors, they are getting the PowerPoint ABC's of military mortuary manners. "Wear your dress uniform," Calladine tells them, and remember that some wives want to kill the messenger. "Give them the news, then get the hell out of Dodge."

Though military wives live with a vague sense of dread that is often described as coming home to see an unknown dark car parked in the driveway, Calladine says the cars used are simply the notifier's own vehicles and that they are specifically told not to lurk about. "If nobody's home, don't sit there like a bulldog waiting for them to come home," he says. "Go get a cup of coffee, check the neighbors to see if you can find out if they're on vacation or whatever."

And be careful, Calladine says. "Make sure we aren't informing the wrong people." This isn't just hypothetical. The same week that Calladine conducted this training there was a helicopter crash at Fort Drum, a routine training accident in which eleven soldiers died when a UH-60 Blackhawk helicopter went down in the forest. "We had the name of an individual who might've been on board who, as it turns out, wasn't. So if we had rushed out and said, 'Oh so-and-so was on this and killed—and then he shows up, we're going to look like a bunch of idiots."

When the *proper* primary next of kin is located, the rest is scripted. Literally. "I have an important message to deliver from the Secretary of the Army, may I come in, Mr. Jones," says a "Casualty Notification Guide for the Casualty Notification Officer," which Calladine offers to his audience. Sample scripts follow:

(1) For death cases: "The Secretary of the Army has asked me to express his deep regret that your *(relationship; son, Robert or husband, Edward; etc.) (died/was killed in action)* in *(country/state)* on *(date). (State the circumstances provided by the Casualty Area Command.)* The Secretary extends his deepest sympathy to you and your family in your tragic loss."

According to Calladine, the next thing most wives or parents want to know is exactly what happened. " 'What happened? How could it happen?' they'll ask. You're not allowed to tell them. You don't know," Calladine says. "Don't commit the army to anything. Even if you know gory details of the incident, you don't give them." Depending on the service more details are provided in the next few days, weeks, or months after investigations are complete.

Giving out these details is the job of the casualty assistance officer. "Sometimes when you tell families about a death there's a wall thrown up instantly," Calladine says. " 'Okay, you've told me, now get out!' that kind of thing. There's that controlled anger against the messenger. We just do what they say and we get out. Then we try to get hold of them later to have *another* person go out and help with paperwork and benefits. That's the casualty assistance officer and that's why we split it into two categories."

Timing is everything. Notification can't be done before Calladine's office gets official, faxed confirmation from the Department of the Army

(DA)—even if he can see the burning hulk of a helicopter crash from his office window. And it must be made within four hours of hearing from the DA but not after 10 P.M.

"Why not past 2200 hours?" one soldier wonders.

"DA policy," Calladine says. He realizes this is, perhaps, an unsatisfactory answer—and scrambles. "We don't want to go in the middle of the night and wake people up and tell them that their loved ones are dead. We, uh, want to wake them up at 6 o'clock in the morning and do it instead."

FOR LAUREN, there is just The Knock. There is her life *pre*-Knock and there is Now. The story of who she is now, and who her family is and will become, begins with the Knock on the door. Any vague "happily ever after" image that she carried in her head is gone. The disorientation sets in. There used to be a line from here to there—this is my life now and if I drift along like this I will end up there—that has been interrupted. The Future now requires conscious thought.

"I've never even been on a date as an adult woman," Lauren says. Death came to her, she insists, out of the blue. "I've never lost anyone young or really close to me before. I never thought about him dying in combat. I thought that he might get hurt in training," Lauren admits. "We've had friends that had gotten hurt and even died in training. It was almost a regular occurrence that people would blow off fingers or have jumping accidents. I expected something like that, but not this."

Death came to her out of the blue, she insists. But she doesn't quite mean that. "It wasn't something that my husband and I talked very much about, primarily because he didn't want to talk about it." She pauses, then remembers something. "A couple of weeks before he left, my five-year-old was upset one night. He kept giving Rob these sidelong glances. I asked him what was the matter. His eyes were welling up and he said, 'I don't want Dad to go. I'll miss him. I'm worried.' I said, 'Why don't you just tell him that?'" Lauren thinks for a moment. "Rob's reaction, well, Rob's a great guy but he really thought he was skilled enough to avoid getting killed, and he said so." Rob started playing with his son, distracting him, cheering him. Lauren considers the scene in retrospect: "Of course," she says, "his death had nothing to do with his skill."

That night before he left Lauren told him, "I don't want you to do this." She's not exactly sure what she meant. "I wasn't asking him not to go, because he didn't have a choice. Much as he loved us and valued our lives, he honestly believed that this would never happen. He thought he was the best, so good at what he did that this couldn't happen. Then some kid with a forty-year-old weapon in a ditch got a lucky shot. And our lives are changed forever."

Death came to her out of the blue, she insists, but it was all around her. "There's been four people in our SEAL community who have been killed lately," she says. "I was at the funeral for the first one [in March]. A woman I knew was sitting in the row in front of me," Lauren recalls. As she looked at the widow, the woman Lauren knew turned around: "It could have been any one of us," she whispered to Lauren. Lauren shivers. "The next week, it *was* her. It was her husband who died next."

Death came to her out of the blue, she insists, but offers foreshadowing. "I went to Hallmark and stood there looking for a sympathy card for this second widow and cried. There were no sympathy cards left by then in our community," she said, explaining that in this small military town where everybody knew everybody all the cards had been bought up. "A few weeks later, when I saw some cards in stock I bought one." With battles raging in Afghanistan and Iraq, she knew she would need it. "I bought one and I saved it," she said. "That card was for me. The next sympathy card was for me."

"EVERY MISHAP IS A STORY, which must be reconstructed in detail," says a ninety-four-page air force directive entitled "Assistance to Survivors of Persons Involved in Air Force Aviation Mishaps." It is a tiny, poetic kernel of *truth* in a passel of jargon-filled fact.

As a reporter, I find myself scurrying around collecting the details about casualties, persuaded indeed that "every mishap is a story" and further convinced that if I find enough details and construct a proper story I, too, might edge closer to *truth*.

Part of that is because the military wives I have spent the past year talking to admit that this fear forms the shadowy backdrop to all their thoughts: What if?

Part of it is because, as a reporter on some Department of Defense press list, I get an e-mailed statement each time a soldier in Afghanistan or Iraq is killed—and some days, even though I know the content from the subject heading, I press *delete*—guiltily because every mishap is a story or every e-mail is a life and opening them is a tiny tribute I sometimes fail to make.

Part of it is because it takes me back to my family's own "mishap" when, on June 13, 1977, my air force father's plane crashed into a potato field outside Brussels, Belgium. I was fourteen. He was a thirty-six-year-old fighter pilot on a "routine mission." The air force told us only that he had died immediately. Within days of his death my mother, suddenly a thirty-six-year-old widow with three daughters to support, was asked by the military to sign a sheaf of standard forms regarding my father's burial, his life insurance policy, the distribution of his veteran's benefits, and a "routine" waiver of her right to sue the military.

My mother signed.

The military treated us well. It paid to ship the body back to the United States and they flew my entire family from Belgium, where we were stationed, back to the States on a private jet owned by aircraft builders Pratt & Whitney. The military covered all funeral expenses, organized a gun-salute and a fly-by, paid for a Belgian Air Force officer to serve as our escort, and activated veterans' benefits immediately.

But it never told us what happened.

LAUREN WAITED THREE DAYS to tell her boys their father was dead. "I was afraid I was going to scare them," Lauren says. "I was so swollen my eyes would hardly open, my ribs hurt and my forehead was bruised from squeezing my face so hard. And that cry, the crying I was doing was not a normal cry. That was not a normal noise. I didn't want to scare them."

The boys, twenty-one months and five years old, had been whisked out—still sleeping—to a friend's house the night Lauren got the news. Wanting to do things right, she'd talked to a psychologist whom the casualty assistance officer had put her in touch with the next day. "How much do I tell him?" Lauren wondered of her oldest child, and the psychologist told her to be completely honest with her children. "I realized quickly that if my son asked a question, he was ready for the answer."

While someone else watched the toddler, Lauren called her five-year-old into the bedroom. "I need to tell you something," she said. She told him that his daddy had been shot and that he had died and that they were really, really sad but that they were going to be okay. "He understood," Lauren says. "Some say kids don't understand, but he does."

Her son went on to talk about his father's death with everyone but Lauren. "I think he really wanted to protect me," she says. On his first day of kindergarten in September he announced to the class that his dad was dead. The kindergarten teacher, who knew this already, asked him if he'd like to tell them about his dad. "He stood up and told the class that his daddy was a SEAL and what that meant and how he went to fight the bad guys and then got shot," Lauren says. "The teacher said, 'You must be very proud of him,' and apparently he just beamed at that." Lauren says, somewhat ruefully, that she heard this from the teacher who called her afterward to tell her about it, and not from her child.

Because she wasn't sure why he didn't want to talk about this stuff with her—whether her emotion scared him—she asked him. "He said, 'No, it doesn't scare me but it makes me sad to see you cry and I want to cheer you up and make you feel better.' He's a very self-aware little boy," she says. "One time he did something and was sent to his room. I sat on the bed and said, 'This behavior is not okay. I understand you're frustrated and angry but there is no one to be angry with. It's not Dad's fault, not Mom's, not

Grandma's.' And he looked at me like I was so full of shit," she says. "Because he's five, and he knows it was somebody's fault."

"The psychologist said, 'He's five years old and he is going to remember all of this, so you should talk to him and take him to everything,' " says Lauren's best friend, Teresa, a navy SEAL wife who was at the house minutes after Lauren learned Rob had been shot, and is like an aunt to the children. "The guys are gone so often, it's hard for a little boy to understand that his dad's not just gone. For him that first week was a fun week and a sad week. He was excited to see people like his grandparents suddenly visiting. Everyone brought him presents and he had all this attention and then he'd remember, 'Oh yeah, my dad died.' "

When Rob's body arrived Lauren didn't want to have an open casket, but she did want to see him. "I brought my oldest son with me," she says. "At first I was worried, I thought it might be really disturbing for him to see Rob's body, but it wasn't. We went in there alone together for a long time. He asked a lot of questions and wanted to touch Rob." Lauren thinks the experience was good for both of them. "It's very apparent when you see a loved one like that, that this is just a shell. There is no life there. Part of the person, the part we loved is not there anymore," she says. "Because Rob was gone so much, I needed to see him and touch him to believe that his death's real because it doesn't feel real sometimes. I know that my son needed that too."

AS LAUREN SPEAKS I fight an impulse to step outside my reporter's neutrality. Then I stop fighting. "It sounds like you did the right thing," I say.

I am getting her words down, but for a moment, I am also looking back at the days before my own father's death and examining them as I have done a thousand times before to find the signs that led up to his accident.

The Right Stuff came out in 1983, six years after my father's plane crash, but there was a scene in it that I recognized: I'd replayed it in my mind a thousand times. In the final moments of the film, test pilot Chuck Yeager (played by Sam Shepard) struggles to keep his damaged plane aloft. He can't. Bang! It crashes onto the runway. He's dead. Or is he? Suddenly out of the smoldering hulk steps Yeager. Unscathed, he walks across the tarmac through the hazy fumes of a plane about to explode. He removes his helmet. He smiles. Invincible.

Roll end credits.

That was my movie, with slightly altered foreshadowing: My parents had been fighting a lot before the crash, so I figured my father wanted to leave us. Maybe those men in blue who notified us *thought* he died when his T-33 went down. But he slipped out. He trotted across the potato field and disappeared into the woods. Then he began a parallel life, moved to Paris, hooked up with a Frenchwoman, had children.

That's why there was a closed casket and we never saw a body. My sister, age fifteen, speculated that it was because he was "burned beyond recognition." I knew otherwise. Although I had the sense not to talk about it, I kept this other *truth* in my head. For years it breezed along parallel, in perfect formation, beside *reality*—two shiny T-birds dangerously close but never converging. A tricky maneuver for a fighter—or a fighter pilot's daughter.

The Right Stuff, I'm thinking. "The right thing," I say to Lauren. "It sounds like you did the right thing, showing him the body."

"Military operations carry with them an inherent risk of loss," the "Aviation Mishaps" manual reminds. "Every commander within the Total Force has an ongoing obligation to ensure that the members under their command are aware of those risks and manage them responsibly. In turn, members owe it to their families to keep them aware of the nature of their duties and the hazards they entail."

It's a tall order. Or is it a warning? Face the facts. This is dangerous work and people die. All the time.

"I've had twenty incidences since Friday," says Fort Drum's casualty director Calladine, talking to me on a Wednesday night in September 2003. "Since October of last year we have performed close to 4,000 funerals and done notification or assistance on nearly 100 people. We take care of serious injuries as well. And not all of these were from Afghanistan or Iraq, but most." In fact, in the past two years, Fort Drum has had several serious training accidents. Aside from the aforementioned helicopter crash, there was a March 2002 live-fire training exercise in which two shells missed their intended target and exploded near a mess tent, killing two soldiers and injuring thirteen.

Calladine, a twenty-eight-year veteran with a background in psychology, is now a civilian who heads up Fort Drum's casualty office. Fort Drum is home to the 10th Mountain Division, 4,200 of whom were in Afghanistan and 1,500 in Iraq, in 2003. But the casualty area also covers Maine, New Hampshire, Vermont, Massachusetts, Rhode Island, Connecticut, and forty-five northern New York state counties—meaning, if a soldier fighting in Iraq is killed and his parents live in New Hampshire, Calladine is the one sending out a notification officer.

Add to that natural attrition, and casualty affairs may be one of the busiest units on post these days. After all, not only is the department dealing with active-duty notification and burials, but it is providing funeral services for thousands of veterans. "World War Two vets are dying off, one every seven minutes, approximately. Korean War vets are dying off at approximately one every twenty minutes. Vietnam vets, at approximately one every hour and a half. And now we're getting into the next war," Calladine chuckles and shakes his head. He is a portly man with slightly graying hair who clearly takes tremendous pride in his work. He preens a bit, a petty bureaucrat in the best sense of the word—one who revels in the details of his job, whose sense of self-worth swells with each efficiently processed ream of paperwork, each set of "remains" tidily disposed of. Although he acknowledges that he's stretched a bit thin these days, and that nobody exactly volunteers to come help out in his office, he's proud of the fact that he turns out polished soldiers. "Initially when I'd request soldiers for the casualty office, it started out being people nobody wanted," he said, referring to commanders who would assign the detail to those they could afford to do without. "But we have taken those people and basically made them the most sought after people on post." He smiles. "They have pride in their jobs. They know how to talk to a colonel. Even though they're only a private or a specialist, they can talk to this colonel and say, 'Sir, this is what you have to do.' And the colonel appreciates it." These soldiers in the casualty department are also hard workers. "Sometimes we have to do twenty-four–seven shifts in this office. Last weekend, I worked thirteen hours on Sunday and three of my soldiers were in working almost straight through the weekend."

It's a time, money, and manpower crunch that has not gone unnoticed by the Department of Defense (DOD)—and it predates the current, fresh set of casualties. In 1999, DOD issued a report to Congress warning that there was a problem. Noting that approximately 1,500 veterans died each day in the country, that one quarter of U.S. veterans (almost 26 million) were over sixty-five years old, and that the number of veteran deaths was expected to peak at 620,000 in 2008, the Defense Department foresaw some obstacles. "At the same time," the report notes, "over the last ten years, the Department of Defense has made significant reductions in its military personnel end-strength. The inverse convergence of the increase in veterans' deaths and the downsizing of the force, combined with higher operational tempo (OPTEMPO), have made it difficult for DOD to respond to the demand for military funerals."

It is also expensive, costing an estimated $191.8 million annually in manpower, travel, and per diem rates for a small, 3-person funeral honors team. Things get even pricier with the high-end funerals, like those done for air force active-duty personnel and Medal of Honor recipients, which use 19-person teams, including 6 pallbearers, 7 members of a firing party, 1 bugler, 4 color guards, and 1 officer in charge. Cumulatively the funerals were proving mighty taxing. In defense lingo, commanders were expressing "concern of mission degradation," which means soldiers who should have been training for battle were out on funeral details instead.

The Department of Defense is struggling to keep pace. In 2003 Delaware's Dover Air Force Base, site of the joint forces' morgue and mortuary, celebrated the opening of a brand-new $30 million Center for Mortuary Affairs. It's a 70,000-square-foot facility that doubles the space of the existing building with 24 stations for autopsies and rack-storage for 380 caskets. And at Arlington National Cemetery, outside Washington, D.C., things have gotten so tight—even before the war in Iraq began ratcheting up the body count—that the cemetery is annexing 60 more acres to give it 350,000 more grave sites. "We have twenty-five to twenty-seven funerals a day, with an average of six thousand burials per year," says Arlington spokesperson Barbara Owens. The added acreage comes in addition to four columbariums that are currently under construction and which are designed to house 1,000 to 2,000 urns each. (The amount of remains hinges on whether each "niche" holds simply the soldier's urn, or the spouse's as well.) "We're always looking at trends and seeing if there is something new we might want to do down the road," Owens says, explaining that the hot funeral in Europe now is the green burial or eco-burial in which remains are cremated, but instead of being housed in urns in columbariums, for example, they're sprinkled in with dirt as a tree is planted. Although this isn't being done in Arlington yet, it remains another space-saving possibility. "I don't think anyone could fathom the thought of Arlington closing," says Owens, "so we're doing everything we can to maximize the area."

So as the numbers of dead continue to mount, the folks in Casualty and Mortuary Affairs rise to the challenge. Every post and base and camp and station continues to refine its "Mass-Casualty Standing Operating Procedures," in case it is forced to deal with the loss of an entire unit or more. And every possible snafu that can be anticipated is addressed, even down to the nitty-gritty details, like spelling out that a commander is required to remove from a soldier's footlocker any items that may cause "embarrassment (pornographic material or letters) or added sorrow if forwarded to the eligible recipient." ("We are required to go through everything that is there," explains Calladine. "If they have a *Playboy* magazine, we're required to look through every page to make sure there's not a letter or bill or whatever tucked in that magazine. Do we wanna give the *Playboy* back? I don't think so. Do we wanna give the image that the soldier was a pedophile? Or a homosexual? We will not give that kind of thing back to the family.")

Just as a unit like the 10th Mountain Division proudly traces its history to the first ski patrols in World War Two, the "diggers" also invoke their rich history. Down in Fort Lee, Virginia, where the mortuary affairs specialists are trained at the quartermaster school, a museum exhibit entitled "Duty to the Fallen: The Army's Mortuary Mission" notes that the Quartermaster Corps "has been responsible for the care of the dead since the Civil War." In recent days its personnel have been deployed around the world to assist in such places as Bosnia, Somalia, Croatia, the Middle East, and closer to home in Oklahoma City and with Hurricane Andrew.

Just as the infantry soldier proudly counts those landing at Normandy as his heroic antecedents, so too, do these "logistics warriors" have their celebrated moments of bitter triumph. "During World War Two, more than 250,000 Americans died and were buried in temporary cemeteries around the world," Dr. Steven E. Anders writes in the September 1988 *Quartermaster Professional Bulletin*. Then called the QM Graves Registration Company, these men were among those that scrambled ashore on D-day with the army. "There they gathered bodies from the beaches, in the water, and inland, actually cutting many from wrecked landing craft submerged in the shallow water," Anders writes. "By the end of D-Plus-2, one platoon alone had buried 457 American dead; by working day and night, the three platoons had been able to clear the beaches of all remains." Other, oft-quoted, moments of professional triumph include the recovery of remains from the *Lady-Be-Good,* a B-24 bomber that crashed in the Libyan desert during World War Two. Seventeen years later, when an oil company discovered some of the crew's remains, the army stepped in and began a recovery operation. The team discovered that all but one of the nine men aboard had survived the crash—and indeed had walked more than eighty-five miles across the desert leaving a trail of clothes and parachute parts in the hopes that rescuers would find them. Instead, a determined unit from Mortuary followed the clues to collect, at long last, their remains.

These specialists tout a record of progress. Fifty-eight percent of those who died in the Civil War were identified. In World War Two and Korea, 78 percent were identified. By Vietnam that figure jumped to 96 percent.

Today they are proud of their near-perfect record of recovery and identification. Their modern battle cry? "No more unknown soldiers."

THE LANGUAGE SURROUNDING a soldier's death runs hot and cold with euphemisms that elevate—*supreme sacrifice, lives laid down, fallen heroes,* reporters write—and ones that detach—*mishap* and *fatality, deceased personnel* or *remains,* the army calls them—but they have a shared nexus: distance. The euphemisms serve as a buffer, a bit of no-man's-land to keep your feelings at bay. They create a distance from the straightforward irrefutability of *death.*

Lauren eschews such euphemisms. She speaks directly about her experiences. "I wanted to know every detail about Rob's death," she says. "I wanted to know where he'd been shot, what his other injuries were, what his vital signs were in the hospital." She refers to a friend of hers whose pilot husband was killed twelve years ago. Even though a casualty officer said that the remains "weren't presentable," her friend gave explicit instructions about, for instance, what her husband should be wearing and which ring he should have on which finger as he was buried. A year later, reading the military's detailed accident report, the widow learned that the only "remains" in the coffin were a single, badly decomposed foot. "Rather than tell her this up front, she had to read about it a year later," Lauren says. "And that sent her all the way back to dealing with his death again from the beginning, reimagining it." For her part, Lauren had an insatiable need for details. "Sometimes, it was 2 A.M. and I had to know, was my husband breathing on his own before he died," she says. "And I'd call the casualty officer right then and, if he knew it, he'd give me the answer. And I can sleep at night knowing that nothing is going to pop up unexpectedly."

There is something bravely defiant in the way Lauren tells her story, as if she knows that protocol dictates dignity and silence, but reality for her—and she suspects for lots of other wives—is that healing comes by somewhat forcefully acknowledging that this death happened. In imagining it, in excruciating and accurate detail, so that she is facing it in its entirety, it is now a part of who she is. And, ultimately, speaking about her husband becomes a way of reclaiming who he is—was.

This makes some uncomfortable.

"Part of why I can do this," Lauren says, referring to her ability to cope and her process of healing, "is that I have great friends around and I can talk about Rob and Rob's death with them. I don't feel like I need to put on a smile for them." Lauren says she feels compelled to talk and sometimes will go from weeping to laughing in moments and feels very grateful that her friends just let her do that. But many of the men Rob worked with, and particularly the men who were there in Afghanistan, don't want to talk about it.

"The guy who was right next to my husband, I'd never met before," Lauren says. "But he came to see me and told me everything, step by step what had happened. And our other friend who took care of him right after he was shot, won't talk to me—can't even look at me."

Lauren understands that it is hard for him to look at her. In some ways, she feels as if she looks different. She knows she *is* different. "It's sort of like when you fall in love for the first time and you feel like you *look* different, like it's written across your forehead," she says. "When Rob died, I felt like I *looked* wounded. I didn't want to go to the grocery store because I felt like everyone could see." It affected her sense of self and identity. "I don't want to live in grief," she says, "or have a scarlet W [widow] on my chest and wear it like a badge for the rest of my life, but it has changed me . . . just like being married to Rob changed me.

"One of the few books on widowhood that I found helpful said, there's no way to go around grief, you have to go through it," she says. "And by telling the story again and again, it's a very cathartic experience. My coping is ugly. People say, 'How are you doing?' But they don't really want to know."

"TELLING THE STORY again and again," Lauren says, and I think of the story of her "mishap" constructed in this retelling of details. I think of her collecting these details to build a solid, three-dimensional story that will sustain her—and her children—over the years.

When these details are missing things get complicated. Details are invented.

In my own case, as I got older, and was forced to acknowledge certain realities, my explanation for my father's death shifted. There was still my parents' fighting. And there was still my aborted conversation with my father in the week before his death when he talked about "making some changes"—did he mean we were PCSing (doing a permanent change of station, i.e., simply moving again)? Did he mean he was thinking about getting out of the air force? Did he mean he was thinking about leaving, divorcing our family? Did he mean, as I later became convinced, that he intended to commit suicide? The conversation my father began in a Serious Tone with my sister and I was never finished. We were interrupted. I don't remember by what.

And then there was the crash.

"What really happened?" I wondered.

Years later I asked a family friend, a colleague of my dad's who was one of the "notifiers" and who delivered my father's eulogy. I am not sure if it is because he was a lawyer for the air force and wasn't at liberty to tell me exactly what happened or if he genuinely didn't know, but instead of telling me how the accident occurred he described "possible scenarios."

My father was doing a practice maneuver called a simulated engine flameout, where he flies, cuts the engine, free-falls for a bit, then restarts the engine and flies off. Either he was hotdogging, let himself free-fall too far and didn't leave himself time to restart the engine, or something went wrong with the plane.

Hotdogging? I didn't know enough about my father to know whether this was plausible—though I was well-versed in fighter pilot mythology that described this as a prerequisite for the job.

Another family friend—also a colleague of my father's who was a quality control specialist for air force jets—told me a few years ago, over late-night drinks, that the manufacturer of the plane my father flew had re-called a part; the part hadn't yet been replaced. He believes it malfunc-tioned.

In the course of researching this book, I learn that there are such things as accident reports—and that families are entitled to see them. So I write to the military and request *all* my father's records.

The National Personnel Records Center sends me a sheaf of papers, mostly employee evaluation forms and citations that went with medals he got in Vietnam in 1969. There is no accident report included. But I pore over the employee evaluations and note that many specifically remark on his attention to safety as both a pilot and an instructor pilot. "Captain Houppert instills an acute sense of safety mindedness in both the students and instructors," a 1972 report said. "Captain Houppert recently demon-strated his outstanding flying ability when the wing tip separated from the aircraft he was flying. By checking the controllability of the aircraft at slow airspeeds, he determined that it could be safely landed and recovered with-out further incident." A few months later, the squadron commander writes about my father's shifts as runway supervisory unit controller, explaining that, "[d]ealing with student pilots who are unsure of themselves, and in fact barely meet skill requirements for solo flight, Capt. Houppert has demonstrated superb performance as a controller. Numerous times he has been called upon to literally talk a student down to the runway and through a landing, averting a major accident and, quite likely, saving the student's life."

The employee evaluations seem to discount the hotdogging theory.

And while there was no accident report among the fifty-five pages of documents, I find a memo dated three weeks after my father's death. The subject is "posthumous promotion" and it says that:

"Captain Houppert had completed a simulated engine flameout approach to the field and radioed that he was initiating a go-around for another approach. It was at this point that witnesses saw the aircraft suddenly roll and start to spin. Capt. Houppert immediately ejected from the aircraft, but the altitude was too low to allow the parachute to deploy."

I was surprised to learn that he had ejected—probably *not* the behavior of someone intent on suicide. This mishap, it appeared, was an accident.

LAUREN BURIED HER HUSBAND on July 7, 2003, the day she turned twenty-six.

Once, in passing, her husband had mentioned that he wanted to be buried at Fort Rosecrans National Cemetery in Point Loma, "one of the most beautiful places in California."

"How am I going to come visit you?" Lauren had asked. "And where am *I* going to go?" He was glib. "You'll go in with me," he had said.

"That was the extent we talked about it," Lauren says. "We were twenty-five and thirty and you just don't talk about that stuff."

Still, she remembered the conversation and when Rob died, relayed his wishes to the navy. "The command said they haven't buried anyone there since the sixties but recently some trees blew down and they had ten more spots," she says. "There was room for him."

Lauren says, that as these things go, she cannot complain; the navy was solicitous, kind, and accommodating. "The command was so generous," Lauren says, explaining that they collected pictures and videotapes of some of Rob's SEAL training and also of him with his family and compiled them onto a DVD for the kids. They blew up pictures of Rob and put his medals on display in a shadow box. "Then they wrote this amazing letter, one to each child, explaining what 9/11 was, who their daddy was, and what he was doing and how he was special to them," Lauren says. They printed the letters on parchment paper and framed them for the boys, so that they will have them when they get older. "They also gave me a beautiful listing of all the guys that were there in Rob's unit so that in twenty years if I or the boys ever want to get in touch with them, we'll have them.

"That's what I mean by the command taking care of us," Lauren says. "And they made it look effortless."

After a memorial service in Virginia Beach and another one in San Diego, where they had also been stationed, Lauren's husband was interred at Fort Rosecrans. "The spot where he was buried was back from the road, on the ocean side. It was peaceful and quiet and you could hear the ocean rushing against the cliff," Lauren says. "It's exactly what he would have wanted."

There were bagpipes and a twenty-one-gun salute and a presentation of the flag. And there were yellow roses. "He was fond of yellow roses," Lauren says, "and he'd bring them to me on my birthday—when he remembered." Lauren's mother suggested the final words for his tombstone, "Devout Patriot," and Lauren concurred. "He would have been so proud."

THE SOLDIER WHO DIES at war is a no-brainer for Casualty Affairs. Or the reporter. Or the public. Unlike the "accidental death on a routine mission" there is an obvious framework to drape the combat death on. The narrative is familiar and straightforward and as old as Homer's *Odyssey*. Words are easier to come by: "You must be very proud of him." "Our country thanks you." "Died in defense of freedom." "Devout patriot."

A combat death provides a bit of protocol for the journey past grieving relatives, supportive friends, tables laden with cold cuts and Tupperware containers of food. Does it help the widow to hear her own sacrifice cast in terms of patriotism? Possibly. Because unlike an accidental death, where one must rail against fate, there is a noble explanation. A sense that you are part of a cause larger than yourself probably *is* somewhat comforting. It is how communities have survived for ages: an individual sacrifice for the sake of the group.

But can that sentiment be manipulated? Amped up? Massaged into policy? And what purpose might be served by ennobling all military deaths so that the rites and rituals are all reminders of this greater cause?

Consider the soldier's accidental death. In 2003 the number of accidental on-duty deaths in the army more than doubled, jumping from 63 in 2002 to 130 in 2003. In Iraq 67 percent of the soldiers are killed in combat, while 31 percent have died in accidents. In Operation Enduring Freedom (Afghanistan and other deployments) the military breaks down the casualty figures into "hostile" and "nonhostile" deaths: By summer 2004, more than twice as many soldiers had died nonhostile deaths (68) as had died in combat (30).

But those mishaps are not a story, Lt. Col. Jon Larsen at the Army Safety Center in Fort Rucker, Alabama, tells me. "Operation Iraqi Freedom is the great news story," says Lt. Col. Larsen, explaining that it is abnormal for there to be more combat deaths than accidental deaths. "The army has traditionally always had more casualties due to accidents than hostile deaths." To Larsen's mind, Operation Enduring Freedom is business as usual. After all, 56 percent of deaths in World War Two were from accidents. In Vietnam, that number had shifted only slightly downward, with 54 percent of deaths from accidents. In Desert Shield and Desert Storm the numbers of accidents shot up, constituting 75 percent of all fatalities there.

Speculating as to why there have been so many more fatal accidents among soldiers in 2003 and 2004, Larsen says the sheer numbers of active duty folk are higher—especially because National Guard and deployed Reserve units are lumped into this figure as well. "And anytime you get three hundred twenty-four thousand soldiers in a place, there are going to be more on-duty accidents," he says, explaining that all deaths taking place in the war zone get tallied as occurring while on duty. "If I am swimming in the Euphrates River and drown, this accident will be characterized as *on duty*. Whereas if I am swimming in the Colorado River one afternoon and drown, it's not considered on duty."

Still, there is an increase in the *rate* of accident fatalities, not just the simple numbers. And on the army's own website, a flashing red flag reminds commanders in 2003 that the army's fatal accident rate is already 400 percent higher than it was last year.

But the specifics of each accident are glossed over by DOD, which ends each casualty bulletin with the vague tagline "an investigation is pending." Of course, DOD *never* e-mails reporters the results of these investigations. But no matter. We, the public, are willing to loosely construe heroism so that pretty much anyone on foreign soil who dies *willing* to defend our country counts—whether or not they were actively engaged in that at the moment. If they were changing a tire on a helicopter and the tire exploded, that counts. If they are killed in a car wreck caused by a pothole, that counts.

Even those who die on U.S. soil in routine training accidents are generously—and automatically—draped in the mantle of heroism. Especially during wartime. While Frederick Calladine prepped his notifiers for angry responses from the families of the eleven men recently killed in the Blackhawk training accident at Fort Drum (one of the worst the post had seen in more than a decade), Maj. Gen. Franklin L. Hagenbeck buoyed the larger community. Lest anyone think the men died in vain—accidentally, unnecessarily—Hagenbeck wrested a proper narrative from the mishap. "These brave soldiers knew they were serving something greater than themselves," he reminded the army community in the *Ft. Drum Blizzard,* the post's house organ. "And your response to this tragedy demonstrates that you, too, know you serve something greater than yourselves: America and all it stands for."

And in so saying, an accident is no longer merely an accident—i.e., an avoidable incident that resulted in a useless waste of lives—but a glorious and generous act on the part of soldiers who gave their lives in defense of America. In the aftermath of such tragedies—where widows and families may misinterpret the word *accident* to mean *avoidable* or, worse, *unnecessary*—the military is quick to blur the boundaries of heroism. He who holds the details spins the "mishap"; one tweak and a catastrophe becomes Serving America and All It Stands For.

Does serving the nation and all it stands for help the grieving process?

Well, if anger is a part of the grieving process, perhaps this gets you through the anger more quickly. There is still anger at the randomness—why out of all these soldiers is my husband/father/son shot?—but there is a Grand Purpose that, if you subscribe to it, allows your soldier to be a martyr for a cause. He died for a reason and the reason is worth dying for. Or becoming a widow for. Or raising fatherless children for.

Where things grow trickier for families is when the war itself begins to seem like an accident, that is, avoidable.

"I think the war with Iraq was completely unnecessary. My husband's death was unnecessary," mourns Andrea Brassfield, a twenty-two-year-old Texas widow whose husband, Artimus, was killed in Iraq in October 2003. Brassfield opposed the war before her husband, also twenty-two, was deployed. She opposed it when he e-mailed her that the Iraqi people hated the U.S. military presence. She opposed it when they brought him back in a body bag. "If it had been Kosovo, I would have felt differently," she says. "But I think this was unnecessary; really it was. His death. . . ." Her voice trails off. She seems unable, unwilling, to complete her thought.

BACK AT FORT DRUM, Calladine continues his presentation before the new notifiers on this first night of the war, invoking the family's "kill the messenger" reaction so often the phrase begins to function as a kind of stutter—"I've seen a guy get flattened . . . just kill the messenger, like it was his fault. They blame the army. They blame anybody. You just happened to be there so you're the one getting punched. Just kill the messenger."

Meanwhile, a few miles away from Fort Drum in the center of Watertown, there is a peace protest going on. It's a tiny affair in this army town, six protesters in all. One of them is an army wife who has given considerable thought to the news the above notifiers bring. "I am well aware when I married a soldier that the ultimate sacrifice might be his life, but I want to be 100 percent sure—and I can speak for a lot of people—that this ultimate sacrifice could absolutely not be avoided," she says. For her an *accidental* death is not acceptable.

Calladine, oblivious to the mini demonstration, hammers home the dangers of chance. Point by point, he ticks off every rule, every procedure, every protocol. Calladine—and the military—aim to organize death to squeeze out doubt. "No sleepin' now, okay?" he says. "Let's roll right into this thing, then we can all go home." He clicks on the first projection:

There's no more effective way of creating bitter enemies of the army than by failing to do everything we can possibly do in the time of bereavement. Nor is there any more effective way of making friends for the army than by showing that we are personally interested in every casualty that occurs.

—Gen. George C. Marshall
Chief of Staff, 1944

"We preach this," says Calladine. "And we live it in Casualty."

Danette

2

MILITARY WIFE:
A Day in the Life

I have flag pins I wear all the time on my sweaters. My entryway is all red, white, and blue Americana. I fly the flag outside my house. When I walk to a soccer game and they play "The National Anthem," *I stop right where I am and I put my hand over my heart. Lately though, I think about the spouses that have gone to Iraq or Afghanistan. I have a hard time hearing* the anthem *and not thinking about the people who've died, or might die. It's a reflective moment. I'm reflecting on people that fought for our country. Or even all the people that serve our country. Patriotism for me means military service to our country. Yes. Definitely. The military. That's the framework in which I view this. For me the military is patriotism.*

—DANETTE LONG

IT IS 5:10 A.M. ON FRIDAY, MARCH 21, 2003, AND DANETTE LONG'S TEEN-age boys are on autopilot as they collate and roll forty-one copies of the *Watertown Times*. One day after the United States invades Iraq, the newspaper has splashed a full-banner headline across the front page, "Iraq Leadership in Disarray after Raid: Saddam's Aides Believed Killed," but the two boys, sluggish, sleepy, and laconic neither notice nor comment on it.

Nathan, sixteen years old, is a large boy. He has his mother's dark hair and roundness but, with his studied teenage lack of affect, is the antithesis of her perky loquaciousness.

His younger brother, Kenny, fourteen years old, looks like a smaller version of Nathan, and speaks for the pair. With some prodding, he maps out the parameters of their work. "I get twenty newspapers to deliver and Nathan gets twenty-one," Kenny says. "Weekends, we have twice as many papers." They wish they were getting more money. "If you don't count tips, we get about forty-six dollars every two weeks."

"Yeah? And what's my pay?" Danette, a round woman with dark hair and round glasses, asks as she bustles in with an eye on her watch and a tone of "hurry hurry" in her voice.

"My undying gratitude," Kenny deadpans.

Danette gives her son a smack in the bum with one of the rolled-up newspapers. He laughs, and the three of them scoop up the bundles and carry them out to the minivan in the driveway.

Danette is joking, but indeed it is not clear who shoulders the bulk of the labor here. The boys sit in the back of the van while Danette drives through the predawn light just illuminating the snow-dotted lawns of Fort Drum's housing areas. Danette stops in front of a house and unlocks the auto-lock doors of the car. One boy pops out and ambles up a driveway to drop the paper. She drives a few houses up. She unlocks the doors again and the other son pops out to shuffle up a driveway. She drives past four more houses, pulls into a driveway and efficiently tosses a paper out her window onto a porch. She backs out of the driveway, backs down the street, and unlocks the auto-lock doors. Then her first son pops back in. She backs up past a few more houses, unlocks the auto-lock doors, and the second son pops in.

She repeats this forty-one times.

And, as she drives, Danette describes her life as a military wife.

＊　　　＊　　　＊

DANETTE IS THIRTY-SEVEN and, like 21 percent of army wives, grew up a military brat. Her father first served in the navy, then he enlisted in the air force, and Danette spent her childhood moving from one place to another, including a 5-year stint in Alaska. Her husband, John, is thirty-nine and is also a military brat. The two met in Sedalia, Missouri, where Danette's father had been stationed at nearby Whiteman Air Force Base. Danette graduated from high school on June 1 and married John on July 27, 1983. She was 17; he was 20. "We came from a small town," she says. "You dated the person in high school that you were going to marry. You got married. You started a family and that's how it went." She had Nathan at 19, Kenny at 21.

Then the moves began. The Longs have lived in Maine, North Dakota, New York, Texas, Oklahoma, Florida, and possibly some other places. (Like most military families, they begin to recount their past by ticking off places on their fingers, grow confused about the order of moves, begin debating with each other who was in what grade or what job, grow alternately confused or adamant about the details, and slip hopelessly offtrack. One afternoon several months later, Danette will try again. "Come on now, how many states have we lived in?" she prods her husband. "Nine? Ten?" But John doesn't want to play: "I lost count a long time ago." He shrugs, disinterested.) Today, as Danette swings through a housing area of pale yellow- and blue-sided duplexes, she explains that they almost always lived on base, or in this case, on post. "Maybe it's because we've lived in a lot of supercold-oriented places and you don't have to pay for heat when you live on base," she says. The minivan's door slides open, and Nathan hops out. It slides closed. She backs up, past a house with a "These Colors Don't Run" red-white-and-blue poster in the window. Past their own yellow duplex with a jockey, dressed in desert khakis holding an American flag out front. Past a dog out for an early morning walk; the dog wearing a red-white-and-blue bandana around its neck, its human wearing a matching red-white-and-blue tuque. Bruce Springsteen belts "10th Avenue Freeze Out" on the car radio, and Danette shifts into drive and says it's not just the free heat that draws her to base housing. "I like the community. The base community feel. You know you're surrounded by people who are basically the same socioeconomic status, the same age, and they have children in the same range usually." She does not say "same values," though that is implied.

"It's true you go those long winter months without really seeing people because, you know, you're kind of shut up in the house in the cold and whatnot," she says, "but in the summer it's different. There is a real sense of community."

What does she mean by "community"?

Danette smiles. "In the summertime here everybody is standing out in their yard until seven or eight at night going, 'Oh, gosh, I really need to go in and make supper. Oh, I really need to get in and make supper.' But you don't want to. Because you're enjoying the companionship and, you know, you see a couple of women over here and you chat with them. And then the guys are walking down there and the next thing you know, barbecue grills are going up and there's a big barbecue and that kind of thing. It's just very communal. And I enjoy that feeling. I like the fact that all of our friends are just a couple of streets over. Where if you live in a civilian community you might have . . ." She pauses and explains that once, down in Florida, they lived off base—mostly because the public elementary schools they would have been zoned for if they opted for base housing were terrible. So they moved to a new subdivision in the private sector, living "on the economy," as it is called.

"When we lived in there we had one older retired couple to the right of us, one older retired couple to the left of us, a couple that had a new baby. Then there were some other people scattered around that had children and whatnot, but they were fewer and farther between. You had to plan more if you wanted to get together with your friends because they just weren't that easily accessible. But on base everybody's just right here." She makes a sweeping motion with her arm, indicating the rows of still-dark duplexes neatly arranged on either side of the van. "Here they all understand. They all know what you mean if you say your husband's going TDY," she says, using the abbreviation for *temporary duty,* which means your spouse will be leaving town for two days or two months. "They're like, 'Ugh, if you need anything let me know.' "

And Danette reciprocates. For example, her neighbor, Michelle, is on her own now. Her husband was deployed the day before to the Middle East, and Danette worries a bit about her. "Maybe I'll see if she wants to join us tonight for dinner," she says.

For Danette this deployment business is old hat. Although her husband missed the first Gulf War—"A little disappointing to him, in terms of his career, but not for me," says Danette. "He complains that it's a little like being on a football team and never getting to play."—he was deployed to Bosnia for six months and has gone on more TDYs than she can count. At this particular moment, he is seven months into his year-long tour in Korea, where he is serving as an air liaison officer.

(Later, when he has returned from Korea, John will describe his job to me: "Every army unit that goes to the field has an air force contingency and it's our job to call in close air support. My job is to be the liaison between the army commander and the air force who has the airplanes. The army says, 'There's some tanks over here, blow them up.' And my job is to get the air force planes the information they need to do that. In Korea, I did the same thing basically, except with a language barrier and seven more layers of bureaucracy." Even though he has a Ph.D. in education and curriculum development, he has only spent five out of his almost seventeen years in the service working in that capacity.)

Before moving to Fort Drum in 2002, the Longs lived in Minot, North Dakota, for three years. That was the longest they'd spent anywhere, but they're hoping to beat that record here. In fact, John volunteered to go to Korea for a year because it meant the family could stay in Fort Drum for two more years. By then, Nathan will have graduated from high school, Kenny will be a senior, and John will be one year shy of twenty years in the service, at which point he can retire with a decent pension—$2,700 a month, plus free health care at the relatively young age of forty.

The Longs are thinking they'll retire right here in Watertown. After eight years of taking classes at four different colleges in Maine, Texas, Florida, and North Dakota (and wrangling with administrators about transfer credits and new graduation requirements each time), Danette finally got her B.A. in 2000. When she landed her first full-time teaching job at the local high school last year, she discovered she loved it—and wants to stay. In the past, meaningful employment was hard to come by. Over the years she has worked as a waitress and an office manager, sold home interiors, and run a family daycare center out of her house. "Those were all just precursors," she says. "Teaching is definitely my favorite."

She gets tremendous satisfaction from working with teens, she tells me, and, as I watch her with her own kids, I sense her perky and pleading methodology. On the radio Bruce Springsteen continues to croon his love songs to labor, and Danette tries to help me engage the boys in a discussion about their own labor history. In the summers they sometimes cut lawns, which can be quite lucrative, she prods. But the boys seem disinclined to talk. The consummate multitasker, Danette's energy and chitchat are inversely proportional to those of her laconic sons, who move with disinterested, sleepy reluctance through their morning.

So as she drives—forward and back—and unlocks the door and deposits her sons, and reaches for a paper and tosses a paper and retrieves her sons, and creeps through the paper route, she cheerfully chats *for* them. "Well at least the weather is nicer now," she says. "There for a while in January we were freezing. I'm really proud of them though. They've stuck with the paper route. I was surprised. When the paper changed from an afternoon to a morning paper, I really thought they would have quit. Of course, if I hadn't been driving them they probably would have." She laughs. She doesn't begrudge them this. Indeed she even speaks of the work as a joint operation. "We still print the address sheet every day," she says. "When we first started I would print it out and then mark, mark, mark, as we dropped each paper, but now I just kind of glance at it and go by reference. But I do print it out every day because occasionally, you know, it's like you get to the end and you have one paper left and you're like, 'Uh-oh, we didn't stop at number twenty-four!'" She pauses for breath. And sighs. "Okay, those were Nathan's two routes. Now we go do Kenny's route, third and final."

By 6:15 A.M. Danette and the boys are back at the house. While the kids go upstairs to dress for school, Danette mixes up a batch of Pillsbury blueberry muffins and pops them in the oven. She fries up some bacon and makes hot chocolate for the boys, which she supersizes in a large Mason jar. When they come down, Nathan in a yellow Adidas shirt and the baggy homeboy jeans that are still the fashion in the suburbs, Kenny in a gray shirt and baggy homeboy khakis, they begin grazing, moving from bacon strips on a paper towel on one side of the stove, to the muffins cooling on another counter, to the hot chocolate settled on the third counter in the U-shaped kitchen. Then they repeat the pattern: bacon, muffins, cocoa, bacon, muffins, cocoa, bacon, muffins, cocoa . . . never bothering to actually sit down.

I try to strike up a conversation with Nathan, who is a senior in high school this year. Lamely, I ask him about college plans. He tells me that he has a friend—"not a girlfriend," he assures me, but a friend-who-is-a-girl. She is a freshman at a state university in Kansas. "I might go there," he says.

The school's nice?

"I guess."

What's he like about it?

"It's big."

Any other schools he's looking into?

"Not really."

At 6:40, the boys amble upstairs to brush their teeth and Danette bustles around the kitchen putting breakfast dishes in the sink and wiping the counters. At 6:45, she hollers for the boys to come on, and at 6:48 they all pile into the minivan again, and Danette drives them to their bus stop a block away.

Observing the 25-mph speed limit (10 mph when passing troops in formation), Danette putters through the housing area, turns on to a main road, and slowly travels across Fort Drum.

• • •

FORT DRUM, near Watertown in upstate New York, is home to more than 11,000 soldiers and 8,800 family members. A model post, recommended to me by the army's public relations team, it has lots of new housing, 2 beautifully designed daycare centers, 3 medical clinics, bowling alleys, craft centers, libraries, 2 sports complexes with indoor tracks and indoor pools, a multipurpose auditorium that seats 850, a teen center with pool tables, a gym *and* a room for a "garage band" (instruments and sound-system provided), as well as a commissary with an espresso shop at its entrance. The army spent $1.3 billion between 1986 and 1992 to create a "new" Fort Drum, with 130 new buildings, 35 miles of roads, and 2,272 sets of family housing units. It is touted as a state-of-the-art post that also has "a foundation in tried-and-true traditional values."

It's a brave, new outpost in a rural region with little to offer in conventional arts and leisure. Some hardworking Better Business Bureau types have stretched to suggest that it has historic value: Did you know that Clement C. Moore was inspired to write "A Visit from St. Nicholas" ("'Twas the night before Christmas") while visiting these parts? Or that the nearby town of Chittenango paints its brick sidewalks yellow every summer to celebrate L. Frank Baum's *The Wizard of Oz?* (Not because Baum was born there but because, well, it's just kind of fun, right?) Or that Laura Ingalls Wilder's husband, Almonzo, grew up in these parts? Fort Drum's *Guide for Newcomers* is full of such tidbits, functioning as both an information booklet and a rhapsodic tribute to New York's North Country for folks who may be somewhat reluctant to embrace a place 20 minutes *north* of the nation's snow capital (which got more than 19 feet of snow in 2004), where the unemployment rate crept up to 14 percent in the 1990s, and where per pupil spending is among the lowest in the state. (These statistics are absent from the *Guide for Newcomers.)*

Located an hour north of Syracuse and a half hour south of the Canadian border, the post comprises 107,265 acres across Jefferson County and is the Northeast's largest military installation. It is divided into three basic areas. There is the developed section of Fort Drum, which includes such basic entities as barracks, administrative offices, training facilities, housing, and the commissary. Then there is Wheeler-Sack Army Airfield, which is a kind of mini airport, mostly used to deploy soldiers and equipment for various missions. (This is where army and air force planes are kept and re-paired in hangars and where soldiers gather in huge, warehouse-like build-ings as they prepare to go to Iraq and Afghanistan—often by civilian airline requisitioned by the army for the purpose.) Finally, the biggest hunk of Fort Drum is pine-barren wilderness—used to train the resident 10th Mountain Division, as well as Reserves, National Guard, and other military units.

Among other things, Fort Drum has become a winter survival proving ground for soldiers—and their families. Although the *Guide for Newcom-ers* optimistically describes winter temperatures as low as 15 degrees Fahrenheit (already bad enough for these army folk who have tended to move here from places like Fort Stewart, Georgia, and Fort Campbell, Ken-tucky), the truth is worse. Winter temperatures frequently drop to –10 and –20 degrees Fahrenheit and annual snowfalls of 10 feet or more often ren-der the roads impassable. One January, Fort Drum Army wife Ulli Robin-son e-mailed me a weather update: "Reeeeally cold up here . . . –38 last week but it's 'warmed up' . . . only –7 today."

In this weather the Fort Drum families scurry from house to car to commissary, if they absolutely must, and try to reassure each other: "They say it wasn't *this* cold last winter, right? How long can it last?" The post's paper, aptly named the *Fort Drum Blizzard,* regularly runs winter survival tips and the Morale, Welfare, and Recreation Department there runs an an-nual Spouse's Safety Day, offering snowblower certification workshops (so that spouses can borrow an army-owned snowblower for the season), cold weather injury classes, and winter driving lessons.

During one week in January 2003 temperatures hovered at about –26 degrees Fahrenheit. At 6 A.M. one morning—*not* having taken a winter driving class—I found myself struggling to steer one of eight cars colliding into each other on a bridge above the treacherous Black River, where ice, snow, and blinding fog from the river sent cars skidding and crashing all over the highway. Despite the fact that two of the vehicles involved were large trucks, that most of the cars were totaled, and that one driver found himself in the river below, no one died. Judging from the efficiency and swift response of local fire and rescue squads, they'd been around the block with this one a few times before. Verification came after that, when I began to notice how many cars bore battle scars. Rust and dents and missing bumpers are *de rigueur* here where almost everyone met, or topped, my accident story with one of their own.

To make the cold worse, in this unforgiving landscape of flat pastures, stunted trees, and low scrub a fierce windchill develops. Folks here call it "the lake factor." Wind gathers tremendous force as it whips across nearby Lake Ontario and it creates a bitter and bizarre landscape. Giant snowdrifts shift the landscape so that gentle hills and valleys emerge from flatlands; trees are not the beautiful snow-laden wonders Robert Frost marveled at in his snowy walk but bleak, black, twisting interruptions in a white desert—the wind whipping the snow off the branches the moment it touches them.

Despite the inhospitable climate, it's not uncommon to pass an outcropping of tents in this wasteland of winter tundra where soldiers, hunkered down at −20 degrees Fahrenheit are carrying out training exercises. The soldiers training in this weather, or even simply standing outside to guard an installation road, are bundled in the kind of survival gear you see on documentaries about the Arctic. They look like ghostly creatures from another planet with giant, white, hard-plastic boots, goggles, and puffy white winter wear that obscures their human form. Even soldiers who work inside in this weather—but need to dart from the parking lot to their car or dash out for lunch—typically wear special, army-issue polypropylene long underwear beneath their uniforms and an army-issue balaclava. With this latter pulled up over their heads, many of the female soldiers look strangely like their Muslim counterparts in Iraq as they scurry around the post.

The 10th Mountain, a light-infantry division, evolved from ski patrols in 1941. The 11,000-soldier division has been sent on operations ranging from battles in Mogadishu, Somalia, to peacekeeping missions in Bosnia, to disaster relief after Hurricane Andrew in South Florida. "Light infantry," as the name implies, means soldiers are traveling light, with weapons that they can carry. The division is a reinforcing combat unit or follow-on force, meaning that it is not typically the first to deploy for battle. Still, the division is designed for rapid deployment via land, sea, or air within ninety-six hours of notification. In the aftermath of September 11, 2001, some of its units were quickly dispatched to guard nuclear and chemical research facilities at Aberdeen Proving Grounds, Maryland, and by October 2, the first of its soldiers were on the ground in the Middle East. The 10th Mountain has spent most of 2003 and 2004 in Afghanistan—with some smaller units from Fort Drum sent to Iraq or Korea.

On the outer edges of the various administration buildings are the many housing areas. The housing at Fort Drum is an experiment for the army. While there are 2,272 housing units on post—arranged in fifteen subdivisions with names like Caisson Courts and Patton Heights—half the army housing is actually located off-post. This is a departure from the usual, clear on-post/off-post housing distinction where families either live in the army's free housing on-post or receive a tax-free housing allowance (ranging from $429 to $1,205 depending on rank and local rent levels). At Fort Drum, there is on-post housing, off-post housing, and a middle category: off-post housing run by the army.

DANETTE DRIVES PAST various housing areas, past administrative buildings, past tanks sitting on railroad cars, and past a guard who stands at the back gate of the post. She exits the post and at 7:05 A.M. she pulls her minivan into the parking lot at Carthage High School where she teaches English. Seemingly plopped down in the middle of the cheapest farmland the county could acquire, the school sits across from a large-scale chicken farm. An ordinary-looking institution circa 1980s—squat and county-budget bland, the school has a unique air quality: Here the school-lunch smell of fried fish (it is Friday) and macaroni and cheese mingles with the omnipresent odor of chicken manure.

Inside Danette's classroom her ninth graders have just finished reading William Saroyan's *The Human Comedy*. The book, set in the 1940s U.S., is a coming-of-age story. When the novel opens, fourteen-year-old Homer Macauley has gotten his first paying job delivering telegrams. Many of the telegrams, of course, come from the War Department, telling families about the death of their soldier husbands, sons, brothers.

It's a good tale under the best of circumstances, and particularly evocative now, the day after the United States has invaded Iraq. Still, though twelve out of twenty kids in this class have parents stationed at Fort Drum, 25 percent of the students at the school are military brats, and more than 6,000 soldiers will be shipped out from Fort Drum to Iraq and Afghanistan over the next few months, no one mentions this personal connection to the literature.

Instead, the students hew to the established ninth-grade curriculum and are charged with writing an essay through the "critical lens" of the following preestablished quote:

> *Literature provides us with the experiences we can't live in our own lives and enlarges our knowledge of the world and the ability to understand and sympathize with others.*
>
> —ANONYMOUS

The students are to use the xeroxed "Task IV Guidelines"—a dull prescription for proper essay writing that spells out in deadly detail the elements that must be contained in each paragraph—and blank eyes turn away from Danette's instruction to hunch over blank papers.

One student raises her hand. "What do they mean by a symbol?" she asks, pointing to the guidelines.

Another fifteen-year-old raises his hand with a question about the quote. "What is literature?" he wonders.

Danette takes the questions in stride. She smiles amiably at her students, defines the terms, and urges them to settle down to their writing. "Remember, no personal pronouns," she says.

TWO MORE CLASSES, lunch in the teacher's lounge, one more class, then the ninth-graders gather in the auditorium to watch an earnest group of college-age New York City actors present an edited version of *The Glass Menagerie*—curiously, the Gentleman Caller, having a real-life broken leg, limps alongside Laura—then a prep period, then school is over. A few errands on the way home, a phone call to touch base with the boys, mail from the mailbox, the dog is let out, and she sits down—for the briefest moment—with a sigh.

It is the first time I've seen her simply sit. For the most part, Danette moves in a constant, capable, cheerful way through her world. Things are in their place, and if there are any reservations about this placement, she hides them well. To her, my questions about military life are an interesting diversion. "I hadn't really given it much thought," she says. "Let me think about that." The military life gives her no more cause for thought than Saroyan's novel did her students. It simply *is*. It is the world she has always known.

But for wives who marry into the military—"muggles," as J. K. Rowling might call them—there is a curious round of new protocols and regulations to internalize: Men are no longer referred to by first names or by "Mr." but must be called "Colonel Weasley" or "Major Granger"; her husband declines to hold her hand—or the kids'—in public lest he need to salute a passing superior; a trip to the cinema begins by standing as a flag flutters across the screen and "The Star-Spangled Banner" blares from the speakers—presumably, even if the movie is Michael Moore's *Fahrenheit 9/11;* a dip in the post pool at dusk is briefly interrupted by "Taps" trumpeted from speakers across the installation and she stands, hand over dripping chest by the side of the pool for the duration. Old civilian friends who want to come by for dinner must be met at the post's front gate so that she can sign them in; school chums coming to a son or daughter's sleepover meet in the Dunkin' Donuts parking lot just off-post and are collected in the minivan to be buzzed past the guards and onto the installation; heavily armed soldiers trot by when she stops for a traffic light; esthetics are for pussys, which means that buildings tend toward the low, squat, flat-roofed, cinder-block utilitarian variety devoid of cornices, gables, or details (basically anything that might collect dust or be hard to duplicate). *Sirs* and *ma'ams* proliferate.

But there are tremendous advantages, too.

If I may return to my *Harry Potter* analogy, there is a scene in the first novel when Harry first arrives at Hogwarts School of Witchcraft and Wizardry and enters the great hall to eat. All the young wizards sit at long, empty banquet tables. Suddenly, out of nowhere, a tremendous and delectable feast is spread out before them. To Harry, who has never gotten quite enough to eat, Hogwarts is heaven.

Likewise, to civilians who may have led a hardscrabble existence the list of perks that come with military life is almost mind-boggling. First, there are the biggies, like job security, a good pension plan, free medical care, free housing (or subsidized if you live off base), free utilities, free marital counseling, free drug counseling, free alcohol counseling, free financial advice, subsidized gasoline, subsidized childcare, food and other necessities sold at cost (plus a modest 5 percent markup to cover logistics and employee salaries at the commissary), tuition assistance or tuition reimbursement, free gym membership, free aerobics classes, free pool membership, and free swimming lessons for the kids. Next there are the modest, yet still significant cost savers. If a faucet leaks in your house, a quick trip to a Family Self Help Center and you've got a replacement, *free.* Want mulch or topsoil for your garden, a new recycling bin, a replacement knob for your door, a new fluorescent bulb? The Family Self Help Center also gives those out gratis. Movie tickets at the base theater run $2.50. Going on vacation? You can rent a camper ($45 a day), a tent ($10 a day), skis for the family ($12 a day), or bikes ($4 a day) at the post rental store. Need a snowblower or carpet steamer? The base lends them at no cost.

In some ways the military is the closest our country gets to creating a benevolent welfare state. The most obvious example of this, of course, is socialized medicine. Even as conservatives insist that a system of socialized medicine would never work in this country, that it would mean inferior care for all, and that we would have to ration resources, the military mini-state has gone about quietly developing just such a system to serve its 1.3 million active-duty soldiers and their 2 million family members. Since 1956, all military families have had full medical benefits through clinics serving every installation. For the most part patients see whichever doctor happens to be on duty. (In my own case, as an adolescent going to my first gynecological exam, I had a doctor with a prosthetic metal hook for a hand doing my pelvic exam. Used to Vietnam vets growing up in the 1970s military community—my gym teacher in fifth and sixth grades had no legs, for example—I took it in stride.) In the military, if patients need a specialist, they get a referral from the general practitioner on duty. If a specialist is not available at that particular base or post, the patient is referred to a local civilian doctor or goes to one of several regional military hospital centers scattered across the country. Even though the military has begun restructuring its entire system over the past few years to cut costs, it has not departed from its basic provision of free health care for all service members and their families. And it has not yet resorted to charging "employees" a share of the premium based on their marital status or number of children, as many private employers do.

The big hidden cost for service members, of course, is that they may go to war and die—or die in a training accident while preparing for war. The big hidden cost for soldiers *and* their families is a demand that they surrender self-determination to the institution. As Spec. Rachel Tolliver, a one-time soldier at Fort Drum, put it, commenting on her inability to be critical of an army policy in the post newspaper, "It's ironic that we're charged with defending all these freedoms we're denied as members of the military."

And it's not just soldiers. "You have probably heard the phrase 'to sign your life away' pertaining to men joining the military?" Fort Drum army wife Heidi Klaus-Smith asked me. "Well, I've come to the conclusion that it's not the men who sign their lives away."

Hers is a rarely articulated sentiment.

And a dangerous one.

Excluding complaints about the difficulties of finding work—about which I heard a lot—most of the wives I interviewed, if they complained at all, wondered about more modest problems: why they couldn't plant a vegetable garden in their backyard; why military housing always seemed to have linoleum everywhere; why they had to move so often; why the poorest members of the enlisted community had the hardest time getting on-post housing; why the military couldn't more closely determine their husbands' redeployment dates; why the military pay didn't match that of the civilian world; why the military made so many bases down south where the schools for their kids were lousy; and why the military bureaucracy was so hard to navigate.

AT 5:10 P.M. I leave Danette's house, agreeing to meet her and her neighbor Michelle an hour later at the mall. We are spending a Friday night on the town at the Salmon Run Mall in Watertown—either to catch a movie or dinner. Lost in my thoughts about which movie we might watch, I make a wrong turn and end up wending my way through one of the post housing areas. Patches of snow still dot the lawns and I pause at a stop sign, watching two girls in pastel parkas race their bikes down the sidewalk. The sun is going down, but they are inspired by this barest hint of spring in the air and they leave their jackets unzipped and stray far on the paths that lead away from the housing area toward one of the main streets. They look to be about six years old, and I marvel at their freedom—a fenced-in world, yes, but one where little girls can pedal as far as their skinny little legs can take them. And moms and dads don't worry about kidnappings or drive-bys or even cars—at 25 miles per hour the margin of error for those who forget to stop, look, and listen is generous.

It is peaceful here. The identical houses and duplexes, equally spaced across the field, look organized, spacious, and clean. There are no dealers on the corners, no graffiti on walls, no sneakers dangling from power lines, no homeless people on the heating ducts—none of the signs of poverty and disorder so common in my New York City home. In this early March dusk many families have turned their lights on and, peering from the dark outside a warmly lit house, I feel lonely and covetous.

Dusk is a bad time when the day's regrets flutter up. *What if?* As usual when I'm reporting, I begin to imagine the world from my subjects' perspective. But this time the ease and comfort with which I assume their perspective is unusual. It feels like coming home. Familiar. The MP at the gate, who salutes the car as I drive in, is waving welcome. The commissary and PX are exactly where and how I expect them. The code necessary for navigating this world is easy to crack. Described by military brat and novelist Sarah Bird as a world of signs stenciled on cinder block that "bark out acronyms, squadron names, unit designations, the whole vast hieroglyphic that orchestrates every twitch of military life," the signage is a detour down memory lane. The slight drawling twang that permeates the linguistic fiber of all military families—partly because so many are genuine Southerners, partly because 118 out of 170 bases are located in the southern half of the country, and partly because the singsong, lackadaisical accent stands for the unflappable soldier or pilot—was a cadence that made my interview subjects my high school buddies. The chitchat, a finely calibrated mix of bluster and sarcasm, was easy to parse, and the quick friendliness from people used to making friends fast, seductive.

And I begin to imagine what would have happened if I had fallen in with the majority of my military brat classmates who joined the service after high school? Or the girls who'd married the guys who joined—a statistically more likely scenario? Suppose I married the love of my life in high school who is floating out there, somewhere in the Iraq-Afghanistan-Saudi Arabia-Kuwait ether as an air force pilot—and this had become my life? Who or what would I have become if I had remained in this particular world?

Peering in the windows, I try to imagine. I try to sift through my nostalgia. This world was *home* to me for so long, it is comforting to be back here. At the same time, I know *home* evolved into a suffocating reality that sent the teenage me hightailing it out of there—Adidas on tarmac—barely looking back. Am I now responding only to the sense of financial security that comes with a military life—security notably absent from a reporter's existence?

To make myself feel better about the choices I've made I try to remember why I fled this world in the first place. I dredge up the teenage me and recall the sense that the cinder-block walls were closing in on me. Even then, I moved through that world as an observer rather than an engaged participant. As a teen, I was adept at picking up on the social cues: I could talk the talk just fine and parlay it into popularity, but the deeper, intrinsic logic of the military culture and its trickle-down effect in my DOD school eluded me. At the time I doubted my perceptions, what I saw was plainly not what others saw.

Revisiting this military community, the same doubts assail me. Everything seems so seductively orderly and predictable and congenial—why not accept it at face value? And around and around I go past the indistinguishable houses, from Fitzsimmons Loop to Dayton Loop to Few Loop, my logic—or lack thereof—as loopy as the winding streets I follow. I normally have an impeccable sense of direction, no tolerance for disorientation. So I pull over and think for a minute (okay—and consult a map). Turns out that there is a method here. All these little residential loops feed onto big loops, which feed into bigger loops (Fort Drum's version of the Washington, D.C., Beltway, perhaps?), but it is only when I see all these little loops in context that a clearer picture of the whole emerges. The loops are purposely designed so you don't *have* to think. You end up where you've been directed. And so I find my way out of the housing area, off the post, and free of my circular, tail-chasing logic.

I hit the highway—rushing now—to catch up with Danette at the mall.

*   *   *

DANETTE, so far as I can see, is one of those people whose life seems crammed with activity. She is in constant motion. She never seems to tire. And, by design, she tells me she is rarely alone.

With her husband safe, comparatively speaking, in Korea, Danette is one of the few wives I visit the week the U.S. invasion begins in Iraq who does not have CNN on as a constant background noise. Liberated from the TV, she has made plans to go to the mall, drop off the boys at a movie, and either catch another movie with her neighbor Michelle, or, if nothing good is playing, go out to eat. As we walk through the Salmon Run Mall, Michelle goes on a rant about some peace protesters she has seen. It is long and involved and indignant and lasts the entire length of the mall. "I don't think those people should be allowed to do that," she says. "Why are those people so upset? Don't they understand what the military has to do?" she says. "Have those people forgotten about the Pentagon and the World Trade Center?" she asks. "How do they think that makes us feel with our husbands over there fighting?" The peace protesters are a personal affront.

Danette says little, but steers us toward a list of posters outside the mall's cinema. Nothing good is playing and we decide to eat at Barkeater's Cafe, an Applebee's-style restaurant in the mall. Once we've ordered we start talking about moving. Danette confesses she's a total control freak and has the whole thing down to a nearly flawless system. Shortly after her husband gets any new orders she begins going through closets to weed out the rarely worn. She labels boxes for the packers so that the packers *unpacking* will know on which bookshelf each box of books belongs, which drawer contents go back into which drawer. It usually takes her about a week to be fully moved in at the new location—and "fully moved in" means curtains up, pictures hanging on the walls, computers and VCRs good to go.

I'm impressed.

Danette admits that this is just part and parcel of being a control freak. "And I would add that I was kind of peeking at your notebook of questions last time when we met—this is the anal side of me—I looked at your list," she confesses, laughing. "I thought, well, when she asks me a question I wanna be ready."

"I live with this all the time!" Michelle says.

"It's my military preparedness," Danette says sheepishly. "One of your questions was, if there was one thing about the military that you could change, what would it be?"

Danette's a little put out that I never asked her the question. And she has obviously been thinking about it in the two months since we last met. "Can I answer it?"

"Please."

"The thing that I would change would be the housing regulations because the people who need to live on base the most are the ones least eligible for base housing," she says. "Low-ranking E-1s, E-2s, or E-3s, whatever, if they're married and have children, can't live in the barracks, of course, but they don't qualify for on-post housing either, in some places." She explains that on-post housing is typically restricted to those with a rank of E-4 or above, and while these very junior families get some stipend to help cover the cost of rent, it is usually inadequate. "Here are your youngest wives and those newest to the military, those most probably in need of support and most financially stressed and whatnot, and they're the farthest from the PX and commissary, from the hospital, from the support of military neighbors who will notice if you haven't put your lights on for a day and ask, 'Are you depressed?' "

Danette knows of what she speaks; she remembers how hard it was in the early days. In fact, she confesses, she was horrified when her husband raised the specter of enlisting.

I'm surprised to hear this; she seems the consummate military wife.

Danette explains: She was eighteen, he was twenty-one and had just gotten laid off from his job working as an analytical chemist for a company in Sedalia, Missouri, their "hometown." "At the time, we weren't sure but we thought I might be pregnant," she says. "And he looked at this as, he needed to have something secure for his family, to be a solid provider. And he didn't like the insecurity of not being able to have guaranteed employment, so he went down and joined. I mean, I grew up military. I can remember when he came home and said he was going to join—I was bawling! Like, totally upset and depressed at the fact that he was going to join the military. Because I grew up in the military and I thought, I don't want to move. I don't want to go through all this stuff." Danette sighs, remembering. "Oh yeah, I was devastated when John said, 'I'm considering this.' " Finally, though, he won her over. "I was like, okay, if you think it's best, then that's what we'll do." She shrugs. "Fast-forward eighteen years and I couldn't imagine any other life."

Danette's Foremothers

COCKTAILS, CLEANING, AND THE COLD WAR:
Coming of Age in This Man's Army

I don't think patriotism is really something you put on. It's just a part of you. For example, at the high school where I teach we have the Pledge of Allegiance before class. Occasionally we have kids that stand up and say, "I don't want to say it," and I say, "You're talking to the wrong person. If you have a problem saying the pledge, you need to keep it to yourself."

—DANETTE LONG

TODAY DANETTE MOVES CAPABLE AND COMPETENT THROUGH THE MIL-itary world. " 'What happened to that quiet girl I married?' my husband wonders sometimes," Danette says.

Her friend Michelle, sitting across from her at Barkeater's, raises her eyebrows, as if to say she is skeptical that Danette was ever—could ever have been—a wallflower.

"Really, I've changed," Danette says.

What does she attribute that to?

"Murphy's Law for military wives: If something's going to go wrong, it'll happen while your husband's TDY [away from home for temporary duty]." She recalls her first experience with Murphy's Law. She had just dropped her husband off to go TDY for training and, within an hour, she had been in a car wreck—not her fault, she says quickly—and totaled the car. "We were young airmen," she says, sharing her husband's designation. "We had no money. We had no transportation. I was twenty-one. Kenny was one-and-a-half months old." Danette says she had to figure out how to buy a car, how to get a loan, how to get herself and the baby to checkups— all on her own. And, while these things happen to other young couples, most would pick up the phone and call a family member to come get them from the side of the road, have Daddy or Uncle Bob help them shop for a new or used car, catch a ride to the grocery store with an old friend. Danette was on her own.

She had to cope, and she did. The experience changed her. "Somehow I went from the quiet wallflower to the gregarious woman that I am today," she says. "And I have to think that a lot of that is due to the experiences I have had as a military wife—having to cope with these things. And that's exactly it.

"My students and I have been talking about that idea with the book we're reading," she says, referring to William Saroyan's *The Human Comedy.* "Here we have the main character, teenaged Homer, acting as the adult male in the family, delivering war telegrams knowing at any time that the message that comes through could be about his brother. And he has to deal with that. And the thing that I try to get home to my students is how you deal with information is what makes you an adult. Not how old you are, or whatever. It's how you cope. How you handle the incoming information.

"And I think that's the exact same truth for the military wife. You know, how you deal with the fact that you have to move, how you deal with the fact that you have to walk into a room full of complete strangers and say, 'Hey, I just arrived today. What's going on?' You know, you have to do that. We actually moved one place and the same day I arrived, I heard they were having a wives' coffee that night. I went. I went because I knew the coffees were monthly and I didn't want to sit for a month without having contact with other ladies. I was tired of my husband and my kids—I'd just spent two weeks driving across the country in a car with them! I found out the address of the coffee and I went.

"Now, reverse that eighteen years, or fifteen years, and there's no way I'd have gone. It was the experiences I had between those two points in my life that made me even able to do that."

"So this was your coming-of-age story?" I wondered.

Danette laughs. "It's not actually too far-fetched an analogy. When you figure that I was only eighteen when he joined up. Yeah. There you go. The military is my coming-of-age story."

IN THE 1940S a rash of how-to literature made its debut, seemingly designed to speed up army wives' coming-of-age. These advice books—written by and for army wives—were marketed as offering tips to help women work the system, but actually spelled out for newlyweds what the system expected of them.

The books and pamphlets prove a useful historical artifact.

Spanning the years from 1941 to the present, this how-to literature provides a revealing glimpse of the issues army wives faced and the standards they were held to during this era. The handbooks are instructive not because women hewed to the advice offered—no wife, even the most June Cleaver among them, could live up to these detailed expectations for hearth, hubby, and homeland—but because they clearly spelled out who constituted the perfect army wife.

The most renowned book in this genre is Nancy Shea's *The Army Wife.* The book came out in 1941, and in later years Shea penned *The Navy Wife* and, when the air force gained its independence from the army in 1947 and her husband, a major, became part of this new service, *The Air Force Wife.*

Because Shea updated her books every couple of years and reissued them for almost three decades—one edition was even issued posthumously—they present an interesting portrait over time. Here we can see how the image of the ideal army wife endures, how it has evolved, and how the army's expectations for wives were spelled out.

Although the books are not published or endorsed by the army, they are clearly quasi-official "wife" manuals. Shea obviously worked in tandem with various official army departments—for example, she added new thanks with each edition, suggesting that the army thought well of her message and continued to work with her to get it out. Thanking a major general, several brigadier generals, and lots of colonels by name, she also specifically thanks the brigadier general who is chief of information for the army and many other divisions and units "for giving particular chapters a final check." Although we don't know how many wives read Shea's books, or whether they acted on her suggestions, we *can* assume that they reflected the army's agenda for wives. As Barbara Ehrenreich and Deirdre English noted in their 1978 book *For Her Own Good: 150 Years of Experts' Advice to Women,* the "experts'" advice can be revealing in and of itself—as a reflection of expectations and, more important, as a chronicle of the effort to control or shape the discourse. Books like Shea's are a way of advising wives how to think about their military experiences.

Shea's books rely on a common formula, one that endures in their contemporary equivalents. The author strikes a maternalistic tone to offer advice to the novitiate. She spells out in nitty-gritty detail exactly what the proper behavior is for every imaginable circumstance—and then backs away from this typical military protocols-and-regulations pattern to reassure the young army bride that she'll be fine if she takes it all in stride, views army life as a grand adventure, and retains her sense of humor.

While it's not clear how widely the books were read—the fact that Harper & Brothers reprinted *The Army Wife* five times between 1941 and 1966 suggests that the book was fairly popular—it's easy to guess how they were used. Some of the dog-eared copies I purchased from secondhand stores were inscribed "Compliments of Officers Mess Club," suggesting that they were gifts to newly married members. Others bore inscriptions like this one:

MARCH 30, 1943

To my darling Rachel, the greatest wife any officer ever had.

All my love, Bob

A close reading, noting what stays in the book and what gets dropped, proves revealing—especially as certain enduring themes emerge.

Of course, some changes simply reflect the passage of time and shared civilian/military cultural trends. For example, the sample menus that Shea offers the new wife grow (slightly) snappier and (quasi-) ethnic as time goes on, evolving from meatloaf to chop suey. Shea's 1942 advice to send the three-year-old army brat to a preschool where "the destructive, the inconsiderate, the selfish, the rude, the crybaby, the unsanitary learn the error of their ways through the anguish of unpopularity," evolves into a suggestion that parents pick up a copy of the kinder, gentler Dr. Spock in 1966. Also, some of the more exuberant, hooray-for-West-Point passages have been toned down. (Perhaps due to complaints from readers whose husbands hailed from the Citadel or Virginia Military Institute?) Where she once crowed that "something about a soldier sings in every girl's heart" and explained that "West Point cadets are outstandingly the best-looking, the most attractive and the handsomest embryo officers in the world" and the "finest cross-section of American manhood," she later hedges her bets. By the time Shea's husband has become an officer in the fledgling air force, she has changed her tune and is insisting that air force officers "represent the cream of American manhood; they are the finest cross-section of young men." Shea reminds her imaginary young reader, Peggy, that whichever fine specimen of American manhood she chooses, he will "appreciate your cheerful willingness to fall in with the system."

Perhaps the most striking deletions occur in a section about overseas assignments. In the 1948 edition Shea holds nothing back as she warns Peggy about being stationed in postwar Germany:

The German youth of today, between the ages of fourteen and twenty-eight, has been carefully and thoroughly educated for world conquest, killing and treachery. No matter how friendly and repentant, how sick the Germans claim they are of the Nazi party, as a nation they have sinned against humanity and they are not to be trusted.

Clearly it was difficult for many families to move into a country as occupiers and try to settle among a people when they had lost family members and friends in the war. But fortunately this problem doesn't plague Shea for long. By 1966, Germany is simply "one of the most photogenic countries in the world," full of modern architecture, flower-filled window boxes, and "quaint, old-world charm." History is now merely "its colorful past."

And speaking of history, there is one thing Shea declares she is ready to relegate to the dustbins. In 1954 she offers a kind of mea culpa. In the section "Army More Democratic," she writes that "it is no longer possible to tolerate even the implication that Army life is merely an officer's life, and I am much embarrassed that I did not include the soldier's wife in my first book in 1941." So in the 1950s she introduces common "Connie," the enlisted man's wife who's got her own exciting challenges to face.

Still, she continues to direct most of her comments to the young officer's wife who is—or should be—trying desperately to play hostess-with-the-mostest to help propel her husband's career onward and upward. With that in mind, tips for entertaining and creating a proper home receive a lot of attention. They are so important, according to Shea, that they should be considered both a business and a patriotic duty.

Every successful business in the world is built upon a system, and without a system a business does not continue to thrive. The Army household is a business, and the Army wife is the business manager.

The keynote of her housekeeping should be "efficiency." . . . Fortunate indeed is the Army wife who has specialized in home economics because homemaking in this day is a highly specialized art, a definite business and a profession.

Shea goes on from here to map out the army wife's chores for the day, and the order in which she should do them, warning her to stick to her schedule and admonishing the poor young brides that "[i]f you stop to finish a detective story, remember to deduct it from your leisure instead of skipping your household duties." And Peggy is on her own. "Don't ask or expect Ted to help you with the dishes. He is working for the government." (It's interesting that even in the 1940s readers bristled a bit at this. Shea admits in the 1948 text that this last suggestion was the only one that garnered adverse criticism in her first edition. Still, she sticks by it. And why not? If she has elevated housekeeping to a profession, why denigrate it by suggesting that any ol' Tom, Dick, or Ted can do it?)

Shea gives considerable advice about servants for the wife who is stationed overseas and can take advantage of the cheap labor, but reminds the stateside wife in 1954 not to despair if she has to do all the work herself. After all, it is her "job."

Learn to enjoy doing a good job at your housework; have respect for your job and a mature pride in your home. There is nothing menial in housework if you have a sincere love for and a genuine interest in your house.

And not only is it Peggy's job, it's a reflection of her character:

Your living room paints your portrait as a homemaker, and is more of an index to character than any palm reading would ever reveal. . . . The moment one steps inside the door of a house one senses something of that atmosphere . . . If you have a maid to answer the door, does she smile when she admits a guest? If you have a dog, teach him to wag his tail in welcome.

While such advice to homemakers was common at the time, the stakes are higher here, Shea tells Peggy in every volume and edition of the text. The disorganized or thoughtless housewife may put her husband's very life in danger. Don't bother your husband with the petty problems of home and family, she says in this 1966 excerpt. His work is sacred. You worry, so he doesn't have to. A distracted husband is a dead husband. (Or, a distracted husband may hasten the death of underlings.) This "truism" endures to the present and, as we'll see, wives in 2004 continue to fret about this—and manage it in different ways. But in 1966, Shea was direct:

His mind cannot be disturbed by worry over unpaid bills, the tension of making it home for a party or "bust," or news phoned him by an unthinking wife that Butch fell out of the tree house and broke his arm. The arm will heal, but a mistake in judgement on the part of her husband may claim several lives. To do his best he must have a congenial, happy home life. His mind must be free for the work at hand.

Again and again, Shea hammers home her conviction that a wife, as "executive officer in the home" has a central mission: keeping up her man's morale. Again and again, Shea hands us science as the essential tool for accomplishing this mission, the science of housekeeping, that is. Thus is the army wife elevated from drudge to professional:

The Army family which earnestly tries to run its establishment on a business basis will find that system and efficiency bring proportionate returns, as they do in a thriving business.

This notion that running a home is a business, studied, examined, and quantified by experts, is not new. Ehrenreich and English's research further reveals the professionalization of housework can be traced back to the beginning of the twentieth century when the "woman question" had folks all hot and bothered. Were women rightly relegated to the private sphere? What did it mean that they were nattering about wanting to vote, to go to college, to get a job?

Ehrenreich and English argue that the answer to the "woman question" was to redirect women's energies toward the home. "The home was an ideal 'container' for aspirations which could not be met in an increasingly stratified society," they write. "[F]rom a middle-class point of view it was a wholesome target for working-class ambitions and from a male point of view it was a safe focus for women's energies." So that smart women didn't feel underutilized as industrialization took over more of their household tasks—like sewing and knitting—experts began urging them to treat it as a business. Ehrenreich and English write:

Domestic scientists set up "Housekeeping Experiment Stations" to discover the "principles of domestic engineering." The scientific housekeeper now saw herself not only as a microbe-hunter, but as a manager operating on principles of industrial efficiency. In fact, by the nineteen thirties, domestic scientists considered "management" to be the major thrust of homemaking, practically eclipsing housework itself.

Of course, as the authors wryly note, this division of labor between manager and worker in the industrial world, concentrating "planning and intellectual skills in management specialists" makes for a flawed model in the one-woman home. (In our case here, poor Connie and Peg must wear both white and pink collars, drawing up proper schedules for efficient housework and then doing the dirty work.) Still, this image of home as factory continued to be evoked as a way of filling the domestic void. "Old work was invested with the grandeur of science; new work—challenging, businesslike—was devised," Ehrenreich and English noted. "If homemaking was a full-time career, the Home would be safe, and 'The Woman Question' would be answered."

Likewise the army had a vested interest in keeping wives from questioning their rigidly prescribed lives, and the "business efficiency" model is clearly one Shea takes to heart in her army wife books. Of course, the military has had a long love affair with efficiency—employee evaluations are "efficiency reports," periodic tests are "efficiency exams," surveys and reports are "efficiency studies." Shea marries these ideas nicely, even linguistically, labeling her housekeeping sections "operation efficiency."

Even though Shea's book didn't surface until the 1940s, which puts it somewhat out of sync with the historical trend documented by Ehrenreich and English, it certainly reflects a typical military lag-time. Never known for being cutting edge, the military community seems to operate in a social and political time warp, slightly out of step with all that is *au courant*— from social trends, to fashion, to music. (A fact that, as military teens living overseas in the late 1970s, my sisters, my friends, and I constantly bemoaned: Why was it the PX would carry only Toughskins when everyone was wearing Levis [and had been for eons]; that the PX offered Wrigley's and Breck but not BubbleYum and Agree; that it carried albums by the Beatles but not the Police?)

In her postwar and early 1950s editions, Shea was also echoing official U.S. government doctrine, which was urging any and all Rosie the Riveters to return to the home.

> *Homemaking is a full-time job, and a wife should not work unless there is a real need for the money she earns. Of course, there are extenuating circumstances, where an aged or ill parent must be supported, but simply to improve one's standard of living or to buy a piano, silver, or a car is not a very worth-while reason, if such work in any way jeopardizes your home responsibilities. If you do work, always remember that your husband and your home should come first, and it is not cricket to expect your husband to accept a slapdash sort of housekeeping.*

She goes on to say that Peggy's work will be at the whim of her husband's boss. After all, "some commanding officers have serious objections, and will not allow it." Peggy should secure permission first, Shea warns.

And Connie, our young enlisted wife, should be getting used to seeking permission for things as well. "I feel it is important early in your married life, Connie, that you, as an enlisted man's wife, understand and accept the relationship, too," Shea writes. "There is no rank among Army wives," she explains, offering up what is now a time-worn cliché among wives, who even today insist this is the case but frequently go on to complain about the uppity officer's wife they once knew who "wore her husband's rank on her sleeve." In Shea's case, she goes on to qualify this "no rank among wives" statement: "Yet a junior wife should always show deference to older women, particularly the commanding officer's wife and the ranking sergeant's wife." (This advice remains relatively unchanged in contemporary "wife" books.) But not to worry, Shea says. "Regardless of her husband's grade, every Army wife has three basic responsibilities":

1. *To make a congenial home.*

2. *To rear a family of which he will be proud.*

3. *To strengthen her husband's morale.*

In other words, your whole scheme of life revolves around your husband, your children, and a happy home. But don't forget to "cultivate some outside activity that will make you more interesting and thereby more attractive."

There is nothing less attractive, according to Shea, than a bored wife—or worse yet, a complainer. She is quick to slight any women who have trouble adjusting to military life. Hers is a daintier version of the "Don't be a pussy!" soldiers hurl at each other, and echoes the macho bravado that is viewed as intrinsic to adjusting to military life. Buck up, she tells her readers in labored metaphors:

Army life is like a three-ringed circus, and Army women must necessarily be versatile. Just being a good equestrienne isn't enough either in the Army or in the circus; in addition, the rider must learn to take the jumps. Sometimes they are easy little low barriers. At other times they are the five-foot-six variety with a blazing arch or water hazard thrown in. This is when the Army woman shows her mettle, for which she will receive no silver trophy, no blue or red ribbon, but all in all she will gain a sense of satisfaction and achievement. If combined with a lot of fun, this adds up to that elusive thing everyone is seeking—happiness.

Turn that frown upside down, she says in 1954, insisting that sheer willpower will do the trick—and reminding poor Peg that her husband's success hinges on her ability to adapt.

If you are unhappy, your husband is eventually going to be unhappy too. It is not wise, even in a jocular manner, to complain continually about the Service, and it is extremely dangerous to discuss service gripes with civilians. . . . To complain to this group about the Army . . . well, just don't. Complaining suggests a lack of restraint, self-control, plain common sense, and maturity. Finally, no good comes to your husband, as such talk reflects on his happiness in his work—and on his choice of a chatterbox for a wife.

Shea goes on to say that an army wife "should be interested in what is going on at the post" and get out and meet "key" people. "In this way she can become an alert, well-informed, and well-integrated Army wife." A contemporaneous book (1956) for navy wives, written by Florence Ridgely Johnson and published by the Naval Institute, illustrates how peers can, and indeed should, reinforce this message:

You share equally with your husband, the responsibility to the Navy. This means accepting the bad with the good, without criticism or complaint, and doing the best you can with the tools at hand. . . . Navy women are, for the most part, a quietly courageous lot. They do

*little complaining themselves and have no respect for the woman who
does.*

Shea concurs, with regularly scattered bits that urge Peggy to be positive, look on the bright side of life, don't whine:

*An army wife never complains when she has to leave the spring
garden she has so painstakingly planted. She smiles and hopes that
the family who inherits it will enjoy her pansies, tulips, and hy-
acinths. . . .*

Interestingly, Shea never veers into the harsher realm of blame. For instance, she never tells Peggy—or even Connie—that she has made her own
bed. That would be an overt acknowledgment of serious hardships, trade-
offs, and compromises. Instead, Shea opts for a subtler approach, suggesting that if the ladies merely tweak their attitude a bit, and adjust their view
of reality, military life can be one grand party.

AT 4:30 ON AN AFTERNOON in November, Danette is gathered for a Friday
night pizza party with her family. She sits in Cam's, a small, brightly lit
pizza parlor in Watertown's central square. Her husband, her sons, and a
friend's daughter she has picked up from school because her friend was in
a pinch are with her. She is pausing—briefly—between the school confer-
ences she conducted this afternoon at the high school and her evening
commitment of volunteering for "Teen Night," an evening of supervised
recreation at the local middle school. As the family eats pizza and fiery
wings, Danette keeps one eye on her watch and the other on her kids, reminding them to hurry, wondering if they have any homework, getting a
handle on their plans for the evening. The consummate multitasker, she
also talks to me, giving me the update on Nathan's college plans.

When I spoke to Danette a few months ago, she told me Nathan had done some research and found out how expensive college is. While his parents think he ought to work for a year and earn money before going to college, Nathan preferred going to Kansas—where the "friend that is a girl" lives—to attend a junior college there. He would establish residency so that the following year he could go to the university and get in-state tuition.

But some vague "something" has happened between Nathan and his non-girlfriend so that by November he has dropped the Kansas plan.

Problem is, Nathan is a C student, and so his options for college are limited.

"Nathan is talking to some recruiters now," Danette says. "He's taking the ASVAB [Armed Services Vocational Aptitude Battery, an aptitude test for potential recruits]. He's been talking to a navy recruiter." She laughs. "I know. I know, you'd think he'd go for air force! But he's thinking maybe a nuclear sub. He doesn't really know. He's having trouble deciding.

"Guess that's one reflection of my parental mistake. I think I've done too much for him for too long. I think it's time for him to do for himself more, and he doesn't know how. We're working very hard on independence these days."

Danette wouldn't be displeased if he enlisted in the navy; it strikes her as better than the army or the marines. "In times like these, I think the navy is the safest place. Because he's just out in a boat somewhere, not on land. That's a personal choice. If service to his country is what he wants to do, who am I to stand in his way?"

"Is that why he's interested in the navy?" I ask.

Although Nathan sits at an adjacent table in the pizza parlor listening to our conversation, he doesn't say anything.

"I don't know," Danette continues. "In today's world, it's not like the fifties where that sense of patriotism was so strong. Whether he's doing this out of a sense of duty or for college money or because it's just a matter of he doesn't know what to do or where to go and the military is a very structured organization, much like home. . . ." Her voice trails off. "It could just be the security that the military brings. Why does anybody join the military? I just have to hope that I taught him well and that he'll make good choices." Danette pauses for breath and then sighs. "I try not to question. I try to just support."

FAMILIES, formally or informally, support the military mission in a variety of ways. Shea was always very direct about this.

By 1950, as North Korean forces crossed the 38th parallel, Shea was telling her young wives that it was time to "gallantly take off our peacetime party dresses and put on the drab sackcloth of grim purpose again." But she most decidedly did not mean that Peggy ought to hustle out into the paying workforce. Indeed, the "grim purpose" Peggy is told to embrace is the American way—as exemplified by normative American 1950s values, which means, of course, even greater dedication to hearth, homeland, hubby, and now, little Butch.

In the aftermath of World War Two, the U.S. government left tens of thousands of soldiers scattered across Europe and Asia as occupation forces, and later, in an effort to prevent the spread of communism. After a long war and years of separation, there was considerable pressure for the military to let wives join their husbands overseas. "Wives were going to the government and saying, either you bring them home or put us over there," says Donna Alvah, a history professor at St. Lawrence University who has studied military families during the Cold War. Even Gen. Dwight D. Eisenhower tried to secure permission to get Mamie over to Europe with him, directing his request to Gen. George C. Marshall himself. (Marshall, chief of staff of the army, turned him down at first, reportedly explaining that if Eisenhower had his wife over there, *all* the soldiers would start clamoring for their wives.) "At the same time, though, there were concerns that this was an 'unnatural' way for the men to be living and this was creating some social problems in local communities," Alvah says. Referring to the soldiers' heavy drinking, rowdiness, and sex with local women, Alvah notes that the government grew worried that this poor image of Americans might undermine Cold War foreign relations. "There was the idea that wives and families would create some normality and settle the personnel down," she says.

In 1946 the military began sending families over to join soldiers—and a secondary purpose emerged. "In the beginning, the families were supposed to represent an alternative way of life to life under Nazism, to help with the denazification and reeducation of the German people," Alvah says. "Then, with the Cold War, attention also shifted to the idea that families can represent the American way of life in both Europe and Asia."

According to Alvah, the military was exploring both "hard" and "soft" tactics. Hard tactics meant, of course, military might. Soft tactics meant the subtler reeducation efforts. The Cold War was, at this point, primarily a psychological contest, and so the U.S. government figured it needed to be fought using cultural resources rather than traditional "hard" ones. This included funding arts through the Congress of Cultural Freedom (a front for the CIA); the financial support and subtle politicization of art by cold warriors such as Nelson Rockefeller (who dubbed abstract expressionism "free enterprise painting"); and the creation of the National Endowments of the Arts and Humanities. Military families also played a role in promoting the good life—that is, the American, democratic, capitalist version.

But this was not without problems. "It was hard for the military, an authoritarian, hierarchical institution, to embody American democratic ideals of liberty and freedom," says Alvah. And if the military were to be a part of this ideological war, it needed to rethink its tactics. "To represent what Americans saw as the epitome of American life, they needed nice American nuclear families and American homes to do that." Thus began one of the biggest migrations of military families abroad—peaking in 1960 with 462,000 soldiers and families stationed at overseas bases.

The American patriarchal family became a kind of unofficial ambassador of American values. Explaining that there was a tremendous fear of communism's "homogenizing influence," and worry that the "heteronormative family, resting on gender difference, would give way under communism to manly women, effeminate men, and perhaps even homosexuality."

Alvah argues that military families became inadvertent foot soldiers in this ideological war. "The American patriarchal family, [in which] wives perform a crucial feminine dimension, organizing the private sphere and curbing male aggression," she says, "served as a foil to communism, in which the totalitarian state obliterates the family and its morality, individual freedom, and gender difference."

In this way Shea's rigid insistence on traditional gender roles in *The Army Wife* serves an ideological purpose. In the 1948 edition she is quite direct about this:

> *It is a hard task for American Army families to move into a hostile enemy country, and take up the long-term guidance of the German or Japanese people in their economic, political and social rehabilitation according to democratic principles.*

At times Shea nearly echoes the government brochures and booklets given to families as they boarded flights overseas:

> *The Army's mission overseas is really a hard one and dependents who are permitted to go overseas are, in a sense, guests of the Army. . . . As an Army family you will have tremendous influence overseas and this influence should at all times be helpful to our national objectives. Army children also are just as much ambassadors of good will as you are. . . . Dungarees or blue jeans with loud Western shirts worn on the streets give the same bad impression that Europeans receive from some of our poorly done movies. We should be extremely careful in our dress to leave a good impression of the American way of life.*

(And to think I attributed the lack of Levis in our commissary on a base in Belgium to a mere fashion oversight.) Shea concludes the chapter by reiterating that "the prerequisites for a successful Army wife might be summed up as follows: she should be gracious, diplomatic, well-mannered, but above all American."

Chapter I "Army Esprit de Corps," of the 1954 edition, also makes it explicit that the housewife is not merely a housewife; she's a player in a high-stakes game. "It is important that Army wives today realize that they have a large stake in their husbands' military career and that by their attitude, interest, and adaptability they also play an important part in our national and international security," Shea writes. "We are no longer mere 'camp followers.' "

And so the "professionalization" of wives' work in the military extends beyond housework to working for the army. Shea's books—and indeed most of the other books for military wives from the 1940s through the present (as we'll see later)—do their best to make it clear that a wife, not exactly a partner in her husband's career, is "executive officer" to her spouse, the commanding officer in the family. The literature then goes on to warn a potential slacker that if she does not toe the line her husband's career may suffer. Clella R. Collins tells us in her 1942 *Army Woman's Handbook:*

> *Wives may lose sight of the fact that their husbands, while in the service, are directly responsible for their wives' actions. It is particularly true in the service that a wife can make or break her husband. . . . Numerous instances are on record where an officer's efficiency has been discounted heavily, where he has failed to achieve positions of trust and distinction, and even where transfers have been made, entirely because of the fact that the wife was indiscreet in her speech or showed too plainly a lack of knowledge of military customs, ordinary social customs, or customs of good breeding.*

It is best, in fact, to think of the army as a mutual career, Shea tells young Peggy. Shea recalls hearing an army general speak to a group of wives on "the unwritten efficiency report":

> *He pointed out that as an officer chooses the military career as his profession, so does a young woman choose a career in the Service*

when she becomes engaged to an Army officer. And as an officer has an efficiency report filed in Washington, just so has his wife an "unwritten efficiency report," unfiled but known, labeled and catalogued through the Service. This unwritten efficiency report may be the means of bringing special assignments of honor to an officer or it may deprive him of an enviable detail for which he has worked faithfully.

It is interesting to parse the logic here: A wife is a "kinda-sorta" employee of the army—albeit an uncompensated one. Technically she's a conscripted subcontractor whose unpaid work reflects directly on her project manager husband. Her husband's "project" happens to be the nation's defense. She owes loyalty first of all to her husband/boss, then to her boss's boss (the U.S. Army), and finally to the big boss's mission, our national defense. It is a triad of obligations that has served the army well.

FAST-FORWARD SEVERAL DECADES, though, and it is clear that the modern military has a problem. Today all the armed services have declared that they cannot, in good conscience, keep any efficiency reports on wives. (In fact, their conscience was prodded by two wives who filed a lawsuit in the 1980s when their husbands were barred from promotions because their wives held jobs instead of doing the requisite volunteer work on post. In 1988, DOD issued a directive forbidding the practice of commenting on a wife's behavior in her husband's job review.) Today, the military agrees that it is not really fair to hold a husband responsible for his wife's actions. The old adage that "a man who can't control his wife or kids can't control his troops" has been discarded. No word of the wife who drinks or the kids on drugs surfaces in any official employee evaluation, as it used to. But what that means, in practical terms, is that the army has to lean extra hard on the remaining parts of its triad to win compliance from families. It must push harder for a wife's allegiance to her husband's particular unit, to the army, and to the nation—manifested through the army and its missions.

What has changed in terms of official military doctrine is not so much the expectations of wives, but rather the method of expressing them. Where the military once used a stick, it now uses a carrot—or a "volunteer-of-the-month" parking space. A new benefit, a compliment, language that ennobles sacrifice and a call for unity of purpose are the new invitations for loyalty.

As Morris Janowitz, a sociologist who studied and wrote extensively about the military, noted in his 1971 book, *The Professional Soldier,* the military itself underwent a sea change in the 1960s. "There has been a change in the basis of authority and discipline in the military establishment, a shift from authoritarian domination to greater reliance on manipulation, persuasion, and group consensus."

Janowitz accounts for this change by saying that the success of highly technical modern warfare relies on highly trained and highly motivated soldiers working as a team. Janowitz argues that this precipitated a shift in management techniques. "In fact, the central concern of commanders is no longer the enforcement of rigid discipline, but rather the maintenance of high levels of initiative and morale."

The change Janowitz refers to was reflected in the military's family policies—eventually.

Throughout the 1960s and 1970s little effort was made to woo wives with additional benefits and support systems. In fact the contrary was true. Wives were mostly left to fend for themselves while their husbands were deployed to Vietnam. The explanation for this was simple: with the draft in place until 1973, the military didn't have to woo anybody. It didn't much matter whether soldiers or their families liked the work when they were drafted to do it.

But today, the military is greatly preoccupied with maintaining soldiers' initiative and morale—and, by extension, wives' initiative and morale.

To do this it adopts a fluid lexicon, mixing and matching its terms so that the words bleed across the soldiers' porous professional and personal lives. The army is a family. The family is a team. "First sergeants in today's Army have a responsibility to establish a partnership with all members of the Total Army Family (TAF)," a 2003 training manual reminds leaders. "Many studies show that soldier performance, readiness, and retention relates directly to family satisfaction with army life. You, as a 1SG [first sergeant] in today's Army, must fully support the Army Family Team Building (AFTB) program."

To train families to be good army families, well acquainted and contented with the ways of army life, the U.S. Army introduced the AFTB initiative in 1994. This program consists of classes, typically taught by experienced wife volunteers, that explain every aspect of military life to the uninitiated. While a smattering of such classes had been offered ad hoc before, this was the army's first systematic effort to make the classes uniform and to mandate that they must be offered year-round at every installation. Referred to as "Basic Training for Army Families," the classes are the first formal indoctrination lessons the army has tried for wives. "The basic philosophy of AFTB is the belief that individuals can function at a high level in any situation with minimal outside support when they have been appropriately trained," an October 2003 army document explains to post commanders. Soldiers are required to take the classes; wives are "strongly encouraged" to do so.

Why? The army spells out its motivation in this 2003 sergeants' training manual:

> *The Army of the future is to be family-friendly. In a real sense, families go to war and family readiness plays a key role. . . . Research and experience prove the critical relationship between unit readiness and family readiness. . . . In summary, the Army is changing its view on the responsibilities leaders have for preparing family members for coping with the rigors of Army life. [First sergeants] today must take the training of family members as seriously as the training of troops for combat.*

Army brass needs to make sure the wives are behind them. In Shea's day, women were assured that being an army housewife was a professional calling they could excel at if they just properly wrapped their minds around the task. Today women are also coaxed to consider themselves professionals—albeit of the unpaid variety—as they are carefully "trained" to recognize and bolster the army's mission.

"BACK IN THE OLD DAYS, the good wife did this and that, and she hosted coffees, and she joined the clubs—and there was a lot more pressure in terms of protocol," says Danette. "But in today's modern society where not every wife is a stay-at-home mom, there's not the same expectations. We still have the wives' groups and stuff, but I think the focus is just to support the wives while their husbands are gone. There are still some strict regulations and control and structure, but not to the degree it was before."

It is almost a year after I spent a day in Danette's life, and we are speaking on the phone. She remains in motion. "Sorry, it might get loud here for a minute, when I turn on the washer," she says, clearly bustling about with her housework as we speak. But she is feeling pensive.

"The most melancholy time of the day for me is the evenings," she says, admitting that, because her husband is TDY for a couple of days she sat up in front of the computer "like an idiot" until 2 A.M. the previous night. "It's always like that for me," she says. "When he went to Korea it took me two weeks to get into a routine again. And going to bed is the hardest part." She laughs. "So I put that off. For days after he leaves I'll stay up till two or three in the morning, falling asleep sitting on the couch rather than going up to an empty bed."

Like all the wives, fear for her husband's safety is Danette's biggest worry. She refers to the old movies in which someone shows up on a rural doorstep with a telegram—and sobs break out. "I don't know. Gosh, anybody who says they don't think about that would have to be lying. The minute they're walking away down the airport terminal you say, 'Is this the last time I'm going to see him?' You memorize his gait, his smile, and every-thing. Just in case."

Danette counters these thoughts as best she can. "In my mind, where he's gone to Korea or Bosnia or wherever, I'll say, 'His job doesn't put him in direct contact with the enemy.' He's more the liaison, working with the people in the tent back at the camp, telling those guys out there what to do. It's not like the poor wife of the sergeant who's out there on the ground with the troops, calling in the information. Maybe it's rationalization on my part." She pauses, but dismisses the notion. "The way I view it when he's gone is, he's not in that position of most critical danger. Whereas if I had a husband who was an infantryman, I'd be beside myself. It could be pure fabrication on my part. We don't really talk about what he does very much. John's a very private person. I don't get into the day-to-day workings with him. It's probably better that way because I don't psych myself out with what I know." The sound of the dryer drowns out her next words.

"What?" I ask.

She repeats. "Ignorance is bliss, isn't that what they say?"

Danette also lets on that other worries bubble to the surface during these late nights of insomnia. "I fear for his relationship with our children, too," she says. "Last year was Nathan's junior year of high school. He has only one more year and then he's off on his own—and John missed most of that entire year, being in Korea." She struggles to delicately phrase what she wants to say. She starts over. "Nathan and John have very similar per-sonalities. I know how to handle Nathan because I handle John. . . ." She trails off and tries again. "I worry, has John been gone so much to the point that later when they're adults he won't have a healthy relationship with his children? Has he been gone so much they won't know how to talk to him or he won't know how to relate to them? I see them talking sometimes, or trying to, and conversation seems to come very difficult to Nathan and John. Or is that just their personalities?" She stops to think. "And then sometimes I think the long breaks might be good, give them a break from each other . . . I dunno. . . .

"I'm a worrier, so I just worry about these things."

Almost as an afterthought comes Danette's third worry: What will these long deployments do to their own relationship? This one is dangerous and is introduced in the third person. "People change over time," she says. "When they're away from each other for a year, you're talking about major changes in people's thoughts, routines, personalities, friends. And those kinds of changes can cause friction." Danette explains that her husband is not a "big communicator" when he's gone. "If he's gone for four weeks, if I don't call him, I wouldn't hear from him. I mean, he trusts that I can handle things, so I guess that's comforting. He doesn't worry, but it can be kind of lonely." She recalls one incident that happened when he was in Bosnia in 2001. "The air force lets you make these 'morale calls' once every two weeks for ten or fifteen minutes—at DOD expense. Well, in Bosnia he took his morale calls and gave them away to some of the airmen that worked under him because they were having some problems at home."

"Were you upset?"

"Fifty-fifty," Danette says. "Part of me wanted to shout, 'Whaddaya mean you gave them away?!' And part of me says, 'You saw someone in need and you did something to help them and I respect that.' And it's not like he didn't contact me via e-mail. So it's not like we weren't in contact. But, well, sometimes you want to hear his voice. I mean, if it was a long time and there was no communication at all, then I would have been bothered." She pauses, but reassures herself. "But if that was the case, maybe he wouldn't have given them up."

At the end of our conversation, as though it had maybe taken her a while to verbalize this, she gives me her final, maybe biggest fear: "I worry sometimes that he likes it too much."

"What do you mean?"

"That year in Korea he just went to work and then went back to the barracks. He didn't have to worry about anyone's schedule but his own. He ate when he wanted, read when he wanted, got up and went to a movie when he wanted." She struggles for a moment to articulate her thoughts. "I worry, what if he decides he likes that world too much? Compared to coming home to moody teenagers and having to accommodate all of us, to eat now and rush here and go there on this family schedule. So there's always that fear: What if?"

She is silent for the briefest moment, then shakes it off. Bucks up. "This life can be a bit manic sometimes. One minute you're feeling depressed because he's gone and then you're going out with friends and just getting on with it. You have to just adjust your personality to it," she tells me. "Some people have a lot of problems with it—it was harder in the beginning—but I do all right." She laughs, cheerful and competent again. "Things don't stay with me very long."

Crystal

4

ALL THAT YOU CAN BE:
Young, Poor, and Alone

Lately Richard has been thinking about staying in the army and joining the Special Forces when it gets time for him to reenlist. A bunch of guys at work told him, if you go Special Forces you're going to be a single man. But I told him when he first got into this, you know, that whatever you want to do, you do it. I don't want to hold you back from what you want to do. I realized from the beginning that having a wife and kid puts a damper on things. And I know the Special Forces guys are sometimes gone eight months of the year. That's hard on a wife, but I understand. I said, "I don't want to hold you back from what you want to do."... I don't really know what we'll do. He comes home with a new idea every day.

—CRYSTAL SOLLOWAY

WHEN I WENT TO MY FIRST WIVES' MEETING AT FORT DRUM I CAME IN with another wife from down the block and everybody's looking at me because, like, I'm in the teenage clothes and all," says Crystal Solloway in her dry Kentucky drawl. On this January 2003 day she sits at the table in her small apartment, dressed in faded jeans and a worn navy blue T-shirt—with a piece of white yarn knotted around her throat as a necklace. She has a stud in her tongue and five earrings in each ear. Around her left wrist she has five green and two brown rubber bands, one of which she pulls down and twirls between her fingers while we talk. "I go to this wives' meeting and I'm in the flared jeans and everybody's looking at me strange." She turns to the neighbor who has brought her to this Family Readiness Group meeting for army wives: "Man, they're looking at me like I'm your daughter. This lady, she said, 'Well, if you wouldn't dress like a teenager. . . .' And I said, 'I *am* a teenager! I'm seventeen, how am I supposed to dress?' "

Crystal gives a low laugh, dismissing the incident as ancient history.

Today she is nineteen.

Today Crystal has accepted her outsider status. Whether it's her age, her inexperience—until moving to Fort Drum she had never lived anywhere outside of Bowling Green, Kentucky—or her relatively new identity as a mom, she feels that she doesn't quite fit in. "I get along better with the single guys in the barracks than the wives because they're more my age," she says.

But then her son, little Richard, who is plopped close to the TV in an easy chair in the exact center of the small living room gives a screech—concretely interrupting any fantasy of a parallel world. Though the child is two-and-a-half, his speech is garbled and completely unintelligible. "I know it's a fire," Crystal says soothingly without even looking at the *Elmo* cartoon where flames have attracted a fire engine. "It's okay. Elmo is going to put it out." She explains that he's seen this video four times today and 400 times since he got it for Christmas a month ago, but he always freaks out at this part. "It's okay," she says, as he runs over and hugs her. Disentangling herself from the chubby arms that have twined around her neck, she picks him up and plops him back down in the easy chair in front of the TV. "He's tired," she says. "He didn't have a nap today, and I'm trying to keep him awake 'til bedtime." It is only dusk. "Two hours. . . ." She sighs.

.   •   •

CRYSTAL SOLLOWAY doesn't love the army. She doesn't love Fort Drum. And she doesn't love upstate New York, in the winter, in the snow, when it's –26 degrees Fahrenheit—as it is on this particular day in January 2003. She doesn't love being cooped up all day in her apartment with a toddler for days on end because she's afraid to drive in the snow and, anyway, her husband took the only working car to work. She doesn't love the meager military paycheck ($1,821 a month). But she loves her husband, Richard, a skinny, twenty-year-old army infantryman with the 10th Mountain Division, whom she's known since she was a freshman in high school.

So here she sits. Mostly alone. Day after day. A dark maroon king-sized sheet has been draped over the picture window in the living room to block out the bitterly cold drafts of air; it also blocks all natural light. The apartment is small—and feels smaller. She goes out, sure, she tells me. In the summer she and the baby take walks to the playground at least once a day if the weather's nice. In the winter she sits tight. "Mostly I clean, or watch cartoons with the baby," she says. But twice a month, on payday, she does leave the house. She loads little Richard up and, in the winter, they make a mad dash for the car—"We don't have a lot of warm clothes because it didn't get like this in Kentucky"—and Crystal runs errands, first stopping to deposit her husband's paycheck, then grocery shopping, and buying what she needs from the PX (a store comparable with Sears in its line of items, its quality, and its prices).

Crystal has come a long way since Bowling Green. She got pregnant when she was sixteen, had little Richard when she was seventeen, married her husband four months later, but really had never been on her own. She and Richard lived with her mother in Bowling Green, and then Richard joined the army. One week after Crystal gave birth he left for basic training. Crystal and their newborn stayed on with her mom.

In the spring of 2001, when Richard got orders for his first assignment at Fort Drum, Crystal and some family friends packed up a U-Haul and together made the 850-mile trek to meet Richard who was already at his new post. When the truck was unloaded in Watertown, New York, and the friends had departed, Crystal, Richard, and the baby were left to set up house together for the first time.

What this means is that Crystal, who could "kind of" cook spaghetti, who had never paid an electric or gas bill, who'd never balanced a checkbook, who didn't have a savings account, who'd never drawn up a household budget or filed her own income taxes, whose grandparents lived down the street and whose mom would sometimes get up with the baby in the middle of the night to relieve an exhausted Crystal . . . was on her own.

She and Richard had a lot to learn. "And Richard's even worse than I am at this stuff," she says. And though she is referring to organizing their financing, she later admits he doesn't care for dealing with the baby, either. (For example, when they make the long trek from Watertown to Bowling Green for holidays, they usually drive down in two separate vehicles. "Richard very seldom rides with me because he knows he's going to be cooped up in a truck with me and a two-year-old for, like, fifteen hours," explains Crystal.)

For a while there, the phone was her lifeline. "If the baby got sick or something, any little thing I didn't know, I'd be on the phone with Mom. 'Okay, Mom, what do I do? Do I give him medicine? Do I wait till it gets worse?' Or, I'd be, like, 'How do I cook this? How do I cook that?' Or if he got really bad diaper rash, I'd pick up the phone. 'Okay Mom, what do I do? You've done this a lot more than I have!' "

Hard as this was, it got worse. Less than six months later, on the heels of the September 11 terrorist attacks, Richard was working extremely long hours and occasionally would disappear completely for days on end while his unit did training exercises. Then one day in October he drove up in front of the house, jumped out and said, "I've gotta get my ruck [backpack]." A kiss, a hug, and he was gone to Afghanistan for the next six months.

At the time Crystal's mother was visiting and was due to leave the following week. The plan was that Crystal, little Richard in tow, of course, would drive her mother back to Kentucky, stay a week, then drive back to Fort Drum. A week stretched into two, two weeks stretched into two months, then two months became six. Somewhere around the middle of this time, Crystal realized that she didn't want to go back to Fort Drum. "I knew one wife down the road here in Watertown because her husband was in the same company as Richard, and I knew one couple in the building, but other than that I didn't know any wives at Fort Drum," she says. "I wasn't real comfortable staying here by myself, especially with everybody telling me the winter gets as bad as it does. And I just didn't want to be up here by myself for that." She shrugs. "So we just stayed in Kentucky."

Neighbors cleaned out the fridge in Watertown and kept an eye on the place (even sleeping there occasionally when they had marital spats of their own), and Crystal had packed enough to get her and the baby through the winter. There was nothing pulling them back.

And certainly the army itself doesn't tug too hard under these circumstances. Many of the young, junior wives do require more social services and more hand-holding during deployments, so the army is happy to see them go. Plus, it saves some costs for utilities each time a wife "goes AWOL" like this. But at the same time, the army would prefer these young and still-impressionable wives remain nestled in the heart of the army culture and so returning to parents during a husband's deployment is vaguely discouraged. (The army says it likes to have wives close by so it can "offer support," but the subtext is that there is something wimpy about running home to Mama in a culture where wimpy doesn't fly.)

In Crystal's case her ties to the community are extremely tenuous; she guesses no one but her nearest neighbors even noticed she was gone. "I didn't want Richard to think I was just abandoning our home," Crystal says. "But I got along a lot better in Kentucky than I think I would have here."

When Richard returned from Afghanistan in March 2002 and Crystal rejoined him at Fort Drum, they were on their own again.

ARMY, AIR FORCE, NAVY, and marine recruiting ads are of a distinct genre. Carefully scripted, they are mini coming-of-age stories focusing on the challenges that make a boy a man. The ads and websites and testimonials—like the armed forces in general—celebrate an accelerated process of maturity. The navy, for example, announces its raison d'être to prospective recruits—"Life. Liberty. And the pursuit of all who threaten it."—on its recruitment website, then offers the tagline: "See how the Navy can accelerate your life." Private Richard Jones offers a testimonial on the army recruiting site that is laced with comments from his mother. He says, "I completed basic training and I proved to my mother and everybody else that I'm becoming a man." He explains how he bonded with his buddies: "We're all family—can't nothing top it." And his mother smiles and nods her head. "A new man," she says.

Conceptually, things like basic training camp are specifically designed to propel the pimply-faced adolescent from a soft, comfortable boy safe in the cradle of family and community to the lean, mean, fighting machine the military wants. "The path is tough, the results, immeasurable," marine recruiters tell prospective recruits. It transforms boys:

> The change is forever. Becoming a Marine is, perhaps, the most difficult challenge you will ever face. But if you stay the course, you will be undeniably different. The uncertainty of youth that led you to the Corps will be gone forever. It will be replaced by the markings of a proud warrior, a formidable opponent and a match for any obstacle life might throw at you.

This should not be taken to mean that basic training makes a person independent. Integral to this transformation is a shift from dependence on the family to dependence on the team. The soldier must learn that he can trust no one but his buddies. The soldier has a new family. A 2004 marine ad puts it this way:

> To belong. This is family. Ours is a kinship as old as a nation, hammered from countless battles and long years. Together we have

known pain, victory, and a trust few others will ever experience. This is our Corps. This is our way.

This notion of shifting alliances, from family to military unit, is considered the very foundation of modern warfare or, in military parlance, "combat capability." General Norman Schwarzkopf, commander of U.S. forces in operations Desert Shield and Storm, described the process to the Senate Armed Services Committee in 1993:

> What keeps soldiers in their foxholes rather than running away in the face of mass waves of attacking enemy, what keeps the Marines attacking up the hill under withering machine gunfire, what keeps the pilots flying through heavy surface-to-air missile fire to deliver bombs on targets is the simple fact that they do not want to let down their buddies on the left or the right.
>
> They do not want to betray their unit and their comrades with whom they have established a special bond through shared hardship and sacrifice, not only in the war, but also in the training and the preparation for the war.
>
> It is called unit cohesion, and in my 40 years of Army service in three different wars, I have become convinced that it is the single most important factor in a unit's ability to succeed on the battlefield.

What this "unit cohesion" means for the young army wife though, is that *her* similarly accelerated coming-of-age story—especially with the frequent and lengthy deployments of late—has a price. The more time he devotes to his unit in the interest of accelerating his allegiance to the army (and, according to a 2002 DOD study, the average workweek for soldiers is fifty-five hours; and 73 percent of them were away from their families for an average of 2.4 months that year, before Iraq), the less time he spends with her. The more time devoted to his army unit's cohesion, the less time devoted to his young family's cohesion. And the deeper he is drawn into the military culture with overnight training exercises, long work hours, socializing with his buddies, six-month to year-long deployments, the more likely she is to be left on her own—geographically far from her family, her community, and her friends.

This worries the military.

Here's why. Every study, every report, every training manual, and every brochure that the army has produced about deployment and family in the last ten years emphasizes that a family's "readiness"—read maturity, competence, independence—affects a soldier's readiness. To ensure a family's readiness, the DOD has decided that what the wives need to properly buck up is their own brand of unit cohesion.

How to achieve this has plagued them.

Back in 1993, when a strong economy had recruiters sweating and falling far short of their quotas, the Army Research Institute for the Behavioral and Social Sciences conducted a study, "What We Know about Army Families," that summarized the Army Family Research Program's previous ten years' work. The study examines the changing demographics of the "army family," the link between army wives' happiness and their husbands' reenlistment decision, and how the family adapts to the army. Among the recommendations, the authors suggested that to increase retention of soldiers, supervisors and unit commanders should "create soldier perceptions that you care about families."

The transparent phrasing suggests the problem is less substance than PR.

To shift wives' perceptions and induce their allegiance, the army decided to bring them more completely into the institutional culture, to not only geographically link their husband's job with their home (life) but to engineer firm social links. In 1987, the army introduced what used to be called Family Support Groups, since renamed Family Readiness Groups (FRGs). (With rhetoric similar to that of the "welfare reform" movement President Bill Clinton endorsed, the shift in language is based on the notion that the military's role isn't really to "support" the wives, but to teach them to be self-reliant.) Modeled on the old, grassroots waiting wives' clubs that existed during the Vietnam War, when wives of deployed soldiers would meet and provide friendship and support to one another, the army hoped to re-create this sense of community. Thus it formalized and institutionalized the FRGs.

What that means in practical terms for Crystal, and other wives, is that there are programs in place to foster bonding—like the FRG meeting where she felt dismissed as a mere teen and didn't go back—as well as a host of recreational activities provided through the morale, welfare, and recreation department on every army post.

What this really reflects is a larger dynamic in the military characterized by military sociologist Charles Moskos as an institutional versus occupational (I/O) dynamic. According to Moskos, who developed his I/O theory in the late 1970s (and authored the "don't ask, don't tell" policy in the 1990s), there was a kind of "quiet malaise" many career officers were noting then in the armed services, "a sense that the recruits were being bought at the margin of the labor market, that officers were driven by careerism, and that reasons for military service had become obscured." The more desirable military that Moskos advocated was an "institutional" military, one where members are motivated by some higher purpose, a sense of sacrifice, a broad commitment to their work, and—this is where the families come in—a world in which wives, clustered in military housing and corralled into prefab social networks would live and breathe army. Dedication to the institution was all-encompassing, twenty-four hours a day. Of course it is much easier—and cheaper—for the military to control the troops within an institutional model. The subtle psychology that encourages self-sacrifice allows the military to commend the soldier for both unavoidable hardships like fighting wars, *and* avoidable ones like better pay, fewer deployments, better housing, better schools.

This institutional/occupational tug-of-war between two competing ideas manifests itself in nearly every aspect of contemporary military personnel policy.

For example, as the military struggles to meet its recruiting quotas and, even more important, its *reenlistment* quotas today, it weighs the benefits of both models. Should it increase the intangible benefits of military life (think *morale,* or *patriotism,* or *unit cohesion*) through groups like the FRGs or would better monetary compensation do the trick?

FOR CRYSTAL AND RICHARD money is a big problem.

Richard is paid $1,579 a month, plus he gets what's known as a basic allowance for subsistence, $242 untaxable dollars per month that all enlisted soldiers get for food. If Richard is out in the field or away for training, which happens frequently, the $242 food allowance is withheld, the theory being that the soldier doesn't need it because he eats in a mess hall then. Soldiers like Richard, who are in Afghanistan for an extended period, can draw both imminent danger pay ($150) and hardship duty pay ($100)— an extra $250 a month. (Of course, they're out the $242 subsistence allowance because the army is feeding them while they are deployed.) What that means for Crystal is that the monthly income is erratic. A best-case scenario: She gets $1,829 a month. A worst-case scenario: She gets $1,579.

Crystal and Richard are entirely typical. According to a 2002 Rand Corporation study 54 percent of army soldiers, whose median age is twenty-four, earn less than $2,000 a month. In the army, nearly 75 percent of soldiers have children—with 88 percent of those kids under the age of five. Sixty-four percent of the armed forces were deployed for more than thirty days in 2001, and only 9 percent described themselves as financially "comfortable and secure." Many families earned so little that they qualified for federal poverty programs. According to a 2001 army survey, 38 percent of spouses reported using WIC (Women and Infant Children—a federal food program for low-income pregnant or nursing women and their infants), free or reduced-price school lunch for their children, or Army Emergency Relief, or food assistance or food stamp programs in the past two years.

In Crystal's case, she used WIC a bit when little Richard was a baby. And, fortunately, she lives in army-run off-post housing, which means she pays no rent, heat, or electricity. But she does have other immutable monthly expenses, like phone bills, car insurance, and a hefty car payment ($400) that total $806 a month. She estimates that food costs her $300 a month. This leaves Crystal, who tries to keep a budget for the family, with $473 to cover all the remaining expenses: clothes for the three of them, money for gas, toys and diapers for little Richard. If the car needs new tires ($200 to $500 at Sears), or little Richard needs to graduate from his crib into a bed ($230 at Ikea), or one of them needs a new winter coat ($60 to $120 at Wal-Mart), the Solloways, who have maxed out their credit card and have no savings, are hard-pressed to make ends meet. If costlier troubles come along—as they inevitably do—things quickly grow dire. At the moment Crystal's car isn't working and they don't have enough money to repair it, so she's stranded at home during the day. "It would be nice to be able to save money so that we had some set aside when things happen," she says. "Like the engine going in my car. It'd be nice if we could fix that." (According to a 1999 DOD survey, most junior enlisted are similarly strapped, with 67 percent reporting savings of less than $1,000 and a monthly disposable income of $104.)

Thanks to a little nudging from her mother, Crystal has begun to seek out some federal assistance programs. Her mother did some research and discovered that little Richard might qualify for Head Start, a federally funded preschool program for low-income families. She had an application sent to Crystal and urged her to call the local Head Start office. Crystal did and, on this January 2003 day she is optimistic, looking forward to a home visit from Head Start and free preschool for Richard.

BY THE TIME I VISIT CRYSTAL in the spring of 2003, she has given up on preschools. She's had a home visit from the local Head Start worker and learns that they don't qualify for the program. The family income exceeds the cutoff amount by $300.

Meanwhile little Richard, who is approaching three, still doesn't speak much and grows frustrated as he tries to communicate in a garbled language that is completely unintelligible to all but his mother. He's recently gotten his first haircut and his pale, near-white hair which had hung down in soft curls to his shoulders is now trimmed short.

I have my camera with me, and when Richard grabs it from the table, Crystal takes it away from him. He looks as if he might cry, and I offer to take a picture of him "with his big-boy haircut."

He freezes and smiles for the camera. But before I can focus, the sound of a plane flying overhead sends him rushing to the couch where he has left a pair of toy binoculars. He picks them up, pushes the sheet that serves as a curtain aside, and peers into the sky. I snap some pictures and watch him, a big boy (nearly as tall as my own six-year-old) as he tumbles off the couch and tries to clamber onto a rocking horse—awkward, as if his body had grown too fast for his motor skills to keep pace.

I wonder aloud whether he could go to one of the preschool/daycare centers on post for free, but Crystal doesn't think so. "Besides," she says, "I've heard a couple of the other wives say they hadn't heard very good things about those daycare centers."

I am surprised to hear this. Not only are most of the DOD daycare/preschools highly rated by civilian early-childhood experts, I have visited one of the centers at Fort Drum and found it clean, cheerful, and well staffed—mostly by other army wives—who appeared competent and kind. The fee is assessed according to a sliding scale based on income and ranges from $42 to $124 per week, with someone in the Solloways' income bracket paying approximately $50 a week for full-time care. (That compares to say, a national average of $130 a week for preschool.) Also, Fort Drum wives whose husbands are deployed get two hours a *day* free. But Crystal, out of the loop and isolated, doesn't know this.

"The stuff about on-post childcare could just be rumors, because the army's well known for that," she admits. "But I just haven't heard good things about it." Anyway, she says, "he's a bit skittish about stuff like that." The woman she knows down the road recently tried to take him to vacation Bible school at her church. "She had to call me to come and bring him home because he was so upset," Crystal says.

Plus, Crystal admits that *she* is a bit skittish. When little Richard was younger, Crystal's mom put him in daycare for a week while she worked and Crystal returned to Fort Drum to greet her husband when he returned from Afghanistan the first time. "When Mom went in to pick him up one day, she could tell he had been crying all day and was sitting in the nastiest diaper," Crystal says. It turns out he was sick and their doctor was afraid he might be dehydrated, so he put the baby in the hospital overnight to monitor him. "He's had enough bad experiences with daycare," Crystal says.

Anyway, she's home with him now, so, Crystal figures, what's the point of daycare or preschool?

It's true that from time to time Crystal and Richard discuss whether she could get a job that might help their financial problems. "I definitely would like to go back to work," says Crystal, who worked throughout high school at a Dairy Queen in Bowling Green. "I loved it when I worked."

But Crystal has a few strikes against her. First, she has only the Dairy Queen job to cite on an application. Second, she never graduated from high school. Third, though she intends to get her G.E.D. (General Educational Development) diploma she hasn't yet. Next, the daycare near her house charges $140 a week for full-time care and, like the on-post childcare, operates only from 9 A.M. to 5 P.M., not the kind of hours she's likely to garner off the bat at, say, Burger King. Her husband's erratic, on-call schedule means that he can't be counted on to regularly pick up his son at 5 P.M. (and what happens when he's deployed, say, nine out of twelve months, like last year?) And finally, she lives in Watertown, where the unemployment rate is high, the local job market is oversaturated with military spouses looking for low-skill service jobs, and the minimum-wage job she's likely to get works out to a pretax income of $1.15 per hour more than her daycare costs of approximately $4 per hour.

Still, Crystal talks yearningly of work. With the blindly cheerful optimism of any teen looking toward a bright future, she says that she's going to get a real job someday. "I plan to do something in the medical field," she tells me. "Since I was in elementary school, I've always told my mom I wanted to be a brain surgeon." Crystal tells me that she stayed on the honor roll for most of high school and she figures she'd be a good doctor. "I get into all the E.R. shows and especially the maternity ward stuff," she says. "But now, I'd just like to get my G.E.D., so I can't see really going into that right now. Maybe when Richard gets out of the service I can go back to school." This is almost too much to think about. "I can't really go back to school right now, especially with the baby and Richard's schedule." She pauses. Thoughtful. And her voice trails off. "But maybe, when the time comes. . . ."

For now, though, Crystal tells me, she has some news: she is pregnant.

CRYSTAL AND RICHARD are both the backbone of the army and the bane of its existence—or in DOD lingo, its "human dimension challenges." Though folks in the service like to say that the force is a microcosm of the United States—by which they usually mean "we've got our share of slackers, trailer trash, and the attendant social problem"—the military is *not* in fact a microcosm.

According to the DOD's annual "Population Representation" report its workforce is much younger than the general population, with 46 percent of all enlisted soldiers between 17 and 24 years old. This is in contrast to civilians, where only 15 percent of the labor force is between 17 and 24 years old. (The marines are the youngest, with 68 percent of the enlisted force under age 25; the air force is the oldest with 37 percent under age 25.) Even among officers, those who have a four-year college degree under their belts, the average age is only 26. The physical fitness requirements, an "up or out" promotion policy that forces the unpromoted out of the service, and generous retirement packages that kick in after 20 years of service mean that most soldiers get out by the time they're 40 years old. To get a sense of what this looks like from the vantage point of someone going gray, consider that a fifth of the civilian labor force is over 50 years old; among the military's enlisted members, only two-tenths of 1 percent are.

When it comes to race, the military is also slightly out of sync with the general U.S. population. Hispanics make up only 9 percent of enlisted sol-

diers but are 13 percent of the young civilian population. African American cans make up only 13 percent of the civilian labor force in the 18- to 44-year-old range, but they make up 22 percent of enlisted soldiers: the army has the highest percentage with 29 percent; the marines, the lowest with 17 percent.

There has been some talk from politicians like U.S. Representative Charles Rangel (Democrat-New York) that African Americans' overrepresentation in the army means that they are disproportionately cannon fodder in Iraq and Afghanistan, closer scrutiny of the figures doesn't bear this out. Not only have African Americans not died in a higher proportion than their Caucasian counterparts in these wars, but African Americans are also slightly *underrepresented* in combat jobs. So while African Americans' overall numbers in the military may be higher, they have been more likely to fill support jobs. According to military sociologists Charles Moskos and John Sibley Butler, the reasons for this are twofold. One, given the inequity of education in our country, African Americans are more likely to get an inferior education and thus to score lower on the military's entrance exam, the Armed Services Vocational Aptitude Battery (ASVAB). That tends to push many into such lower skilled support fields as food preparation and maintenance. Two, those who do make decent scores on the ASVAB have more say about what fields they want to pursue in the army—and they make different choices. Some studies have shown that African Americans enter the service for slightly different reasons than Caucasians. An amazing 50 percent of eligible young African American men (i.e., those who met the physical and educational requirements) actually applied to enter the armed services in the 1980s. There is speculation that because they face more discrimination in the civilian job market, African American youths find the military is an attractive alternative. For these soldiers, the draw may be less gung-ho patriotism than career training and skills that they can later apply in the civilian job market. If so, opting for the infantry may appear less attractive than, say, a job in computer programming.

Meanwhile, when it comes to gender parity the military is, not surprisingly, severely skewed. Only 14 percent of enlisted soldiers are female com-

pared with 47 percent of the civilian labor force. While direct combat positions remain closed to women, 92 percent of the career fields across the services are open to women. How "direct combat" is defined can vary. The air force has opened up the highest number of jobs to women (99 percent), and the army has opened the fewest (91 percent). In actual numbers, the air force has the highest proportion of women serving (19 percent), while the marines have the lowest (6 percent).

When it comes to education, most enlisted soldiers have a high school diploma (96 percent) but only 28 percent of them have a college degree. Among officers—where college is a prerequisite—all of course have degrees.

Geographically the military isn't quite a microcosm of the country either. Forty-three percent of recruits come from the South, while only 15 percent are from the more populous Northeast.

When it comes to class, the DOD says most of its soldiers come from slightly lower socioeconomic backgrounds than average Americans but that the armed services basically mirror the population as a whole—up to a point. Not surprisingly, those in the top quarter of the nation's income and education bracket, for example, doctors, stockbrokers, lawyers, and politicians, are not sending their sons and daughters for active duty in the army (only four out of 435 members of Congress that voted us into Iraq have kids in the military). A mere 8 percent of new recruits come from families with a father or mother in the "professions."

Given all the above, it's clear that the military is *not* a microcosm. So when folks invoke the term—"We're just a microcosm of the rest of the country," Fort Drum public affairs specialist Rachel Tolliver tells me. "The military is, in many ways, a microcosm of our society," retired General Wesley Clark frequently reminds the press—what *microcosm* really means, I think, is that the military views itself as representative and ordinary. *Microcosm* isn't a reference to the actual demographics, it's a reference to Thornton Wilder's *Our Town*—Grovers Corner, U.S.A. The military sees itself as an extension of the vast American middle class—with middle-class values, middle-class incomes, and middlebrow tastes.

But keeping soldiers and their families convinced that they are card-carrying members of the middle class has taken some fancy footwork over the years. Making sure that service members reenlist, especially when the economy is strong and jobs are more plentiful, has occasionally meant coughing up some pay raises.

According to Col. Mike Jordan, U.S. Air Force (Ret.) of the Military Officer Association of America, military pay has swung back and forth on a pendulum over the past four decades. During the Vietnam War, when the draft was in place, the military didn't have to entice anyone with a competitive salary. "With the advent of an all-volunteer force in 1973, the military's pay tables had to be reconstructed so that we could attract and retain the right quality to sustain an all-volunteer force," Jordan says, marking the first effort to bring military wages up close to those of civilians. Obviously, most of the jobs weren't directly comparable—there aren't too many infantrymen, fighter pilots, or tank drivers in the private sector—but researchers and advocates looked at education background, training, and experience to develop a new pay scale and successfully made a case for Congress to approve pay hikes.

But in the mid-'70s Congress capped the pay raises so that by 1980 military pay rates once again dropped way behind those of private-sector employees. Referring to the servicemen recruited during this period of low retention and relaxed requirements (66 percent of new recruits had a high school diploma in 1980, versus 92 percent today), Jordan invokes the term *hollow force.* (Military sociologists also note that this period saw a spike in drug use and crime, a drop in morale, and a sense that "the best and the brightest" had left the services, with test scores and education background of new recruits slumping dramatically.) "There were huge retention problems, especially among those enlisted men and officers who had already reenlisted one time," says Jordan. To address the problem, Congress agreed to two massive consecutive pay raises of 11 and 13 percent in 1980 and 1981.

But instead of gradually keeping pace with comparable incremental raises after that the military once again fell behind until, in 1987 and 1988, the joint chiefs of staff complained that retention was a problem and insisted this was due to the poor pay. (The U.S. military is legally forbidden to unionize, so members must vote with their feet. Other Western countries, notably Germany and the Netherlands, have unionized militaries. German soldiers earn overtime pay and are tried in civilian courts, rather than courts-martial, when necessary.) At that point Congress not only authorized significant pay raises again, but the military also restructured and targeted the raises so that those in the middle ranks got the most substantial ones. Since 1988, military pay has risen as much as 30 percent for some soldiers.

Today, military pay is about 4 or 5 percent behind that of the private sector in the Employment Cost Index, a way of measuring the rate at which wages grow in the private sector. This is a vast improvement over 1998, when military salaries lagged by 13.5 percent.

Still, Jordan acknowledges that comparisons with civilian pay rates can be tricky, especially at the lower end of the spectrum. "When you look at a person who graduates from high school and goes to work flipping burgers at McDonald's versus the one who enlists in the army, the latter is paid better," he says. "But when the soldier has two or three years of intense training under his belt, you really ought to assess this in terms of someone having a year or two of college—or technical-school training. And if you look at that person five, six, or seven years down the line, when they have several years of experience on top of it, it's not right to compare them to mere high school grads. If you look at their pay then and compare it to someone with two years of college, then they're way behind."

Further complicating this straight comparison is, of course, the work they do. Leaving aside the occasional massacre—like the 1984 San Ysidro, California, customer who gunned down twenty-one McDonald's employees and customers—working at McDonald's is rarely life threatening. Typically, in the civilian sector there is a built-in monetary acknowledgment when a job requires workers to occasionally risk their lives (for example, among police or firefighters).

In the case of Crystal and Richard—and the 140,000 other soldiers de-

ployed at any time to Iraq, Afghanistan, Haiti, or Korea—Congress has decided to acknowledge this risk, but within the narrowest parameters. Soldiers who are deployed for more than six months get additional combat
pay. Once they're stateside, their *willingness* to sacrifice their lives loses its
monetary value.

How much is soldiering worth to us? In 2002 the military asked the
Rand Corporation to study whether its poorer enlisted families were ade-
quately paid. Were they really suffering, and if so, why? In its report Rand
hedged. It's not exactly a question of whether they're deserving or unde-
serving poor, Rand said. It's a question of whether or not they're really
poor. "Military members are still twice as likely as civilians to have financial problems," Rand admitted. But it insisted that "financial problems are
not strongly related to family income." Instead, "[t]his finding suggests that
financial problems are shaped by spending patterns and management skills
rather than by income itself." Pay increases are misdirected: the problem is
poor management, not poor pay.

ON A HOT SEPTEMBER AFTERNOON, when Crystal is eight months pregnant,
she sits at the table in her apartment fanning herself with the folded TV
section of the *Watertown Times*. Richard, now three years old, is stationed
in his usual spot in the easy chair before the TV, sprawled out, wearing only
a diaper. Occasionally he shouts out a jumbled set of sounds to the cartoon
characters who skitter across the screen, but mostly he lies still, staring im-
passively. (Tomorrow he goes for his first day of preschool at Benchmark
Family Services, a neighborhood center that Crystal describes as a "preschool, daycare, and early intervention center." Though Richard made too
much for them to qualify for Head Start, Crystal has decided to take her
mom's advice about preschool and send him to Benchmark for half-days,
three times a week. It costs $180 a month, and her mom has offered to help
pay if Crystal finds she can't swing it.

Crystal doesn't say she is looking forward to the break from twenty-
four-hour single parenting, but she looks like she could use it. Dressed in

jeans and a light blue T-shirt, a slight sheen of sweat on her face and a hint of circles under her eyes, Crystal is looking more tired than I have seen her before.

She hasn't slept well the past two nights.

The night before last, a neighbor down the road said there was an emergency battalion meeting for the wives' Family Readiness Group because two soldiers from their unit, the 1-87 (1st Battalion, 87th Regiment) had been killed and one injured. "She said she knew they were from Richard's unit but didn't know what company they were from," Crystal says. Crystal offered to keep the neighbor's daughter so she could go to the meeting; the neighbor offered to fill her in when she got back. "Don't worry," her neighbor told her. "If Richard had been killed or injured, you'd have heard by now." Still, Crystal would feel better if there were names.

Crystal had immediately turned on CNN but found no mention of the attack. She tried to concentrate on her neighbor's reassurance that she would have heard by now if Richard had been hurt and the neighbor's knowledge that the battalion wasn't all together in one place. "There was some relief to know that not all of his unit was together and maybe he was far away at the time," she says. "I don't want to be rude, but it was one thing I was hoping for." Meanwhile, she kept waiting for the phone to ring. "And I didn't know, would the phone ring telling me there was something wrong, or would the phone ring with someone telling me he's okay?" As more time passed she took comfort in the fact that she'd heard nothing. "If it had been Richard, I'd have heard by now," she kept telling herself.

Finally Richard called at 1:00 A.M., approximately thirty-two hours after Crystal first got word of the deaths. "He knew the guys who had been killed, but he wasn't anywhere near the area where it happened," Crystal says. She sighs, and again fans herself with the paper.

Two weeks later, on the morning of September 29, Richard's unit would be directly involved in an ambush.

That morning, while Richard and the rest of the 1st platoon hung out in the mess hall in Shkin, Afghanistan—Richard complaining to his buddies that a letter he sent to Hugh Hefner asking for a special tour of the

Playboy Mansion for his unit had been rejected—the 2nd platoon is out on patrol. It is attacked. When a Humvee returns to the base with a wounded 2nd platoon soldier, Richard and other members of the 1st clamber aboard and rush back to join the firefight. For the next twelve hours the soldiers would battle across a ridge; at the end of the day nineteen-year-old Pfc. Evan O'Neill, one of Richard's buddies, is dead.

But for now Crystal remains ignorant of the pending battle. She gets a phone call from Richard once every week or so. She tries not to watch the news and start worrying in between calls. Truth is, she's not that big on watching the news anyway. "I'm a soap addict, actually," she confesses.

Today she's worried about how she'll survive while little Richard is at preschool three mornings a week. "I'm going to be, like, what do I do? I'll be lost for a week. I guess I'll watch my soaps and do my latchhook," she says, referring to a new latchhook rug kit that will evolve into her favorite 100-acre-woods resident, Eeyore. "There'll be nobody's diapers to change or anybody to make food for." She sighs, perhaps forgetting that by the end of the following month she'll have a newborn to diaper and feed.

Still, she's not worried. She thinks she's evolved into a pretty good mom—and indeed, she does exude a calm competence with her son. "Before, I did not have patience whatsoever," she says. "We've learned how to deal a lot better. . . . Being with him twenty-four–seven, I can't pawn him off on my mom when he and I are having a bad day. Now I either go to my room and sit and count backwards, or I take him for a walk so we're not cooped up together." She says she's also gotten a lot better at not giving in to him when he has a tantrum. "Sometimes I pretty much wanna scream myself, but I've learned when I can comfort and when I need to let him cry."

When I ask how her husband is with him, she answers instead how she *hopes* he'll be one day. "I think when he gets older he'll mature into a family man." According to Crystal, some of her family and friends think he's not the best father. "I keep telling everyone it's not that he's a bad husband or father, it's just that we're so young," she says, admitting that when she first had the baby he wouldn't hold him or feed him. "Richard had a really bad childhood and stuff. And he's really young. Everyone says to me, 'You're really young, too.' Richard can just get up and say, 'I'm leaving' when he gets fed up, but I can't do that," she says.

Crystal, who clearly falls on the nature side of the divide when it comes to the nature–nurture debate, sees her own parenting as instinctive; she hopes Richard's will be acquired. Rather than seeing her circumstances— basically single parenthood much of the time—as pushing her into an exclusive role, she credits biology for her superior parenting skills. "I think guys just have a harder time picking things up than females," she says. "I'm not as worried about it as everybody else." She says her husband is doing a lot better than she thought he would. "He was a teenage dad. I'm sure that was scary, 'cause it was for me. But moms have got that maternal instinct that bonds you to kids. And dads don't have that. They have to learn. Everyone just expected Richard to fall into place like a regular father would. But I expect when he gets older he'll want to do more with the kids." She is arguing with an unseen interlocutor and worries the topic in circles. "I think it's the age thing with Richard. Once he gets older he'll realize the family thing is okay. I know Richard is doing his own bonding at his own pace. I tell everyone when Richard totally cuts off from the baby and me, then I'll worry. But I see him making an effort. I'm actually, I'm not too worried about it."

In the middle of this discussion, little Richard has spilled his juice on the floor and has torn himself away from *Blue's Clues* to point out the spill to his mother. As Crystal pulls herself off her chair with a huff of effort to clean it up, Richard clambers over to get a good look at my laptop. I am reminded that I was going to give Crystal copies of the pictures I took of him a few months back and apologize that they didn't turn out. Richard's eyes had those peculiar red spots.

Crystal says, "Don't worry about it," and settles back into the chair, relieved to be sitting again in this heat and happy, perhaps, to have ended the conversation about Richard's parenting.

Outside the sun is streaming down, but Crystal has kept the dark sheets that she uses as living room curtains closed, trying to keep the apartment cool on this Indian summer day.

The apartment, of the cheapest construction, is drafty in the winter and hot and stuffy in the summer. Because the army is paying the electric bill, residents aren't allowed to use air conditioners—even if they could afford them. Crystal complains and laughs about an upstairs neighbor, Spec. Rachel Tolliver, who is trying desperately to muster some asthma symptoms so she can get a special medical dispensation to acquire and use an air conditioner. ("It's cruel and unusual punishment to deny us air conditioners," Tolliver will later explain, insisting that she's just trying to do some preventive care, because if she doesn't get the unit "the heat probably is really gonna kill me.") Crystal, though, is complacent and cools herself with her paper fan, trying not to move her very pregnant self around too much, and consoling herself with the thought that she has only one more summer here, only slightly more than a year left in the army. "Richard's ETS is January 2005," she says. "And don't ask me what ETS stands for because I don't know. I just know that's his get-out date."

Crystal says her husband is thinking about becoming a U.S. marshal when he gets out. "I'm not absolutely positive what they do, but apparently they have jurisdiction anywhere in the U.S. and they escort prisoners on planes and stuff." Richard is young, has a high school diploma and no college, but Crystal says he's confident about his chances of getting the position. "How many twenty-two-year-olds do you know who have had two six-month tours in hostile fire zones?" he asked her.

On the other hand, he's also been talking about going to U.S. Army Special Forces school, the elite unit specializing in unconventional warfare, which he's told Crystal will require committing to at least two more years in the army.

What does Crystal think about more time in the army, more time here?

She shrugs, making a sweeping gesture around the apartment—claustrophobic and antiseptic with bland, industrial-style carpeting, cracked linoleum in the kitchen, small and unframed windows—all repeating in a vista of identical homes no matter which window she peers out. She looks, not unhappy exactly, but worn down.

THE SOLLOWAYS' sprawling apartment complex sits in the middle of one of Watertown's civilian neighborhoods of modest homes. After wending your way past an eclectic mix of wood-frame and small, brick houses, you enter Mountaineer Estates, a privately owned and operated collection of apartments and duplexes that the military has leased for a decade. Presumably the "mountaineer" bit is a nod toward Fort Drum's 10th Mountain Division; the "estates" is a transparent aspiration.

There are 244 units at Mountaineer Estates, with the bulk of them going to the army's youngest families, who sit at the bottom of the army pay scale. For example, 71 percent of the units house junior enlisted and junior noncommissioned officers (NCOs), many of whom have a base pay of $2,000 a month. A few of the buildings are duplexes and are set aside for twenty-eight officers' families, but most of the fifty-six two-story buildings house boxy, two-bedroom apartments—two apartments upstairs, two downstairs.

The housing area looks like any enlisted housing area—which is to say that the trees are sparsely planted, the grounds are unimaginative, and the communal areas, pockmarked with bare patches, indicate that the playground is well used, if not particularly well maintained. The buildings of course are identical; two-story structures so nondescript with their brick-and-aluminum siding (is it beige?) that I must consult my notes to summon up their color, only an hour after I've gone (and this was the seventh time I'd visited).

On this sleepy September Tuesday at the Mountaineer Estates, I leave Crystal and little Richard in the apartment and make my way across the grounds. Today is the last official day of summer vacation; school starts tomorrow. With most of the men in this entire housing complex gone—deployed to Afghanistan with the 10th Mountain Division two months ago—there is lethargy in the air, a feeling that the impetus is gone for these mothers of young children to hew to a schedule of grocery shopping, cleaning, and cooking. Three young moms sit around a child's pink plastic picnic table puffing cigarettes as if the bench were a barstool and their Sprites gin and tonic. A gang of girls bike back and forth from the end of the cul-de-sac to the stop sign, using a stack of discarded moving boxes as a kind of midway jump ramp. Movers pace themselves in and out of an apartment with a chair, a box, a dresser. Two women sit chatting on a bench overlooking the playground. In front of them two toddlers push matching plastic lawn mowers across the grass.

In 2001 the army decided to survey these wives—or others like them at various posts across the country. It turns out most families don't think much of the housing the army makes available to them: 37 percent of army families were dissatisfied or very dissatisfied with their housing. Among the problems they cited were the poor or substandard condition of the property and the poor quality of local schools. Further, 35 percent said they were dissatisfied or very dissatisfied with the respect the army shows spouses. Another 37 percent said they were dissatisfied or very dissatisfied with the concern the soldiers' units had for families. Twenty percent are, in general, dissatisfied or very dissatisfied with the kind of life they can have in the army.

When it comes to Fort Drum in particular, a 2004 survey of 800 families here and a series of focus groups indicated that they too had complaints about housing and developed a wish list. They wanted more storage space, more playgrounds in better locations, and, given the length and severity of Watertown winters, some indoor play space. James Corriveau, who is heading up a housing initiative on the post says Fort Drum is going to be building lots of new housing—and this time it will be "sensitive" to a desire for more attractive neighborhoods.

He also hopes to address another common complaint: the rules that govern nearly every aspect of the families' private lives. While the army has a vested interest in creating a "total institution"—meaning a seamless world that bleeds effortlessly between work and home—wives are most outspoken about this particular issue. And it's not surprising.

Fort Drum's "Resident's Guide to Family Housing," given to each new-comer, is a 129-page document of *will be*'s and *never*'s. "Grass will be cut frequently enough to maintain grass below four inches in height," it says. "Grounds around building will be kept free of litter, debris and clutter that might pose an eyesore to others," it says. "Bare spots on lawns will be re-seeded and holes filled in when needed," it says. "Avoid drinking Kool-Aid in carpeted areas," it warns. "Sponsors will ensure their children do not leave bicycles or toys in the street or on the sidewalks." "Holiday lights will be lit only from dusk till 10 P.M. and should be removed by the second week in January." "Pets will be leashed and under the control of a responsible family member 12 years of age or older," it says. Dogs are mandated to get an identifying microchip inserted in their ears. A two-pet maximum adds that "Litters will be disposed of before 90 days of age."

Clotheslines, trampolines, fences, waterbeds, ceiling fans, gardens, painting, and wallpaper borders are not permitted—except with special dispensation (home improvement request form for fences, written permis-sion from the Facilities Management Section for waterbeds, excavation permit for requisite umbrella-style clotheslines, etc.). Energy conservation is required ("Wash only full loads of clothes"; "run your dishwasher only with a full load and then let them air dry rather than going through the drying cycle"; "microwave meals when possible.")

And be forewarned: "The Chief of the Housing Division, his designee, or the Command reserves the right to conduct inspections of family hous-ing in order to ensure a healthy, sanitary environment." Then, when it's time for families to move, there's a white-glove inspection. "But it's a bogus inspection because the army goes in there and paints everything anyway," Corriveau says. (Usually it is the wives who are left with these chores. "My husband is *always* conveniently sent out of state during our cross-country moves," says Fort Drum army wife Veoletta Hayward with a rueful chuckle, echoing a comment I heard over and over from wives.) With typical mili-tary thoroughness, a vast and detailed checklist tells residents what they need to do. They range from the common-sense mandates of "carpets will be vacuumed, then either steam-cleaned or shampooed," to the kinds of tasks that even *überhausfrau* Nancy Shea doesn't require in her exhaustive *Army Wife* guide to domesticity:

> *Radiators, ductwork, heat vents, and grills must be wiped down to remove dirt, sediment, and stains. Baseboard heaters will be dismantled to remove build-up of dirt, dust, and animal hair and put back together prior to inspection. Grillwork for heaters or humidifiers will be removed, cleaned of any dirt and dust, and then reinstalled.*

"Clearing quarters inspections have always been something that nagged at military families," says Fort Drum's Corriveau, who hopes to change things over the next few years. While there isn't literally a white glove, the inspection is traditionally meticulous. "And this comes at an already stressful time for families who are ready to pull out of town for good, but here you are down on your hands and knees scrubbing under the stove first," says Corriveau.

Families surveyed also complained about the lack of privacy. Not only is noise a problem—especially when the duplexes are set up so that one couple's headboard is likely to rest against the party wall where their neighbors have their headboard—but the emphasis on common space means a lack of exterior privacy. "Families want their own backyards with fences," Corriveau says, "so they can sit down and have a private evening outside away from their neighbors' sight."

To further complicate the blurring of the private and public, colleagues and neighbors, work and homelife, one person per area is appointed by the post commander to serve as a leader of that particular development. "Usually it's the senior green-suiter who's in charge of discipline in the area," says Randa Ortlieb, who works at Fort Drum's Housing Division, explaining that the highest ranking officer lands the job and his wife often volunteers to become the area "mayor," the one that supervises how the community center and picnic areas will be used and represents the area in community meetings on post. The soldier is required to solve disputes on anything from complaints about late-night noise to those about dog excrement on communal land. It's extra work for the family involved—typically dealt with in the officer's or NCO's "off" hours. "Sometimes the senior green-suiter doesn't want the job," admits Ortlieb, "but they're appointed by the garrison commander, so it's not a question of 'wanna,' it's 'you shall.' "

"Congratulations on your appointment," a form letter sent by the garrison commander says. "I trust you are a troubleshooter and problem solver who knows where to go for help." A kind of Big Brother of Housing, the officer is ordered to do such things as "visually monitor energy conservation in assigned area and bring to occupant's attention such wasteful practices as exterior lights left on during the daylight hours, doors, windows, and garages left open during the heating season, and excess watering of lawns." He is further reminded that "your role as Area Coordinator is an important part of ensuring our military families live in safe and secure homes. I challenge you to make a difference."

Depending on the collection of residents, these "coordinator" jobs can be either insignificant or substantial. But in any case, even the noncoordinator, junior families in the community tend to chafe under what they feel is an ever-watchful eye of a superior—who shouldn't know or care whether they leave their kid's trike out in the driveway or have a rowdy party Thursday night.

How these regulations are enforced can vary. Danette Long once received a written "warning" because her boys left a baseball bat out on their front lawn overnight—and the base had a three strikes, you're out policy; other times she knows the kids have left stuff in the yard and there have been no repercussions.

In some ways, the labyrinth of rules echo those in the country's hottest, new, planned communities—where uniformity of exterior alludes to uniformity of values within. I am reminded of Disney's model town, Celebration, a collection of 8,000 faux-quaint homes built in 1996 by the Disney Corporation. One of the first experiments in what is known as new urbanism, Disney built an entire town from scratch, including schools, a town hall, stores, and a library—then developed a vast list of rules for its residents. Families wanting to live in pristine Celebration had to sign a covenant, which spelled out everything from the kinds of shrubs permitted in the front yards to the kinds of curtains that could be hung in front windows. Though Celebration sits in central Florida a few miles from Disney World, it hews to a vision—architecturally and meteorologically—that is pure New England; in the fall, colored leaves are trucked in to be scattered on the sidewalks, and in the winter fake snow falls from machines discreetly placed on lampposts.

The more apt, though less common, term for this building trend is *neo-traditionalism.*

Like Disney World itself, where all the messy realities of life are tucked away in subterranean corridors—food deliveries, trash pickup, employee locker rooms, kitchens discreetly out of public sight—fantasy rests on façade. Coming from New York City as I do, where people live their lives on the street—playing cards, barbecuing, pissing, kissing, fighting—Celebration is a foreign country. Described in the original brochures as a place that "takes you back to that time of innocence," I am struck by the yearning. And the logic that spurs its articulation. Celebration is a place where trim lawns and tasteful shutters are symbols of clean living, where rules mandating that the fences be picket and the play equipment nonplastic fuel illusions that Norman Rockwell's imps frolic inside, where cleanliness is still a virtue—invoked in opposition to the messy moral relativism that clutters things elsewhere—and where complementary and orderly exteriors are to be read as shorthand for a harmonious world within.

In many ways military housing communities—heavy on the same rules, though shy on most of the amenities—are Celebration wannabes.

MEANWHILE, back at Mountaineer Estates, *real* leaves blow around the trunks of its scrawny, token trees. And on this November day a lower-case C celebration is going on. There's a new baby in the house.

Matthew James Solloway was born on October 29, 2003. Weighing 7.5 pounds, he arrived after a relatively short labor.

Crystal's mom rushed up from Kentucky, when Crystal's doctor said she was two centimeters dilated—driving sixteen hours through the night—but Crystal didn't go into labor until a week later. Once Crystal's contractions started around 2:00 P.M., things progressed rapidly and Matthew made his appearance at 10:20 P.M.

Little Richard spent the night with the upstairs neighbor, Rachel Tolliver. Crystal's husband was still in Afghanistan. Crystal's mom, Beth, went through labor with her.

Crystal was glad to have her. "I mean, when my mom was still in Kentucky and was all freaked out I'd go into labor without her, I said, 'Don't worry.' It wasn't so scary as if it was my first time and I was doing it alone," she tells me in November, when the baby is three weeks old. "I told her, 'It's going to be weird being by myself, but if you can't make it, I'll be okay.' "

Across the living room a new piece of furniture has been added. Just about a foot behind the central recliner is a new white bassinet. When mewling cries emit from it, Beth hustles out of the bedroom and picks up the baby. "What's the matter? You wanna look around? What's the matter?" She puts the baby over her shoulder and begins to pat Matthew's back.

"My mom saved up all of her vacation time," Crystal says. "She had three weeks saved and she's using one extra week, unpaid." Beth smiles at Crystal.

Crystal knows she's lucky to have a devoted and supportive family that pinch-hits as best it can given the distance between them. She mentions that one of Richard's aunts also came out from Michigan the weekend she gave birth—new baby clothes, burp cloths, car seat, baby swing, and stroller in tow. "And me and my mom have always gotten along really well," Crystal says. "She's just crazy over the grandkids."

"I am," Beth agrees, a picture of tender efficiency as she paces the living room, cooing at the fussing newborn.

As for Richard, he called Crystal from Afghanistan the day after the baby was born to congratulate her, but he's recently called back with bad news. He thought he'd be back in December, but the return date has been changed to January or February. In fact, due to a change in army deployment policy, Richard will remain in Afghanistan for nearly a year this time. It will be May before he is back; his new baby will be seven months old.

Meanwhile, Crystal's gotten another bit of bad news. "Richard's preschool teachers asked me if he had vision problems, because he holds books so close to his face," Crystal says, acknowledging that she and her mother had wondered the same thing, given how close he likes to be to the TV. At the teachers' suggestion, Crystal took him to a pediatric ophthalmologist this week. Turns out he has a condition called ocular albinism, which means his eyes don't have melanin pigment. This is an inherited defect. Women carry, but don't get it; their male offspring have a one in two chance of acquiring it. (Crystal's brother has it, too, and is "legally blind," having gotten his first pair of glasses when he was not even two years old.)

According to the National Organization for Albinism and Hypopigmentation, this lack of pigment can manifest itself in various ways, ranging from a serious reduction in visual acuity to nystagmus ("an involuntary back-and-forth movement of the eyes") to "crossed or 'lazy' eye," to "sensitivity to bright light and glare." Interestingly, the organization also notes that it can cause slight, usually temporary developmental delays and, because the children's depth perception is impaired it can affect their coordination. Because the person's eyes don't block out light, flash-lit photos typically depict them with red eyes.

MEANWHILE, though Crystal will probably not be here to enjoy it, the army has announced that Mountaineer Estates will be history by 2008. Twenty years and millions of dollars later, Fort Drum has acknowledged that its housing experiment has failed. Neither off-post nor on-post housing is working the way planners had hoped.

Off-post the complaints are loud. When the army began to enter into agreements with local builders for long-time leases of apartment complexes like Mountaineer Estates, it touted the program as a way of integrating army families into the local community, spreading out their spending dollars, and lessening the burden of absorbing all those army brats in any one school district. But with some families as far as twenty-five miles from the post, it's been a real hardship for the soldiers to get to work on snowy days and a hardship for their isolated families—some in towns so small there was not even a gas station. Security has sometimes been a problem, as these mini-army communities fall under civilian police jurisdiction—suffering under cash-strapped local budgets—and there was a series of rapes a few years back. Also, the families are far from the army services that would support and seduce them. So, as the army's leases expire over the next few years, it is abandoning this non-working experiment. In the case of Crystal's Mountaineer Estates, which was leased for 20 years in 1988, the army will completely phase families out by 2008. There is now a joint military-civilian panel looking at options for the 2,000 privately owned apartments the military is returning to local owners. But with the military renting the apartments for $1,000 each when comparable space in the Watertown area runs closer to $600 a month, it seems likely the owners will take a serious hit—if they manage to rent the apartments at all.

Meanwhile, even Fort Drum's on-post housing has failed to win hearts and minds. Residents have complained that it's cramped, lacks privacy, isn't soundproof, and needs storage space and proper ventilation.

Not to worry, says Corriveau, the one overseeing the new Residential Community Initiative at Fort Drum. With this experimental program, the military pairs with a private company and creates a new, jointly owned private company. The new company allows the military to borrow money to finance building—something it was not allowed to do before the 1996 congressional approval of the Military Housing Privatization Initiative.

Since most military housing is fifty to sixty years old, was built on the cheap and is now falling apart, the military has plans to add more than 138,000 new units over the next five years. Many of the units are being designed in the "new urban" tradition, model communities for model families. The air force and the navy have closed deals with private companies, and the army is already working with new partners at Fort Hood, Texas

(5,900 units), Fort Campbell, Kentucky (4,255 units), and Fort Bragg, North Carolina (5,580 units).*

For its part, Fort Drum is hooking up with Lend Lease Actus to borrow $329 million for building. The deal is slated to close February 2005, with building beginning immediately after. Not only will there be 1,244 new homes built over the following five years, but the existing two-bedroom apartments will be converted to larger duplexes and there will be new community centers, bike paths, parks, and open spaces. "This is what the army's all about now," Corriveau tells me, showing me plans for charming, New England-style homes with porches and dormer windows and picket fences—nothing like the bland cookie-cutter duplexes that proliferate today. "Some of the FRGs [Family Readiness Groups] have complained that you can't build unit cohesion and camaraderie if families live thirty miles away from the post, so we're bringing them in closer to help address that." The houses will spread out in waves around central community areas like playgrounds, swimming pools, community centers, housing offices, maybe a golf course. Reminding me that the army "enlists soldiers but re-tains families," Corriveau says, "we're building for the three Rs: readiness, recruiting, and retention."

These will be model communities and every aspect of their design is being carefully considered. Intrinsic to the new urbanism American dream, apparently, is that commandment of capitalism: Thou shalt covet thy neighbor's life. "These houses will promote retention," Corriveau says. "Because the junior enlisted types of homes will look out across the green at senior enlisted and they'll say, 'I want that.' " Persuaded that envy and the military hierarchy can motivate families, Corriveau says the buildings will hammer this home. "The houses will say, 'See what happens if you stick with the army!' "

To bring all this about at Fort Drum, the army has hired the services of Looney, Ricks Kiss—the same architects that built Disney's model town, Celebration.

*   *   *

WHEN MATTHEW IS A FEW WEEKS OLD, Crystal drives down to Kentucky to spend Thanksgiving with her mother. Thanksgiving spreads into Christmas, Christmas into New Year's, New Year's into St. Patrick's Day.

Five months later, when I try to visit Crystal in March 2004, no one answers the phone at her apartment and her voice-mail box is full. Later, the upstairs neighbor, who has a key to the apartment and has been bringing in the mail, tells me Crystal must still be in Kentucky because no one has heard from her in months. When I track her down in Bowling Green, Crystal says the engine in her truck died again. This time it needed to be completely replaced. Because she was strapped for cash, her brother and his girlfriend's father have been working to install a new engine. That took some time. Then, just when they finished, her transmission went. So the truck's back in the shop getting a new transmission. When that's finished, then she's "definitely" heading back up to Watertown.

Meanwhile, little Richard's gotten his first pair of glasses. "I don't know if he hasn't gotten used to them yet, but he doesn't like to wear them, not too much," she says. "When he's watching TV sometimes, we'll put them on him," she says. She uses "we" the same way an old married couple automatically does—but to refer to the parenting team of her mother and herself. "He'll wear them for about thirty minutes, then take them off. Then we'll try them again. But when he goes to play, we take them off of him so they won't get broke or anything."

She hasn't spoken to her husband in a couple of weeks, but he was still making occasional murmurs about reenlisting. "But only if they're offering bonuses!" Crystal says, laughing. He wants to reenlist to stay in Watertown. For her part Crystal thinks she'd like to go to Texas or Louisiana. "I've never been there, but I hear they're nice places."

Crystal's coming-of-age story is still evolving. Whether she will "be all that she can be" remains to be seen. All the elements of her story are lined up. Just as the army brags that it takes a boy and makes him a man, so, too, do the hardships of army life seem to take a girl and make her . . . what? A wife. And a mom. At the moment, that's where Crystal's identity and aspirations lie.

Near the end of our time together I ask Crystal to revisit her own dreams. She has backed away from wanting to be a doctor. "Maybe I'll be a nurse because I wouldn't have to be on call a lot—with the kids to take care of and Richard away all the time, that'd be hard." Adjusting her expectations downward to accommodate the reality of Richard's army career, seems logical. How she'll feel in twenty or thirty years is still a question but for now, Crystal doesn't even name this *sacrifice*. "I do want to get out there and do something," she says, burping a sleepy Matthew over her shoulder. "I'm just not for sure what."

Tabitha

THE RULES OF ENGAGEMENT:

Domestic Violence in the Military

TWENTY-THREE-YEAR-OLD TABITHA CROOM WENT MISSING OCTOBER 4, 1999.

Lieutenant Charlie Disponzio got notice of the young woman's disappearance as he arrived for the night shift at the Cumberland County sheriff's office in Fayetteville, North Carolina, on October 6.

"I got a strange missing-person case today," Lieutenant Disponzio's co-worker, Sgt. Rick Obriant, told him. Apparently Jimmy Newsome, the owner of Jim's Candy Corner in Fayetteville, had found a purse in the Dumpster behind his store. The woman's keys, wallet, credit card, and checkbook were all inside. Turns out she couldn't be reached at her apartment, her family hadn't heard from her in two days, that she'd missed work.

"Do you have a picture?"

Lieutenant Disponzio was suddenly alert. He knew this person. "That's Tabitha!"

The picture Lieutenant Disponzio looked at showed a slim, young African American woman that he had known since she was a girl. Charlie Disponzio had served in the army with her father, Jessie Croom, and had watched Tabitha grow up.

Disponzio and Obriant spent the next few days trying to piece together Tabitha's movements—who had seen her last and where. They interviewed her family, her friends, her coworkers.

They learned that Tabitha had worked until 11:30 P.M. at her job at the Omni Cinema on the night of October 4. Usually her boyfriend, Forest Nelson III, a thirty-two-year-old Special Forces soldier stationed at nearby Fort Bragg, came into the lobby to pick her up from work. But on this particular night, he had parked his red Ford Escort in the back of the parking lot and waited for Tabitha to come out. One of Tabitha's coworkers, emptying the trash outside, told detectives he saw her get into Nelson's car.

Shortly thereafter, one of Tabitha's neighbors recalled seeing Nelson's car pull up and park in front of her apartment.

At 11:45 that same night, Tabitha's friend Maria Davis called and spoke to her on the phone, wondering whether she still felt like going out to Bennigan's as they'd discussed earlier. Tabitha said, yeah, she still wanted to go. She was going to jump in the shower first. Maria, who lived nearby, said she would be there to pick up Tabitha in fifteen minutes.

Twelve minutes later Maria showed up. Tabitha was gone. No note. No phone message. Nothing.

WHEN THE INVESTIGATION OPENED, it was a simple missing-person case. Trying to piece together what had happened—had Tabitha just taken off or had she met with foul play?—the detectives questioned Tabitha's boss, Tianna Oliver, at the movie theater. Oliver told detectives that she worried when Tabitha didn't show up for work; she had immediately called Tabitha's apartment and left a message on the answering machine.

When he learned that Tabitha had missed work, Lieutenant Disponzio also became concerned. "I know Tabitha and she's very work-conscious," he said. "She even worked two jobs sometimes, when she had to. She was a good girl when it came to being reliable." Tabitha had also once worked as a dancer at a strip club. Disponzio described her fondly as having "a bit of a wild side," but insisted that "she would never not just show up like this for work."

The detectives began to question Tabitha's friends. "They all described Tabitha as very friendly and couldn't imagine anyone wanting to hurt her," Disponzio said. "But they all stated that Tabitha was afraid of her boyfriend, that he was very controlling, that he hit her, that she had been trying to break up with him but was afraid to totally break it off because of what he might do to her."

Indeed, twice in the past month, police had been dispatched to Tabitha Croom's apartment when she called for help; police logs refer to domestic disputes with her Special Forces boyfriend, Nelson. But because Tabitha had declined to file formal charges against him, no restraining order had been issued.

This time, when detectives brought Nelson in for questioning, he was cool. Although he sat in the station for nearly three hours, much of it alone in a room while detectives monitored him on a video camera and filled out paperwork, he never moved, Disponzio says. Hands palm down on his thighs, he stared straight ahead at a spot on the wall. Lieutenant Disponzio recognized the stance—and the tactic. It was one soldiers learned in a survival course called Survival, Evasion, Resistance, Escape (SERE). Nelson, a Special Forces psychological operations soldier, was trained to give nothing away under enemy questioning. Nor did he here.

After a few hours he was released.

On December 26, nearly three months after Tabitha disappeared, her badly decomposed body was found by a Fort Bragg couple out for a walk with their dog. When the dog unearthed a human skull, the couple called the post's military police. More remains were found. Tabitha's belly button ring, what detectives describe as "a bit of meat bearing her tattoo," and scraps of one of her silk camisoles were also discovered. The next day, with some comparative DNA from Tabitha's mother, the body was positively identified.

Tabitha had been buried approximately 400 yards behind Forest Nelson's barracks.

THE MILITARY HAS A DOMESTIC VIOLENCE PROBLEM—or, as the army says, a "spousal aggression issue." Rates of domestic violence in the military are two to five times higher than among civilians, depending on which study is consulted. According to DOD figures, there were 18,000 cases of abuse reported in 2001, with 11,000 of them substantiated by the military. That's a rate of 17 per 1,000, compared with 3 per 1,000 among civilians nationally. The army consistently shows the highest rate, followed by the marines, the navy, and then the air force.

In the 1990s, the military quietly watched as its domestic violence rates shot up from 19 per 1,000 soldiers in 1990 to 26 per 1,000 soldiers in 1996. Then, in the following 2 years, 3 soldiers stationed at a single Kentucky post, Fort Campbell, were charged with killing their wives or girlfriends. Bad press put the military on the defensive. Congress demanded statistics detailing the scope of the problem. There was an investigation, and in 1999 Congress ordered the military to reexamine its domestic violence policies and programs and stem the tide of abuse. It appointed a panel to report back with recommendations.

Then, in the summer of 2002, the army made headlines across the country when four military wives at Fort Bragg were murdered, allegedly by their husbands or ex-husbands, in a six-week spate that forced the military to grapple quite publicly with the problem of domestic violence in its ranks.

Today the military admits it has a problem but insists it is not as bad as it looks. It argues extenuating circumstances. The numbers *seem* high but that's because the military has a disproportionate number of couples who are young and poor—and statistically domestic violence is higher in this group. Still, even the young-and-poor excuse is suspect. Among experts that's a hotly contested "fact." Are the young and poor really more likely to engage in domestic violence, or do the national statistics simply reflect which portion of the population is more likely to come into contact with the system via shelters, free legal clinics, welfare, social services, and the courts?

Meanwhile domestic-violence advocates assert that the military's numbers are even higher than DOD says. The military defines domestic violence narrowly: it only counts when the actions are directed against a current legal spouse—and half of the 1.5 million enlisted soldiers are unmarried, quite possibly living with girlfriends, dating, or busy "not asking or telling." Also the statistics are not uniformly categorized and collected. Not only do definitions and data collection vary from post to post and service to service, but many women have reported that they are afraid to seek help from the military, turning instead to local civilian hotlines and shelters. These victims would not show up in military statistics.

Worse, domestic-violence experts say, is the lack of accountability. Of the rare offenders in the armed forces who are actually kicked out, or counseled out, 75 to 84 percent are given an honorable discharge according to the Defense Department. Although a current breakdown of lesser punishments is unavailable, the military reported in 1998 that less than 5 percent of alleged offenders are even tried in courts-martial. According to the Domestic Violence Task Force's 2001 report, not only is punishment lacking but the military police are inadequately trained to investigate domestic violence. Further, lack of confidentiality keeps many military wives from coming forward. (For example, if a military wife seeks help from a social worker on post, word of the domestic violence goes right to her husband's supervisor who typically confronts him; the husband can then go right home and—undoubtedly furious—confront his wife.) Also, fear of adverse effects on their husbands' careers keep wives from coming forward to ask for help.

In sum, civilian domestic-violence experts tend to dismiss the military's response to domestic violence as largely ineffective. There is a quote they toss around: "Military justice is to justice as military music is to music."

I FIRST STUMBLED onto Tabitha Croom's murder while reading an exhaustively reported 2003 *Denver Post* article about domestic violence in the military; it was the only article to mention that the prime suspect in Tabitha's murder was a Special Forces soldier. The local Fayetteville newspaper covered Tabitha's disappearance and the recovery of her body—but then dropped the story for the next four years; the national press never learned of it.

This was a stroke of luck for army brass.

After all, by 2002, the national press corps was crawling all over Fort Bragg in the aftermath of the four domestic-violence murders there, and the army's public affairs operation was busy reassuring the public that the military took domestic violence very seriously.

"Did they?" I wondered as I trooped along with the media mob from one orchestrated press conference to another in the aftermath of the murders. As a truly gated or closed community, the army has a unique advantage when it comes to containing a story. Reporters are physically barred—by men with guns—from access to the many potential subjects who live and work on post. (In fact there is one gate where the public can, with ID, a car inspection, and a stated mission, occasionally get onto Fort Bragg; I did this but was later kicked out by a public affairs official who learned I was there.) Meanwhile, a public affairs representative canceled all but one of my scheduled interviews.

Frankly this was perplexing. Fort Bragg already had four murders splashed on front pages across the nation. Clearly the cat was already out of the bag. Could this PR fiasco possibly get any worse?

Two years later, I had my answer: Tabitha Croom. Here was a murder successfully kept under wraps by the army for more than four years—a person simply disappeared.

How had she disappeared? Both her person and her story? What happens to the story of her life and death when the military with its vast discretionary powers declines to find and name her murderer? If it doesn't explain her demise—let alone categorize Tabitha's death as *domestic violence?* If the army doesn't finger her boyfriend as the perpetrator or prosecute anyone for her murder, does her death make it into the annual domestic-violence tally? (In 1999 the military listed only one murder by an "intimate partner," and it wasn't Tabitha's.) Is Tabitha Croom an anomaly, the *only* murder the military has managed to keep from official tallies and the press? Is hers the sole instance where commanders managed to disregard troubling facts, like Tabitha's 911 calls the month before? Or that Nelson's first wife once showed up at a Fayetteville hospital with gunshot wounds in her stomach that she said were acquired when a gun she and her husband were struggling over went off?

Is there something more the military might have done, or should be doing to address its "spousal aggression" issues? To indicate that it takes domestic violence as seriously as its leaders profess?

Fayetteville seemed as good a place as any to investigate.

FAYETTEVILLE'S FORT BRAGG, like some evil nexus in a Stephen King novel, is a perennial site for domestic-violence murders.

Of course the town most recently made headlines with the aforementioned rash of murders. But it has a long and rich history of domestic violence—and all kinds of hate crimes. As recently as January 2002, police say, Shalamar Yune Franceschi was killed by her ex-husband, a Fort Bragg soldier who had just gotten out of the service five days earlier (he was out on bail after being charged with kidnapping and raping Shalamar). In 1995, three army soldiers attacked and killed an African American couple allegedly as part of a skinhead initiation rite there. In the summer of 1993, Fort Bragg soldier Sgt. Kenneth French entered a Fayetteville restaurant ranting about Clinton and gays in the military and shot and killed four diners. Recently, the area ranked eighteenth nationally in per capita murders.

The place first blipped onto my own radar screen in the early '80s, when my college journalism professor, Joe McGinniss, treated us to stories about a Fort Bragg-based Green Beret doctor, Jeffrey MacDonald, who had been convicted of killing his pregnant wife and children. McGinniss had covered the 1979 MacDonald trial in-court and behind the scenes, and was about to release his scathing indictment of the man in his bestselling book *Fatal Vision*. Far more interesting than any of the mundane writing topics we undergrads could dredge up on our isolated college campus, were the stories McGinniss would regale us with about the duplicitous Green Beret and how the army fumbled the initial murder investigation in 1970, how its crime labs lost crucial evidence, how the crime scene was trampled and compromised. Ultimately, McGinniss believed the overworked army investigators did their best to try and nail MacDonald, but army brass, after lots of bad press and a hearing, declined to indict him for the murders and honorably discharged him instead. (MacDonald was later tried in the civilian courts and convicted of two counts of second-degree and one count of first-degree murder.) McGinniss described Fort Bragg as a bleak place, and, indeed, when I visited it myself in the fall of 2002, pursuing a new set of domestic-violence murders, I was inclined to agree.

If Fort Drum, the army's model town, is Disney, Fort Bragg is pure Robert Crumb. While Drum's buildings bear the spit-shine appearance and architectural uniformity of a model railway village—albeit one built by an architect whose appreciation for cinder block, small windows, and aluminum siding was perhaps excessive—Bragg is grungy, cobbled-together slipshod, with some beautiful old brick homes from the turn-of-the-century knocking up against miles of flat-roofed, cheaply constructed institutional buildings from every decade since. Not only is Fort Bragg, which opened in 1918, one of the oldest operating army posts, it is by far the largest—with 45,000 active-duty soldiers, 9,715 civilian employees, 10,501 family members, and an average of 8 new babies born on post every day. It is so large and so old that it spills out of its official 160,000 acres into the surrounding region, and its evolution and economy are so intertwined with Fayetteville's as to make the two nearly indistinguishable.

This is a mixed blessing. For both.

Fayetteville is a mean, cheap, hard town—a landscape dominated by strip malls, strip clubs, and pawn shops. It is a town where the Stop-n-Go's will charge 27 cents for a glass of water on a hot day ("Water's free but the cup ain't, lady."), where most of the wages hover near minimum, where the ATMs still offer $10 increments, where the annual crime report places domestic violence murders in a category called "lovers' quarrel," and where the sheriff warns in writing—although there's no law against it—that he'll probably approve as "reasonable" no more than five gun permits per individual. There were 19 murders in Fayetteville in 2002, approximately 1 every 19 days and one quarter of them due to "lovers' quarrels."

It is also a town where history has a way of repeating itself. In the '60s it was where most soldiers on their way to Vietnam shipped from; today it's the last stop on U.S. soil for thousands of soldiers being deployed to the Middle East. Fort Bragg is home to the U.S. Army's Special Operations Command, to the Special Forces (Green Berets), and to the 82nd Airborne Division, a division that can be deployed anywhere in the world in eighteen hours and is known, by members and outsiders alike, as the All Americans.

Fayetteville is a town where the southern charm has dissipated in the hazy car fumes along Bragg Boulevard—a stretch of busy road that takes you from the commercial heart to the military hub. There, on the western edge of Fayetteville, the strip malls thin and bits of scrub pine begin to appear in vacant lots. Suddenly the ratio of camouflaged-clad to blue-jeaned shoppers spikes, berets replace baseball caps, barbed-wire fences rise along both sides of the road, and Fort Bragg's gates appear. On cars here the bumper stickers tend to endorse the National Rifle Association, Jesus, or the army, depending—it seems—on the type of vehicle. Minivans have a bumper sticker all their own: "Army wife: the toughest job in the Army."

IN THE SUMMER OF 2002 it was more dangerous being an army wife than a Fort Bragg soldier. That June and July, when four Fort Bragg army wives were killed by their husbands in a six-week period, the domestic violence casualty rate at the base exceeded the casualty rate for Fort Bragg husbands then engaged in a war in Afghanistan.

The trouble began on June 11, 2002. That afternoon Green Beret Sgt. Rigoberto Nieves, who'd just gotten a special dispensation two days earlier from his commander to come back from Afghanistan to deal with "personal problems," talked with an ex-neighbor. According to *Vanity Fair*, the neighbor implied that twenty-eight-year-old Teresa Nieves had had an affair while her husband was overseas. Rigoberto returned home and asked his wife to come into the bedroom. While Teresa's sisters and their kids hung out in the living room—they were there to help with a recent move to a new home—Rigoberto locked his wife in their bedroom, took her into the bathroom and shot her in the temple. Then he shot himself. At 10 P.M., as the Nieves' six-year-old daughter began to ask for her mother to put her to bed, Teresa's sisters knocked on the bedroom door. When no one answered and they found it locked, they called the police. When police officers broke through the door they discovered the two bodies.

On June 29, a month after returning from Afghanistan, MSgt. William Wright, age 36, an 18-year army veteran serving in the Special Forces, fought with his wife who was seeking a divorce. She had asked him to move out, and he had; he was staying in the barracks. But he'd returned at 7:30 that morning to talk with his wife, who was still in bed. As they argued, he allegedly picked up a coffee mug and knocked her on the head with it, bludgeoned her with a baseball bat, and strangled her. When his eldest son, 13, knocked on the door asking for his mom, Wright told him that she had a migraine. He then allegedly shoved her body into his parachute bag and buried her in the woods. When he returned, he took his three sons, 13, 8, and 5 years old, fishing.

Three weeks later Sergeant Wright confessed to killing his wife. He led the police to her shallow grave in the woods.

On July 9, Sgt. Cedric Ramon Griffin, an army cook who had never been to Afghanistan or Iraq, was accused of stabbing his wife, Marilyn, more than fifty times, then setting the family's house trailer on fire while his two daughters, age six and two, slept inside. The girls somehow fled and survived. According to press accounts, prosecutors in his capital murder trial intend to suggest he was trying to stop his wife from reporting his adultery to his superior officer (technically against the "officer and a gentleman" regs, but typically overlooked by the army). Griffin originally confessed to the murder, but then contested the confession in pretrial hearings—asserting that he hadn't been read his rights. Homicide detectives say he had not yet been arrested when he confessed, and that is why they hadn't yet read him his rights. As of publication, his confession had been ruled admissible and his trial was pending.

On July 19, Fayetteville cops got another murder call. A couple was found dead in their new home just outside town. After being back from Afghanistan six months, Sfc. Brandon Floyd of the secret Special Forces antiterrorism unit, Delta Force, shot and killed his wife, Andrea, and then himself—leaving behind three young children. Andrea's family contends that she was very unhappy in the marriage, that Brandon had become very controlling, and that she was seeking a divorce. She had recently driven the children up from North Carolina to Ohio to stay with her mother. Her mother, Penny Flitcraft, speculated to reporters that Andrea had probably raised the topic of divorce. Brandon exploded and shot her. Then killed himself.

At the time, Fort Bragg garrison commander Col. Tad Davis tried to downplay the murders by pointing out that before this spate, the post had not had a domestic violence murder in two years.

IN TRUTH, even this poor record was suspect—a matter of semantics and parsing the fine print.

After all, twenty-four-year-old Shalamar Yune Franceschi had been murdered in Fayetteville by her ex-husband only six months before the recent spate of murders—but technically this was not Fort Bragg's problem; her husband had already been out of the army for five days before killing her.

And, of course, there was the little problem of accounting for Tabitha Croom's body.

Although Tabitha was a civilian, her body had been discovered on federal property. This complicated things for both the military and the Cumberland County sheriff's office. "If we could show the crime actually occurred in the county, regardless of where the body was found, we'd have jurisdiction over the investigation and prosecution," said Lieutenant Disponzio of the sheriff's department. "But since we could not immediately prove where the crime occurred, Fort Bragg had jurisdiction."

What this means in practical terms is that a team of criminal investigators pursued the murder, but Fort Bragg brass got to decide whether or not to prosecute. So, in January 2000, sheriff's detectives were joined by the U.S. Army's Criminal Investigation Division (CID) and the FBI. "CID did an outstanding job on the investigation and we cooperated with them," said Disponzio. "That's why, originally, everyone was comfortable with Fort Bragg taking over. The military court-martial has looser rules of evidence. They'd have an easier time pursuing this."

But as time went on, Disponzio grew discouraged.

Although the evidence was only circumstantial, according to Disponzio, the investigative team agreed that it all pointed to Special Forces soldier Forest Nelson as Tabitha's killer. Tabitha had told friends she was afraid of Nelson, that he was jealous and controlling. Tabitha had called the cops on Forest Nelson twice in the month before her death over "domestic disputes." Nelson admitted driving Tabitha home and walking with her to the door of her apartment (he denied entering the apartment, detectives say). A neighbor saw Nelson's car there the night of the murder. The murder appears to have taken place during a twelve-minute interval between the time Tabitha's friend Maria called the apartment and when Maria arrived there. There was no sign of breaking and entering in Tabitha's apartment. Nothing was stolen from Tabitha's apartment. She appears to have left wearing only a camisole. Forensics experts determined that she was probably not shot; there were none of the chipped bones that usually accompany such murders. The lack of other trauma to the body pointed to suffocation.

The sheriff's office and military investigators had both taken Forest Nelson in for questioning, but he denied involvement and stayed quiet.

Nelson, a soldier in the 9th Psychological Operations Battalion, never admitted to killing Tabitha—but also never denied it, says Disponzio. He parried questions like, "Did you kill Tabitha?" with responses like, "Why would I kill Tabitha?"

And thus far the military had been able to keep things quiet. Although news of Tabitha's disappearance and the later recovery of her body had made the local paper, news that the primary suspect was a Special Forces soldier had not. Apparently Fort Bragg was determined to keep it that way.

"CID ran into a brick wall when it came to getting somebody in Special Operations Command to prosecute the case," Disponzio said.

Why?

"No reason was ever given to me or any CID agent I know who was working the case. They worked very hard and did everything they could to try and get this prosecuted."

While army investigators believed they had enough evidence to put Nelson on trial, the case was not pursued "due to lack of evidence." Today Fort Bragg says it is still investigating the murder. "We work hard to ensure that before a charging a soldier with a crime, the evidence on hand will stand up to the 'beyond a reasonable doubt' standard," says a Fort Bragg spokesperson. Nelson's commander at Fort Bragg decided the case did not meet this criteria.

And that's what makes military justice very different from the civilian courts. Commanders are granted vast discretionary powers. This is similarly true, of course, of civilian district attorneys who are deciding whether or not to pursue a case. There is always some tension between cops and lawyers; the former are more likely to push for a trial, the latter more likely to hesitate until they are sure they can win a case. But there is a difference here. Military commanders are not lawyers—and, when deciding whether or not to convene a court-martial, they may make decisions that have little to do with how persuasive evidence will be to a judge or jury. Indeed, one might argue that the commanders have a vested interest in *not* pursuing a case like Tabitha's. Military courts-martial were created with a primary goal: maintaining control in the ranks. Justice was secondary. And while commanders have a broader social mandate to maintain law and order on post, they have tremendous leeway in interpreting this. In other words, it is perfectly legal for any commander to consider a host of intangibles when weighing a decision to indict. Is it counter to the good of the organization, to unit morale, to the army, to air its dirty laundry with a nasty domestic-violence murder trial? Is the death of a young, African American ex-stripper worth the loss of a committed, and highly, expensively trained soldier?

The questions that winter of 2000 were many.

In this case, because the Special Forces commander decided not to convene a court-martial, Nelson went free.

AS FORT BRAGG DRAGGED ITS FEET with Tabitha Croom's murder investigation, the Defense Department was facing a public relations disaster. Its fighting force had been increasingly beating their wives. Only days after Tabitha's body was found, Congress ordered the formation of a Domestic Violence Task Force to investigate the military's response to domestic violence and make recommendations for improvements.

The twenty-four-member task force made its first site visit in September 2001. It elected to go to Fort Bragg. The panel, half civilian and half military, met with Fort Bragg commanders, first sergeants, military police, and social workers to talk about, among other things, "offender accountability." While there is no mention of specific cases, the panel did make some observations. "There was a consensus that holding domestic-violence offenders accountable for their violent behavior must involve more than simply sending them to the Family Advocacy Program for clinical intervention," notes from the meeting read.

Two months later, on November 19, 2001, Deputy Defense Secretary Paul Wolfowitz issued a memo to military leaders. "Domestic violence will not be tolerated in the Department of Defense," he ordered. Noting that there were more than 10,500 domestic-violence incidents substantiated that year, he declared that "domestic violence is an offense against the in-

stitutional values of the Military Services of the United States of America."
He then called upon the leaders at all levels of DOD to act decisively.
"Commanders at every level have a duty to take appropriate steps to prevent domestic violence, protect victims, and hold those who commit it accountable," he proclaimed.

Acknowledging that the problem is likely to be even worse than the
numbers suggest, Army Vice Chief of Staff General John Keane sent out his
own memo to army brass a month later. Worried about a decline in incident reporting, Keane said, "We believe this reduction may be partly
attributed to fears of an adverse impact on career progression and under-
reporting by Commanders and Senior Noncommissioned Officers."

Meanwhile, the Defense Task Force on Domestic Violence's offender
accountability working group was raising similar questions: "Should a
commander's discretion to act be limited in these matters?" the panel wondered in its meeting notes from Fort Bragg. "Is a more punitive stance
called for?"

Apparently not.

In early 2002, against this backdrop, Fort Bragg's Special Forces commanders gave Forest Nelson an honorable discharge, allowing him to re-
sign from the military.

"Mr. Nelson reached the end of his service obligation with no discredit
on his performance," explains a Fort Bragg spokesperson.

SIX MONTHS AFTER THE ARMY LET NELSON GO, the whole domestic-
violence issue exploded—with the well-publicized four domestic-violence
murders in the summer of 2002.

The army was quick to say that none of the men had a history of domestic violence. But what this really meant is that the army has no record.
And many of the specific details of the murders—and the role the army
might have played in preventing them—will remain a mystery. Nieves and
Floyd shot themselves right after killing their wives. Bill Wright hanged
himself in a North Carolina jail nine months after he was arrested, before

his trial and several days before his death penalty hearing was scheduled. Cedric Griffin confessed, contested the confession, and alone among them, will be standing trial.

After local reporter Tanya Biank broke the story of the four army murders in the *Fayetteville Observer,* the national press was all over the story with everyone from the *New York Times* to the *Washington Post* to *60 Minutes, Vanity Fair, Glamour,* and *Oprah* weighing in with big stories and flashy headlines decrying "Fort Bragg's Deadly Summer" and "The War at Home." Some of the explanation for this is simple. The media love a good murder story, and when the press can collect murders into a "trend story," editors go orgasmic. But something else was at work here. With the recent invasion of Afghanistan, hundreds of reporters across the United States who had never decoded a single military acronym for their readers were suddenly immersed in the garbled vernacular. Their eyes were trained on a military waiting for war—and in these first forays into the military community they were puzzling over its culture, traditions, and their significance.

How the press covered the story is telling.

Most reporters went right for the sexy theories, as if oblivious to the motives of those promoting them: defense attorneys seeking exoneration for their clients, say. The most sensational explanation for the rash of murders was that Lariam, an antimalaria drug given to soldiers during their recent deployment caused them to become psychotic and murder their wives. Despite the fact that more than 25 million people had taken Lariam over the preceding seventeen years with no murders attributed to its use (not to mention the fact that these guys weren't lashing out at their fellow soldiers, but waited until they got home to go after their wives), the army sent a team of epidemiology specialists to Fort Bragg to investigate. (Lariam does have a substantial list of psychological side effects ranging from depression and aggression to psychotic reactions and hallucinations.) "Is it possible that the less than 1 percent affected could have been clustered at Fort Bragg?" investigators wondered. But several weeks after looking at all the data, studying the men's previous behavior, and talking to witnesses, the investigative team determined the drug was not to blame. Seems this was ordinary, garden-variety domestic violence, common as khaki in these parts.

But the press was not buying it.

Next, reporters began to question whether post-traumatic stress syndrome might be to blame. "Study Links Combat, Domestic Violence" UPI announced. "Four Soldiers' Wives Slain in Recent Weeks, and Authorities Say the Husbands Are the Killers. At Fort Bragg, Some Wonder if It's a Cost of War," said *The Virginian-Pilot.* Sometimes, the press became so enthused about its theories that it flipped the subject and the object of the story, making the soldier perpetrators into the victims. For example, Sean Hannity and Pat Halpin introduced their Fox News segment on domestic violence by asking, "Is the war on terror taking a toll on American soldiers?"

Others used the medical model to blame stress. For example, an Associated Press report, filed a week after the murders, began by noting that a soldier's life is filled "with challenges and difficulties, from basic training to the battleground." This is standard. "But it's rare that those stresses have the deadly consequences that have shaken the Army at Fort Bragg," the reporter notes.

For its part, the military points the finger at the frequency of deployments and reunions. "Our most important resource is the soldier—and the family—and you can't separate the two," Col. Tad Davis, who was the garrison commander (a sort of mayor of the post), told the *New York Post* in the aftermath of the murders. "If the family is not ready [for deployment], then I would submit to you that the soldier's not ready." One of the "stresses" families encounter, as noted before, is the quick independence demanded of wives when their husbands are deployed. Just as quickly, this newfound independence can threaten soldiers who return home and want to take charge again, says the army. To address the problem, the military offers advice, classes, and literature dedicated to helping the *wife* anticipate her husband's insecurities, smooth over them, and gracefully reintegrate him into the family. ("Reassure your spouse that they are needed, even though you've coped during the deployment," says one 2004 DOD guide for spouses. "Be calm and assertive, not defensive when discussing decisions you have made, new family activities and customs, or methods of disciplining children. Your spouse may need to hear that it wasn't the same doing these things alone. . . ." etc.)

Meanwhile, as the army and the press try on various explanations, soldiers have their own theories.

FAYETTEVILLE IS THE HOME of the Special Forces Association National Headquarters, a veterans' organization that is an advocate for its members and serves as a hangout spot for its retired soldiers. It is a low building that screams "government-issue prefab" and sits near the local civilian airport where takeoffs and landings provide a comfortingly familiar aural backdrop.

Inside, on a warm September day, two Green Beret vets sit in a cozy gingham-and-calico country kitchen–style lounges. Much like Stalter and Waldor, the two wizened Muppets who heckle from the balcony, these men pass the time, chew the fat, and bust the chops of those who come and go through the nearby door. And, yeah, they have a couple of theories about those Fort Bragg murders.

"For one thing, in our day, when they put you out of the field, you had four or five days of stand-down time before you saw your family," says sixty-five-year-old Lorenzo Robbins, a retired Special Forces sergeant major who served in Vietnam (twice), Thailand, Okinawa, and Korea over the course of his twenty-five years in the army. "These days, they pull a man from combat and set him down at the supper table twenty-four hours later." In their day, they had their own pre-reunion debriefing: "Took you time to get from your camp in the jungle home—so you got drunk, let off steam and came home with a hangover." He laughs. "By the time you got home, you didn't feel like doing anything!"

Don Davis, a seventy-year-old retired sergeant major with the Green Berets, says it's not the homecomings that are a problem for the Special Forces today, but the coming home—and then going again. "Sometimes you're home just long enough to let the wife run your dirty clothes through the wash," he says. Both men laugh. Neither one's wife had a problem with this schedule, they assure me.

"Well, it probably cost me a divorce," corrects Robbins. He shrugs his thin shoulders. "But I didn't kill her, like some," he says, referring to the recent murders. "She wasn't worth it!" he jokes. "The reason she gave me is 'You're gone all the time.' I had a daughter who was six years old when we divorced and of those six years, I'd only spent eighteen months with her at home."

They're not alone. He points to an adjacent room where five other vets are hanging out around a card table. "Hell, all those guys in there were divorced while they were on active duty," he says. He ticks off their names on his fingers, while Robbins nods, and occasionally corrects with "divorced twice" or "third divorce."

The one exception they can think of is James C. Dean, seventy-three, retired master sergeant and the secretary and administrator of the Special Forces Association. They call him in from the other room. "That's right," Dean confirms. "Twenty-one years in the army and married almost fifty-four years." He removes his black "POW/MIA" baseball cap to scratch, then puts it back on. "In fact, come to think of it, it's our anniversary tomorrow."

For his part, Dean thinks this stuff about the stress of combat causing these men to shoot their wives is bullshit. "I do not believe in any way that they shot their wives because they had just returned from combat in Afghanistan," he says. "The reason they shot their wives is simple"—he takes a drag of his cigarette and exhales slowly for dramatic effect. "Infidelity. The press is missing a hell of a lot," he says. "*Infidelity* was a cause in every one of those four cases."

I agree that infidelity is a drag, but wonder why they didn't divorce their wives instead of shooting them.

"The infidelity could've been really bad," he explains. "In one case, I understand it went on over eight years."

·   ·   ·

THE DEFENSE DEPARTMENT TASK FORCE on Domestic Violence studied both the causes (the subject of infidelity did not surface) and effects of domestic violence. Its assessment was harsh in the three reports it sent to the secretary of defense. The group chastised the military in its 2002 report for its "unintended inclination to minimize the severity of domestic violence incidents." Noting that DOD classified most incidents as "low-level," the task force wondered whether its definitions needed fine-tuning.

"For example, the air force system is a very medical model," says Deborah Tucker, a civilian domestic violence expert and co-chair of the task force. "And in the air force, it's not considered a 'severe' case unless a victim is hospitalized overnight. So even an injury that's considered felonious and that might be treated in a hospital emergency room, but not involve an overnight stay, would be classified as 'moderate.' " In this scenario, a soldier who strangles his wife until she passes out and lands in the emergency room, wouldn't have the incident declared *severe*. (And, with the "medical model" giving way to an "insurance model" today, overnight stays are increasingly rare, even after surgeries.) "When someone is strangled to the point of unconsciousness, in many books that's considered attempted murder. But with the military, it is often classified as 'moderate.' " Noting in understated jargon that strangulation cases "have high potential for lethality," the task force suggests that the military's definitions of severity might be "out of step with common accepted practice."

Meanwhile, the panel found lots of little things—quick-fix solutions—the military can do, and seems quite willing to do. For example, civilian orders of protection (court orders that forbid batterers from being around their victims) were not enforceable on military bases, which are federal property and under the jurisdiction of military police. A mere technicality in the law, the military—and Congress—quickly changed it. And in these hundreds of papers generated by the Defense Department's three-year task force—the military is adept at generating reports—the tone is conciliatory. The documents are full of concessions graciously granted by an organization with an image problem: Sure, we'll get our counselors better training.

Sure, we'll run more public service announcements. Sure, we'll coordinate our efforts with the civilian agencies and local law enforcement.

But where Secretary of Defense Donald Rumsfeld digs in his heels is revealing. The military will not agree with the task force on the *definition* of domestic violence, nor will it acknowledge that there is typically a "primary aggressor" in a domestic-violence situation. This is not mere semantics.

When called to the scene, if there is confusion about who is responsible, military police are likely to arrest both partners in the "fight." But the playing field is not level in most cases; statistics show over and over that batterers hit and that women who can "fight back" or defend themselves.

"It is important to define the problem not just as an act of physical violence," says Tucker. "Because when you actually try to understand what physical violence is, you see that it is just another tool in the batterer's kit to exercise power and control. He'll use economic means [not putting her name on the checkbook], or the kids, or emotional means to get what he wants." Explaining that batterers often isolate their victims to make them dependent and trapped, Tucker says multiple means are employed to achieve this. "And when a person has already used violence in the past, then even if he is not currently beating her, his threats carry the implicit knowledge that he might." Further, Tucker insists, if a wife fights back we *can* make a distinction between her behavior and her husband's.

In a heated, back-and-forth argument the task force chastises the military, explaining that 50 percent of victims of domestic violence use violence against their abusers at least once, but that does not mean that they are engaging in "mutual combat." One person is using violence to coerce and intimidate the other; one person is less able to stop the violence being inflicted; one person is suffering greater injuries, more fear, and more anxiety, the task force explains. It warns that the military's inclination to "blur the boundaries between the law enforcement and clinical responses to domestic violence" is "dangerous." The military wants to frame this as a "relationship problem," and send its members to "couples counseling" rather than arresting them because they are breaking the law. The violence is minimized then, and the abuser is less likely to be held accountable, legally or even administratively.

In civilian communities today, most states have "mandatory arrest" policies, which means that cops are supposed to determine whether an assault occurred, determine who is the "primary aggressor," and make an arrest. When this notion was first introduced, cops resisted. "They would say smugly, 'Well, both parties used force, so we arrested both,' " Tucker explains. The military continues to do this, resisting the "primary aggressor" notion. "The military wants to treat this as a gender neutral issue because they have been trying to welcome women into the armed services and figure out how to teach themselves—and the rank and file—to see women as equal," she says. But with domestic violence things are not usually equal.

"Unfortunately, the military developed its programs and did its domestic-violence training with social workers, chaplains, and military brass twenty-some years ago when the issue was poorly understood," says Tucker. At the time, it was not unusual to call this a "relationship issue" and hand it over to the therapists. Even today, batterers in the military are typically ordered into anger-management classes and couples counseling—both considered largely ineffective by most civilian experts.

"Domestic violence is not something that happens because you're feeling upset today," says Julie Fulcher of the National Coalition Against Domestic Violence. "And these anger treatment models are not very successful because this is not an illness, it's an attitude. It's about people feeling like they're entitled to do this to their wives." These men don't beat their wives because they can't control themselves, she insists, they do it because they feel powerful and because they *can.* "The day you start seeing these guys go after their commanding officer because they're pissed off and they just can't control their anger, we'll rethink our theory," she says.

Still, in the military this continues to be dealt with as a communication issue. It's seen through the prism of couples counseling. "And then there is an assumption about mutuality in violence," says Tucker. "Making this a 'he said/she said' problem."

Indeed Fort Drum's chaplain James Watson explained it this way: "The most common couple violence we see is often mutually initiated." An example? "Often the soldier is trying to leave the room because there is an argument and he's afraid he can't control his anger. And the wife wants him to stay and address the situation. And he shoves past her and that's when the violence might happen."

In fact, the typical scenario for a soldier who is caught battering his wife might go like this. A wife tells a therapist or counselor at the post's family center that her husband hits her. When she leaves the office, the person she has confided in immediately picks up the phone and calls a supervisor to report an alleged domestic-violence issue. The call makes its way up the chain of command to the husband's boss and to the post commander. The husband's boss confronts him and arranges a meeting to hear the husband's side of the story. (Probably, the husband calls his wife, or returns home in a rage, exacerbating a bad situation.) After a series of meetings that include the post commander, someone from the post's Family Advocacy Office, the soldier's supervisors, and perhaps others, the team decides whether or not domestic violence has occurred (usually without speaking directly to the victim). Treatment is recommended—typically anger-management classes conducted at the post's family center and maybe a recommendation for couples counseling.

In more extreme cases, if the shouting and screams are loud enough to alert neighbors, the military police might be called. They would then file a report and set the above wheels in motion.

If the family lives off-post and someone calls the cops, police might arrest the batterer and give the wife a domestic violence hotline number or tell her about a shelter. The wife might seek a restraining order, a court order that forbids her husband to see her or come around their house. But depending on the ad hoc arrangement local law enforcement has with the military post, news of this off-post 911 call may or may not make it back to the soldier's supervisors.

It is a system fraught with problems.

"They think they're helping but they're not," insists a twenty-seven-year-old I'll call Tameka. Tameka says her husband, until this week a soldier stationed at Fort Bragg, beat her for six out of their seven years of marriage. She has reported the incidents and taken the recommended couples classes with him, but it hasn't helped. "The military talked to him a lot over the years about the violence, but there was a lot of change in command," says Tameka, explaining that new bosses and frequent moves masked the severity of his violence. "It was always a new person, a new commander each time an incident occurred."

Tameka, who left her husband the day after we spoke, sought help finally from the local civilian domestic-violence shelter in Fayetteville. According to Crystal Black, director of the local domestic violence program, CARE, the agency sees lots of military wives. And the women face a unique set of circumstances.

Tameka felt the military didn't consider her safety the first priority. When her husband was slated to go to Korea for a year's deployment, she was happy, planning to use the time to get a new job, a new apartment, and leave him for good. "But they kicked him out of the army instead," she says. He was furious. "He said, 'See, you kept calling the cops on me and now see what you've done? I've lost my job.' He's real mad. They could've let him go for a year to Korea. I believe they failed me—and him."

In fact Tameka's story shows the complex position in which the military finds itself. As the abuser's employer, domestic violence advocates want it to act decisively to punish abusers—but at the same time, lack of confidentiality for victims and erratic decisions by commanders can make things worse. Is there a way for the military to hew to a "no tolerance" policy *and* make victim safety a priority? The military says it's between a rock and a hard place. Domestic-violence experts insist there are a few basic steps the military can—and should—take now.

For example, if a woman goes to her chaplain, she probably assumes that she is having a confidential conversation. "But chaplains are not always clear about their privilege or about their options to refer to both military and civilian resources to assist victims and offenders," notes the task force in its 2002 report. Clarify the issue, the task force says.

While civilian courts typically order abusers into twenty-six-week programs; the military's treatment programs average only twelve weeks. And, in fact, civilian domestic-violence experts make a distinction between "treatment programs" like the military's anger management classes, which they have found to be largely ineffective, and what they call "batterer intervention."

"These intervention models are all about holding batterers responsible for bad behavior and for making changes," says Julie Fulcher. Even though she acknowledges that these programs are nowhere near 100 percent effective, she says the ones that work best have heavy-duty oversight. "The men have been ordered by the courts to attend the programs and are carefully monitored by a probation officer to make sure they are attending, participating, not continuing to engage in violence. They check with the victim to make sure the violence has stopped and there is a realistic threat of, 'you're going to jail if you don't shape up.' "

It is not clear whether the military truly understands that sending a strong message that domestic violence will not be tolerated must mean it holds offenders accountable—legally—for their actions. Tabitha Croom's case makes this plain.

After her boyfriend, Forest Nelson, was honorably discharged, he married a woman in the navy and moved to the Washington, D.C., area, where she was stationed. With his clean army record he got a job as a security guard. In one final attempt to keep the case from being shelved, Cumberland County's Lieutenant Disponzio requested a meeting in the fall of 2003 with the military investigators, the FBI, and his own department to determine what else could be done. The group enlisted the help of the navy's cold-case squad. "They reviewed the case and came to the same conclusion we did, that Forest Nelson killed her," says Disponzio. The cold-case squad decided to re-interview Nelson in March 2004. Based on that confidential conversation, the cold-case squad realized Tabitha Croom had been murdered off-post, on civilian territory. Because the trial is pending, the Cumberland County sheriff's office would not comment on specifics of the March 2004 interview, but Lt. Disponzio immediately drew up an arrest warrant for Forest Nelson.

Nelson was arrested in Washington, D.C., on March 24, 2004. He was extradited to North Carolina two weeks later and, as this book goes to press, is awaiting trial for murder in the state's civilian courts. Nelson's attorney, Gerald Beaver, declined to comment on the case.

"A LOT OF US have been following domestic violence in the military for a long time," says Fulcher. She and other civilians working in domestic violence have been monitoring it not only because there are enormous problems there, but also because the military holds tremendous promise—as a powerful institution and the nation's largest employer. "The military is all about indoctrination," says Fulcher. "They've got lots and lots of psychologists conducting studies and contracting with them to ferret out how to best get soldiers in the best mind-set to do the job the way they want it done. They expend tremendous effort getting the military person to do the right thing and think the right way." What would happen, Fulcher wonders, if they directed some of that energy toward ending domestic violence? "They could send a powerful, straightforward message that, when it comes to domestic violence, we're not going to look the other way."

But Christine Hansen, who runs the Miles Foundation, an advocacy organization for military victims of violence, despairs of that ever happening. "Oftentimes, the military's response is to put domestic violence in the context of military readiness or mission," she says. "The focus isn't victim safety, which we as a society have determined is paramount. Instead, the military asks, 'Is this service member a good sailor, soldier, airman? How much time and money have we expended in training this soldier?' " Victim safety is considered in these other contexts. "We have had military commanders say to us, 'Don't you understand there is a war going on here?' " she says. "Our response is, 'Don't you understand there is a war going on in this home?' "

LOVE TRIANGLE:
You, Me, and Uncle Sam

Patriotism? I mean, I'm really, really proud of my husband and that makes me feel very patriotic in some ways. When I hear "The National Anthem" that makes me very emotional, makes me think of him. I almost cry every time. I know where he's been and what he's done. And it's wonderful. People here in Watertown, if he's in uniform, they come up and shake his hand and say, "Thank you." That's just heartwarming to me. It makes me feel wonderful and privileged to be a part of this military community.

On the other hand, I don't agree with the idea that if you don't agree with the war in Iraq, you're unpatriotic. . . . Patriotism doesn't mean to follow a leader like sheep. It might even be more patriotic to question. My husband is a soldier, but I don't get offended when people question the war. I have my own questions sometimes. . . . But what are you going to do? Especially once the war is started? Before it started I was much more critical, but now, you know, support our troops!

—Ulli Robinson

ONE DAY AFTER I HAD RETURNED FROM A VISIT TO WATERTOWN, where I was interviewed by an army reporter for the *Fort Drum Blizzard* ("Author Visits Fort Drum to Research Book"), I received an e-mail from an army wife, Ulli Robinson, who had read the piece:

> I am a spouse myself and just made it through my husband's first deployment. . . . My husband left for Afghanistan within 2 weeks of our arrival at Fort Drum. There I was. New place, new people, new weather, new puppy (a well-meant good-bye gift from my husband. His famous words before deploying, "It will be house-trained before I get back, right honey?"), a house not completely moved into, no pictures on the wall, boxes to unpack, no job, no close friends or family, and a master's thesis to finish.

It is no small indication of the kind of person Ulli is that by the time her husband returned from Afghanistan nearly six months later, she not only had pictures on the wall of her apartment, but she had many friends, a job as a newspaper reporter covering education at the *Watertown Times* (her first reporting job), had learned to drive in the deep snow up here, had finished her master's thesis, *and* house-trained her puppy.

Twenty-seven-year-old Ulli is nine years younger than her husband John, an army warrant officer. Warrant officers are a small group of soldiers nestled in a tier between enlisted soldiers and officers. Unlike regular officers, largely trained to be managers and generalists who move around from one position to another, warrant officers are specialists who develop an expertise and typically stay in the same narrow field their entire careers.

Ulli, who was born in Germany, met John at a university in Hawaii in 1998 when they were both working on their graduate degrees. They dated for two years and were married in 2000. They left Hawaii a year later, had some short, temporary postings in the United States while John underwent additional training, then arrived at Fort Drum in Watertown, New York, on

March 20, 2002. Two weeks later, on April 5, 2002, John shipped out to Afghanistan.

Ulli, who sounds more American than I when she speaks—all flat, Midwestern vowels and colloquialisms—was relatively new to army life and completely new to Watertown, but she's a quick study. Though technically more of an outsider than Danette or Crystal by virtue of her German nationality, Ulli is one of the most outspoken "insiders" I meet. By this, I mean that by the end of her two years in Fort Drum, she actively situates herself within the official army culture—religiously attends Family Readiness Groups, participates in coffee groups, volunteers for the unit—with all the fervor of a recent convert.

But she didn't begin that way.

When she first arrived in Fort Drum, Ulli struggled with her new identity as an army wife, she tells me one afternoon as we sit over coffee at the Borders cafe in Watertown's Salmon Run Mall. "I felt very alienated," she says. "I felt very different from other people I would meet at work." Sometimes she simply didn't tell people she was an army wife or that her husband had been deployed. "I didn't want people to feel sorry for me," she says. She also felt that she wanted to be accepted and seen as her own person. Ulli pushes a flyaway strand of her blond hair off her brow. She looks at me intently through her round, wire-frame glasses, and I am struck by this comment. Her face, round and open, meshes with her personality. She is so frank, and bright, and honest it is hard to imagine her hiding *anything*. "There were just a lot of circumstances I didn't want to put out there," she says.

Aside from feeling uncomfortable with the label "army wife" or "husband deployed," she was terribly lonely. "I would call my parents and say, 'God, there's nobody to talk to!' I'm a real social person but I just don't know people yet. Somebody could break in here and kill me and nobody would know except for you guys in Germany because I don't answer the phone for a couple of days."

It wasn't easy to meet other army wives. Most of the soldiers in her husband's unit had already been deployed to Afghanistan or Bosnia for months and were about to return. Out of sync with the emotions and plans of the larger group of wives who were excitedly preparing to welcome home their husbands, Ulli didn't click right away with the group. Her Family Readiness Group was operational, but it was marching to a different drummer.

So Ulli moved into her small, split-level apartment in central Watertown, went to work, shopped, and ate alone. She had quick, occasional chats with one neighbor while she walked the puppy, but mostly she had only her own thoughts as company. "And that's a really odd feeling," she says. "A very lonely feeling."

Finally she got a break. "One of the photographers at work came up to me one day and he's, like, 'You want to come over for dinner? I was just thinking, you're all alone and you might enjoy some company.' And I was, like, 'Oh man, that is so nice!' And that was the first time somebody asked me over."

It took Ulli three months to meet people and settle into her husband's deployment. "Eventually I learned to say, 'Okay, if I miss his phone call, it's okay. He'll call back,' " she says. "But in the back of your mind you're always waiting. Then the phone rings and your heart races and you run for it, and you pick it up and . . . it's your mom. And you cry."

Meanwhile, Ulli had lots of time and a vested interest in the unfolding political situation—a political junky in the making. An avid reader of American and European newspapers, she was outspoken about U.S. intervention in Iraq—to me, if not her military friends. "I'd be happy with just some solid evidence that Iraq supported these terrorists," she says in March 2003. "But I haven't seen anything yet." When it comes to American efforts to muster up allies for its invasion of Iraq, she's disgusted. "America's acting like a bully, 'This is what we think and you have to think what we think.' And *this* is our diplomacy!" she says. She's on a roll. "Our diplomacy is 'We're going to bomb the hell out of Iraq and that's what we've been planning to do all along. If you don't agree, too bad!' "

"I'm not the biggest Bush fan," Ulli concedes. Still, she owes him a favor.

Once, the highlight of her year, Ulli got to talk to John *and* see him—thanks to George W. Bush.

The president, on a goodwill tour to Fort Drum in July 2002, was scheduled to participate in a video-teleconference attended by ten wives on the post and their respective husbands in Afghanistan. This was an opportunity for the army to show off its newest family-friendly technology, a teleconferencing line where select families could occasionally talk to deployed soldiers. Typically there is a seven-second delay, and the image can be a bit fuzzy. But this time no one was complaining.

Ulli and nine other wives filed into a row of chairs set up in front of a large-screen monitor. Four seats away from Ulli was a reserved chair marked "POTUS" (President of the United States). Army officials, government officials, and Secret Service agents milled around in the room with the wives waiting for the president to arrive. When Bush entered he shook hands with each of the women. Then he reminded the women why their husbands were sent overseas. "We have to do this," he said. "This is for freedom."

Though not a fan of the president or his policies, Ulli seemed likely to forgive him just about anything that day. "He is very kind," she says. "I mean he had tears in his eyes when he talked to us wives. And I was very surprised. Wow, maybe he does care?" Ulli laughs. "And the president was so cute." When Gen. Franklin Hagenbeck, confused by the seven-second delay, stood with his 10th Mountain soldiers in Afghanistan and accidentally cut the president off in a rush to speak to his wife, Judy, the president merely laughed off his apology. "Who am I to interrupt a husband and wife talking?" he said. "You go right ahead."

From the "private" teleconferencing moment, the president left to give a public speech to thousands of the division's soldiers assembled nearby. He told them they were doing a fantastic job. Then echoing a familiar refrain, he said he now also knew that "spouses were doing a fantastic job as well, making sure their husbands hear only happy voices and news during phone calls and in e-mails; the tears and frustrations can be saved for later."

THE NO-MORE-TEARS PROTOCOL is both promulgated by the army and ac-
quires a life of its own. You only have to hear once that "a distracted soldier
is a dead soldier" to start weighing your words and recrafting the e-mail
narrative that goes out to your spouse. The phrase is an oft-repeated warning and a powerful disincentive for wives tempted to share their "frustrations." (And as noted earlier, the dictum dates back to the early *Army Wife*
in which Nancy Shea reminded women that even if little Butch falls out of
a tree and breaks his arm, there is no need to bother hubby with a phone
call: "The arm will heal, but a mistake in judgement on the part of her husband may claim several lives.")

And the moratorium on worrisome news goes both ways.

Husbands are also advised not to speak too freely—not necessarily because of national security concerns, but to protect wives from the harsh realities of war. This holds true even when the husbands are back. According
to a *New York Times* reporter who sat in on a Fort Riley, Kansas, mandatory
training session for returning soldiers, the men are warned against total
honesty with their spouses:

> Instead, they are counseled to take their spouses on dates, to buy
> ice cream and go on outings to Chuck E. Cheese with their chil-
> dren, to come home with unexpected bouquets (corsages work,
> too), and to talk with their mates, but without telling "all of what
> you saw over there."
>
> "Ladies need affection," Colonel McClure announces. "Take a
> lesson, gentlemen. Learn an adjective or two. That's conversation."

McClure, an army chaplain, says that the men will be asked if they shot
anyone, then they'll be asked how it felt. "Don't let them get to that follow-
up question," he says. "That one hurts." Leaving aside the question of what
this does to a relationship when both partners are being urged to censor

their experiences, their fears, and their reality, there is a more immediate problem: Does it work?

Wives don't stop worrying about their husbands because they're kept in the dark. (And vice versa.) The dark simply serves as a blank canvas on which to project a host of worries, several women told me. (For example, one wife said she appreciated it when her husband informed her that he was headed out on a mission for several days. Of course she worried, but she would have worried more, if he e-mailed her every day and then suddenly his messages ceased for ten days.) But the army sees things differently. To the wives it says, "Hush." To the soldiers the army says, "Don't worry, we're looking after your families."

FAMILY READINESS GROUPS are the heart and soul of the army's new family-friendly reforms. As mentioned earlier, the FRGs are groups of families from a particular unit, company, or battalion, that meet regularly. Often the unit commander joins them.

In practice FRGs function in different ways. For example, FRG leaders—typically the commander's wife or another high-ranking spouse—might call a meeting for families before a deployment to let spouses know, if possible, where the soldiers are going, how long they will be gone, how they can communicate with them while they are away. Then, while the soldiers are deployed, the FRG has regular meetings—with some FRGs more active than others. The meetings might take place with an invited speaker—say a chaplain talking about the emotional cycles that accompany a deployment, or how to mitigate the impact of deployment on your kids. Or the wives might get together to make a salable cookbook or a quilt—as some wives at Fort Drum did, each offering a panel with their loved one's name on it. If a unit is attacked and word gets out via CNN before official military channels, the FRG might activate its "phone tree," whereby wives call each other to quell rumors and relay the latest official information they have received. Or, there might be potlucks to organize, or fund-raisers to plan, or newsletters to put out. Because the army pushes the FRGs to provide all kinds of events and activities for soldiers and their families, but does not pay for these "morale-building" events, wives spend a lot of time and effort in fund-raising.

ULLI HAS some time on her hands. Without kids and with her husband deployed more than he has been home, she eventually became active in her FRG. While she is not the leader of the group, she volunteers a lot of her time and is a "key caller." Key callers are those asked to make calls to other wives in the unit if there is information the commander or his wife want to get out. These phone trees can be activated for a range of reasons. Sometimes the FRG leader wants to alert everyone to bring something to the bake sale on Saturday. Sometimes Ulli is supposed to just call and check in with the wives on her list to make sure all is well. Sometimes the FRG leader wants to send out a message from her husband in Afghanistan that the deployment has been extended another three months. (Though this hardly seems the bailiwick of volunteer wives, it is not uncommon.) Ulli wasn't thrilled to be the bearer of *this* bad news. "But they read me the official letter," she says. "I took some notes and I called all my ladies." In Ulli's case, she also goes beyond making these regular calls to the wives on her list to volunteer for fund-raising, planning, and other morale-building functions.

When we speak on March 19, 2003, the day before the United States invades Iraq, Ulli has been an army wife for almost three years and has been at Fort Drum exactly one year and one day. She has made friends with lots of other army and air force wives and has been drawn into the community. "I just feel more comfortable now with my FRG," she says. "And it has become more important for me to go to those meetings now because my husband's second deployment is coming up."

This deployment has her worried. More worried than his last tour in Afghanistan. "I feel very restless. I'm not calm," she says. She feels a need to prepare, to anticipate the loneliness. "I already tell my husband, 'I want to call those wives in your unit right now.' Some of them I know. Some of them I haven't met yet," she says. "But I'm just scared. I just need to know which husbands in the unit are leaving, so I can find those wives and know who is here that I like and who I can talk to. After all, Nina will leave at some point," she says, referring to her best friend whose husband is about to be transferred. "Everybody will leave."

For Ulli the FRGs are working just as the army hoped they would—on many levels. "We have a commander's wife who is extremely welcoming, very loving," Ulli says. This wife is the head of the FRG and is a proper mother hen. "She actually came up to me the other day because she was very concerned about another spouse who doesn't come to any of the meetings," Ulli says. "She said 'It's very odd and it just makes me sick to think she might think she's not welcome.' I said, 'I know that's not it, for a fact. She may just be one of those people who don't care much for the military setting.' " Ulli makes a distinction. "There are some spouses who really don't care about the unit and don't want to do anything. That's fine. It's just not their interest." This is *their* loss, Ulli insists. "For me, it's just important to have somebody to call when you need help," she says.

In her case, that moment came when John was on his way back from Afghanistan and she could not get straight answers from anyone on-post about where she could go to meet her husband. One sergeant told her one thing, another told her something different. No one would go out of his way to verify their information. "There was so much disinformation," Ulli says. Obviously it was "hugely important" for the families to be there to greet their husbands after this six-month absence, but no official source could tell them where to go. "The army did such a crappy job," Ulli says. "Oh God. I was getting this close to calling the general's wife!" She holds thumb and forefinger a hair apart. And in fact Ulli called her FRG leader—who had no answers. Then she called her commander's wife—but got the commander instead, on the home phone. He directed her to a redeployment meeting that night run by the chaplain for wives of returning soldiers. There she ran into the general's wife, Judy Hagenbeck, who directed her to someone who actually had answers. Then Ulli activated the phone tree to let the other wives know exactly where and when they could meet their husbands. "I was there that morning when he got back and there were all these wives and everybody's happy with their kids," Ulli says. "My husband would have felt horrible if I wasn't there—it's been six months!"

The system worked. But why was it necessary? Suppose the army just picked up the phone and made it *their* job to see that wives got accurate information? And what happens to the wife who chooses not to participate? Does anyone ever break ranks?

ON MONDAY, October 27, 2003, Fort Drum army wife Veoletta Hayward did just that.

A brand-new writer for the *Watertown Times,* Veoletta complained in her bimonthly "Military Spouse" column that commanders and their wives try to "shove the FRG down our throats." She went on to insist that "very little gets accomplished" in FRGs and to expose the "animosity between enlisted men's and officer's wives." She wrote that once, when she was told by a first sergeant's wife that she was "required" to attend an FRG meeting and refused, the woman put her husband on the phone. "I very politely explained to him that I was a civilian and that he couldn't order me to do anything," Veoletta wrote. "He then asked to speak to my husband and proceeded to order him to attend the meeting." A military wife for seventeen years—first as an enlisted wife and later, when her husband was promoted, as an officer's wife—Veoletta shared her observations with this military town: "What I have come to learn is that the day a woman says, 'I do,' to her soldier husband is the day she becomes U.S. Army property, property the Army is not always happy to possess."

Veoletta was burned at the stake as a heretic. At least it felt that way to her. "They tore me up for two weeks," says Veoletta, who met me for coffee shortly after the piece ran. She produced dozens of e-mails and letters to the editor, which she had received berating her for "bitching." "Some letter writers said I would have been executed in some countries for this!" she says.

"After reading this article, I was embarrassed that she had even mentioned the military and the Family Readiness Group in such a negative way," wrote one military wife, Emily Rossi, in a letter to the editor. "How could she, as a military spouse and an American, talk so negatively about the military?" For Rossi, questioning military policy was tantamount to questioning the value of democracy. "I would never verbally bash any organization that stands for our very way of life," she wrote.

One army wife, Allison Allen, commended the first sergeant and his wife who had insisted Veoletta attend the FRG meeting for "encouraging participation." She suggested that Veoletta didn't have what it took to be a real insider. "Sometimes gut and grit is the difference between the successful Army spouse and the one pretending," Allen wrote to the editors. Those who complain about army life, Allen implied, simply aren't trying hard enough (the old shut-up and buck-up subtext): "The Army isn't for everyone, but it is what you make of it." She concluded her letter: "I am proud to be an Army wife, to love a soldier, proud of my soldier and of the life that we have created. I believe that makes the Army happy."

And here, Veoletta concurs. "Those women who responded to my column said the army does genuinely care about us," says Veoletta. "Why else would they create those organizations? I say, 'That's *why* they created those organizations, to keep the wives out of their hair.'"

Because Veoletta kept her maiden name, the army itself didn't immediately know just whose wife she was. When her husband heard that army brass was making inquiries he was furious. "His response was to go down there and say, 'Here I am, you got a problem, talk to me.'" This further pissed Veoletta off. "I said, 'You can't do that! I'm a big girl, remember? I can take care of it on my own.'"

But Veoletta *was* shaken. She knew her column would cause a ripple; she did not know that it would be a tidal wave. She even fretted that because her photo runs with the column, she would be recognized on-post. "The first time I went to the commissary after the letters started coming in, I was nervous," she said. She really did have to tell herself to buck up. "I decided that was stupid. I'm not a wimp. And when people asked me if I was the one who wrote the column, I said, 'Well, if you liked the column, yes, if not, that was my evil twin.'"

For Veoletta it has been a rough couple of weeks. Even away from the reprobation on-post, among colleagues at the *Watertown Times,* she has been slammed. "One of the letters was even written by a reporter at the paper," Veoletta said ruefully.

Sadly, she says, the response she got to her column has made her much more cautious. "And I hate that," she says, admitting that it drove her to alter the ending of the column she penned that day.

What bothered her most about all the letters and e-mail she got, was the way that her criticism of the FRGs was twisted to suggest that she didn't participate simply because she was lazy and, worst of all, unpatriotic. Not only does Veoletta volunteer forty hours a week at her ten-year-old son's school and as a Boy Scout leader, where she was the Hiawatha Seaway Council's volunteer of the year last year (as a friend of hers pointed out in the one positive letter to the editor that ran), she considers herself *extremely* patriotic. She plucks at the red-white-and-blue sweater she is wearing, tells me that her entire house is decorated in red, white, and blue, and that three days after September 11, she painted a fourteen-by-seven-foot flag on the side of her garage that faces the road. She points out that her husband left to fight in Afghanistan on their son's tenth birthday and that she supported him. And he may be headed back there again soon. "I'm a Republican who supports President Bush," she says. Then adds the caveat that she's a little uncomfortable with what is going on now in Iraq—even though she was all for the United States in Afghanistan.

As Veoletta segues into the mounting casualties in Iraq, she begins to cry. She tells me that the column she was writing today was very difficult to compose. "God, I can't do this," she says, wondering if she should just stop writing the column. "That's why these women who are saying I'm unpatriotic or an uncaring human being are so wrong." She wipes her tears away fiercely with the back of her hand. "Thinking about those very young men and women dying over there just kills me," she says. "Of course, I try to prepare myself for my husband not coming home sometimes. But I don't know how we prepare."

In the end Veoletta did finish the column. And this time she tried to wear her patriotism on her sleeve. "The sacrifices soldiers make for the American people is incredible. They willingly swear to protect and defend the Constitution of the United States at all costs, even with their very lives," she wrote. Noting that the "men are deployed more than they're home," she concluded on a personal note: "When my son was a toddler he would run to any man in uniform calling, 'Daddyyyyy.' It broke my heart."

· · ·

> *I am not even sure Mrs. Hayward and I are part of the same Army family. In the Army I have known, commanders most definitely care. I have never felt or been treated like a "pain in the rear." Her statement that the Army only pretends to care about us, but would be happier if we didn't exist is unfair. Many spouses volunteer much of their time to programs and in offices on-post and keep those programs running. . . . It sounds like Mrs. Hayward might have had a bad experience with her FRG and it is true that every FRG is certainly different, but it is also true that an FRG is only as good as the people in it.*
> —Ulli Robinson,
> in a letter to the editor,
> *Watertown Times,*
> November 3, 2003

When we get together in November 2003, a day after I've met with Veoletta, Ulli brings me a copy of her letter to the editor—and she is steamed. "I was offended by the term she used, the way she said 'when her husband plays war,' " Ulli tells me. "That offended me when 8,000 to 10,000 Fort Drum soldiers are deployed to Afghanistan or Iraq. They are certainly not playing!

"And I thought she gave FRGs a bad rap. I think you should encourage younger wives to give it a try, when you're an older spouse like that." She pauses for breath. Barely. "It was so negative. She may have had a bad experience. I'm sure that happens a lot. But I'm concerned that a young twenty- or twenty-two-year-old reads this and gets this picture of FRGs right away. I mean, mine is great. Nina had a great FRG." She'll make a minor concession. "Okay, I've met snobbish wives where rank matters, but there are so many more that are not like that."

Ulli was so irritated by Veoletta's column that she talked to Veoletta's editor at the paper. The editor seemed blindsided, surprised by the level of controversy this one measly column had drawn, Ulli says. "I explained to the editor that it's kind of like the army is your family. For me, the army is my extended family. And especially if you participate in FRGs, it really feels like someone did a tap-dance on your toes." (She is so steamed the idioms are tripping her up.)

"It's hours and hours of volunteering in your spare time, and this comment really ticks you off." And Ulli worries for the FRG's reputation in the aftermath of this column. "This thing has spread, too! I've heard from people at other posts who had seen the column. The army is a funny place. Rumors spread pretty quickly."

In some ways, Ulli is one of the army's family success stories. She's an outsider on many levels—foreign, civilian, new to the military community—who's been made to feel she is an insider. The FRG, by making her part of this unit, has provided meaning and direction. Not only has she been drawn into the group, thoroughly persuaded of its value, but she wants to bring others in. "I've been pretty disappointed that none of the wives on my list ever show up at meetings." She sighs, discouraged. Ulli believes they're really missing out. "There are all kinds of things we're doing to try and draw people, to promote togetherness and support, especially during deployment. It's so disappointing that so many people don't bother to show up."

•   •   •

THE ARMY CONCURS. "During Desert Storm, we learned that families and units did much better when there was an active FRG and when families were really connected to the FRGs," says Delores Johnson, who heads up the Army's family programs.

Based on this discovery, the army—in its perennial quest for uniformity—decided to standardize its approach to the volunteer groups. There is now training for the volunteer wives who lead the groups. There are hundreds of pages of material explaining how such groups ought to be run. There are dos and don'ts and "useful tips" that spell out in excruciating detail how the volunteers can beef up their efficiency. There are, for example, nineteen suggestions for phone calls. "When placing a call, be ready to talk when the person answers," wives are told. "Hang up after the other party does," they're reminded. There is advice about homecomings: "Welcomes should be enthusiastic," wives are told. Ironically, given the army's penchant for acronym soup, the instructions define common terms. "Friends are the people you can talk to, have fun with, and share the tasks of everyday life," the handbook explains.

Ultimately the goal of the FRGs is simple. "Good information and friends who provide each other needed emotional support and shared labor to meet daily tasks," the handbook states. "These are the very things that army spouses need to cope successfully with all of the phases of Army life."

Are FRGs a success? "Absolutely!" says the army's Delores Johnson.

But the numbers tell a more complicated story.

According to a 2002 army survey, only one-third of military spouses are even aware that FRG and Army Family Team Building (AFTB) programs exist at their installation, with only 25 percent reporting that they had attended an FRG meeting in the previous year. Asked why they did not attend the meetings, spouses reported lack of time, inconvenient hours or locations, or "no need." Officers' wives were more likely to participate— and to assume leadership positions. Enlisted spouses had their reasons for ignoring the meetings. "[They] are more likely to report that they want to keep their lives separate from the military, are uncomfortable with FRG leaders/members, and that their member spouses do not encourage them to participate," the report noted.

Some wives, like nineteen-year-old Crystal, just don't see the point. Fewer than half rated the programs as "helpful" or "beneficial." Further, the study revealed rank-related discrepancies: "The belief that FRGs are run well and offer good help is much more common among officers than enlisted spouses.

Less than a third of the spouses were satisfied with the support that army leaders gave families. And wives actually think things are getting worse. In 1987, for example, 46 percent of spouses were satisfied by the support NCOs in their solders' units showed families, but by 2001 that number had dropped to 34 percent. (There was a comparable drop among officers' spouses.) And only a quarter of spouses believe the leaders in their spouses' units are concerned about the welfare of a soldier's family.

This is very bad news for the military. Only 57 percent of spouses say they would be satisfied if their soldiers were to make the army a career in 2001, whereas 70 percent liked the idea in 1991. Twenty-two percent said they would like to see their soldiers get out as soon as they had served their time.

What is going on?

The answer is alluded to in the 2000 leaders' handbook for FRGs (then called Family Support Groups, or FSGs) where the impetus for the groups is laid out:

> The Army recognizes that helping families is its moral obligation and in its best interest. Families that can cope with (and in many instances actually enjoy) Army life are more likely to contribute to the community, allow their soldiers to do their Army jobs well, and encourage their soldiers to remain in the service. . . . Hence, the Army mandates that each unit commander establish and support an FSG.

How can the army *mandate* a volunteer organization? It's a question rarely articulated, but one that both sides clearly struggle with.

IN 1968, when I was in kindergarten, my father graduated sixth in his class of fifty from pilot training. That meant he had a lot of options about his career. The air force started at the top of the class and let the new pilots choose their plane. When my father's turn came, he chose the A-1 Skyraider, a plane that was used only in Vietnam.

He came home and told my twenty-seven-year-old mother. She was furious. "I screamed, and yelled, and cried," she says. She doesn't remember what he said. "I know he didn't say, 'Sorry,' or 'no, I won't go, I'll change my plane.' " My mother wept and crawled under the dining room table and wouldn't come out. Eventually my father called some friends, who came over and finally coaxed her out. "I felt like he was deserting us and going off to die," my mother says.

My father spent 1969 and part of 1970 in Vietnam, flying support for search-and-rescue missions. If a plane was shot down and the pilot survived, my father's job was to go in first and try to clear the area of enemy artillery. He wanted to do this. "He saw it as a necessary thing that he had to do for himself and for his military career," says my mother. "But a good part of the reason he went was for himself. It was the only time in his flying career that he could really fly without a million regulations and restrictions—because when he flew there, the main restriction was just 'come back alive.' "

My mother remembers the sense of despair she felt then at being left all alone in a civilian community to worry about my father's safety. (Throughout the Vietnam War wives were typically kicked off base for the duration of their husband's Vietnam tours.) At that time, she was working full-time as a substitute teacher, paying the bills and raising three girls age five, seven, and eight.

"Around October, five months after he left, I thought I couldn't stand it anymore," she says. "I thought I was going to have a nervous breakdown, so I called the base hospital to see if I could talk to somebody. It was just very scary, not knowing if he was going to come back, and it was a lot of pressure taking care of you kids, taking care of everything. I felt like I needed someone to talk to, some help, some direction." She was told that there would be a three-month wait before she could get in to see a counselor. She pushed. They directed her to a local waiting wives' club, which met at the chapel on base.

"That group might have saved my life," my mother recalls. Her waiting wives' club at Selfridge Air Force Base near Detroit consisted of fifty to seventy-five wives who got together regularly. They went to the theater together, went out to dinner, and chatted and bolstered each other's spirits. "It was emotional support for us because we were all going through the same thing and we could just talk and commiserate," she says. It wasn't an official body. It wasn't attached to any particular unit. There were no key-callers or phone trees. There were no fund-raising drives. There was no work or busy work to be done. But for my mother, in 1969, this waiting wives' club was a lifeline.

FAST-FORWARD THREE-AND-A-HALF DECADES and I am sitting in on a Family Readiness Group meeting at Fort Drum.

On this Wednesday evening in March 2004, Fort Drum's Headquarters and Headquarters Company, Division Support Command, Family Readiness Group gathers in a conference room. Although army brass insist that FRG attendance spikes during deployments, and although this unit of 200 is currently deployed to Afghanistan, the FRG leader Catherine Young describes this turnout as slightly *better* than average. Seven wives and three kids show up for the meeting.

The women sit beneath fluorescent lights around a long conference table and are joined by five uniformed NCOs and officers attending in their official capacity.

The meeting is indistinguishable from any PTA meeting. To spare the reader the details I proffer this synopsis. There is an announcement about a reunion briefing in two weeks. The husbands are expected home in a month or so, and wives are encouraged to attend the briefing to learn about readjustment.

There is a discussion about an upcoming potluck. Sparks fly over bring-what-you-will versus thematic. The latter wins. It's a Mexican potluck. They need volunteers to call the other wives and tell them to come and what to bring. Some wives volunteer.

Next agenda item: a fund-raiser. The women have been assigned a day for a bake sale at Fort Drum's main administration building. They will be there from 10 A.M. to 2 P.M. They have decided they will serve lunch. What will they serve? They vote on tacos.

But just as they're about to move on to who'll bring what and who'll staff the booth, a "senior wife" (as the army likes to call its experienced family members) offers yet another helpful tip to the FRG leader. "I think baked potatoes would be good," she asserts.

No one wants to say no to the senior wife, so the discussion is reopened. It's all very cordial and conciliatory. There is a new vote. The inventory expands: tacos *and* baked potatoes will be offered for sale.

They need volunteers to staff the booth. A few women volunteer. They need women to provide the food. Some of the same women, and one additional one volunteer.

They need people to volunteer to bring baked items to the sale. Two women volunteer.

The aforementioned senior wife pipes up. "Remember each item has to be individually wrapped and contain a full list of ingredients," she says.

There is a collective groan, "Aww no."

"Yes," she insists, explaining that it is army regs. There is a discussion of whether there could be a single list of the ingredients posted for, say, all the brownies there. This is determined to be against army procedure.

Next item on the agenda is a morale-boosting summer party for the unit. The pros and cons of weekday versus weekend, and a daytime or a nighttime event, are discussed. What time will draw the largest crowd? The senior wife says that the time is probably irrelevant since the returning colonel will probably insist on attendance. "It's what we call mandatory fun," she says.

As with many such meetings, parsing the group dynamics can be a livelier diversion than the agenda and often proves more revealing. Here the senior wife, whose husband is a lieutenant colonel with the company and who has served as an FRG leader in the past, keeps interrupting the young, newly appointed FRG leader, Catherine Young, who is less experienced and whose husband is only a captain. ("The executive officer's wife, who had been running the FRG just moved," Young later explains to me. "I was asked to volunteer.") Each time the senior wife interrupts—authoring the Baked Potato Amendment and spearheading the push for full disclosure of ingredients—Young defers to her.

Next the group discusses plans for a welcome home event; their husbands are expected back from Afghanistan in the next month or so. It can't really be called planning a welcome home party, because the army actually discourages any full-fledged parties, telling the wives that their husbands will just want to go home and be alone with their families. And while you could call this a "welcome home ceremony," it would be stretching things to suggest the wives have any role in planning it. The army takes care of that.

At Fort Drum these ceremonies—oft rehearsed—are executed with smooth precision. First, the Pine Plains gym is converted into a parade ground. A massive mat is rolled out across the basketball courts to protect the floors from street shoes and combat boots; banners are strung across the painted cinder-block walls, folding chairs are set up for families and colleagues. Then a mini-band of four soldiers is tasked to play Sousa medleys. Soldiers hand entering children small American flags to wave. A few tables of snacks are set up in the corner.

The day before this, I had attended yet another such welcome home ceremony on-post. On this March 2004 day, 119 soldiers from the 642nd Engineer Company have just returned after spending a year in Iraq. At 1:00 P.M. the soldiers file into the middle of the gym and stand at attention.

A chaplain prays, thanking God for the safe return of the 642nd. "We thank you also for the sacrifices of families," he says. The band plays "The National Anthem." Col. James L. Creighton comes to the podium and asks the audience to applaud the 119 heroes standing before them. Since they left on March 23, 2003, the company built over 100 helicopter pads, did force protection, conducted site surveys for future building projects, built a water tower, and built a 3,000-man detention center, among other things. "We're proud of you and what you've done," Creighton says. "And thank you very much to the families of soldiers who supported them here." Everyone present sings "The Army Goes Rolling Along" ("First to fight for the right, and to build the nation's might," etc.) and the 10th Mountain song "Climb to Glory" ("We are proud to be in the Army of the free, climb to glory, mountain infantry," etc.). By 1:14, the ceremony is over and soldiers are dismissed to their loved ones' congratulatory hugs.

Because the local media are always there, and the national media are occasionally there, the army has carefully orchestrated and scripted the homecoming. Indeed, in this particular instance, since the soldiers have actually been home for four days already, this is more a reenactment for public consumption.

Why bother?

The event is an Army public affairs department wet dream. Press attendance is encouraged. Journalists, TV cameras, and photographers come in droves. Visuals are controlled and grandly patriotic. Reporters toss soldiers gentle softballs like, "How does it feel to be home?" The evening news inevitably runs shots of soldiers hugging ecstatic wives. Press favorites: A returning father who is meeting his infant for the first time (bonus points for twins), a father in uniform greeting his returning soldier-son, a child—holding aforementioned flag or wearing daddy's desert khaki cap—in uniformed daddy's arms.

These homecoming images are the ones the army hopes will supplant the flag-draped coffin that the public saw on yesterday's front page. To that end they are rigidly scripted.

What the families are left with are the inconsequential details. The

FRGs can make homemade banners if they want, but the army has already got banners to string across the gym walls. The FRGs can decorate if they want, but the army has already arranged for streamers, bunting, and red-white-and-blue balloons. The FRGs can bring food, but the army has already provided light refreshments.

In this case, the FRG gathered around the conference table in the HHC office decides to table the discussion for now.

Though there are only seven wives in attendance, the traditional party game of raffling off something—in this instance, a basket of St. Patrick's Day goodies one of the wives has brought—is adhered to.

The meeting is adjourned.

SOMEWHERE BETWEEN my mother's experience in 1969 and the FRG meeting I attend in March 2004, something appears to have been lost. As these groups creep toward ever-more official status, wives have lost their autonomy. The Vietnam-era clubs were in their heyday during the burgeoning women's liberation movement, which was propelled along by consciousness-raising groups. Did the military consider the wives' clubs similar fertile (dangerous) ground? At the time the military mostly ignored them. Today the military takes a different tack.

Today, the army has decided that it is in its best interest to bring these groups under its wings, to keep tabs. Army commanding officers are evaluated on the success of their FRGs; they attend all the meetings, or are supposed to; they are required to approve the content of FRG newsletters; and they have the authority to appoint and fire the "voluntary" FRG leaders, to whom they give regular employee evaluations.

THE ARMY, which likes to think it can mandate its way out of a paper bag, is puzzled by wives' passive aggression here. ("How come those ladies won't come to our meetings and play nice?" it wonders.) Some lack of clarity about just whom the army's FRGs are designed to help may be part of the problem.

Is the goal to help wives cope during deployments? Or is the goal to help wives buoy their husband's spirits instead of bothering them during deployments? Conflating these two different aims brings on some of the problems that, for instance, couples counseling does. Is the goal saving the relationship, even though that may be against the best interests of one of the partners or is the goal to help an individual find happiness?

The FRG's confused mission sends mixed messages to wives. Nowhere is this clearer than in the deployment literature the military puts out. An air force chaplains' guide puts forward the familiar trope that "candid and clear communication spouse-to-spouse, as well as parent-to-child, is important in preventing relationship regression." But flip the page and the chaplains are warning couples not to be *too* open:

> Carefully select problems to be discussed in letters. Many day-to-day problems will work themselves out without creating undue concern on the part of the spouse away or at home.

A page later, families are told to "share feelings as openly and freely as possible without indulging in self-pity." Spouses (read "wives") are given tips on how to cheer husbands with frequent letters and tapes that evoke hearth and home (reminders of what they're fighting for). The chaplains suggest wives send the service member copies of her diary so he knows what's up. "The importance of daily activities should not be underestimated," wives are told. "They are tangible pieces of 'life at the other end of the letters' to partners."

Homecomings are notoriously rocky. One Fort Campbell soldier explained why he thought he and his wife were having trouble since he got back from Iraq. "Over there, I was in charge of people," he told a military reporter in March 2004. "I came home and felt like it was the same thing, but my wife has her own way of doing things." The chaplains' guide addresses this. "In fact, returning service members frequently have difficulty adjusting to the new independence of their spouse and/or children at home as well as changes in household rules," it warns. "The returning spouse/parent may feel unwanted, and those at home may have difficulty with the re-balancing of family leadership roles." *Leadership*, a term more aptly applied to a battalion than a family, surfaces a lot in this literature. "Successful reintegration," as the army calls it, means reestablishing conventional family hierarchies.

Because the language is, per DOD regs, gender neutral you have to read this deployment guide carefully to see that much of the compromise and accommodation being urged falls on the wife. (Suggestions about coping with loneliness by pursuing "self-expressive interests like redecorating the house" offer some guideposts to the presumed gender of the subject.)

However, it gets tricky.

While the wife may be the one being "counseled" in this guide, she is not the *client*. Vagueness about just whom this advice is designed to serve is clarified in some of the chaplains' own mission statements. The Army's I Corps Ministry Teams say that the chaplains' job, among other things, is "[t]o advise the command in matter of religion, morals, morale, and ethical issues in order to support the unit mission." And here, once again, I find myself captivated by the military's fusion linguistics. The ministers state their mission: "Operate a state-of-the-art spiritual power projection platform for the war fighter." At Fort Drum, God and the army even share the same motto. "God is there to strengthen you to be all that you can be," the chaplains explain on their web page.

The air force chaplains describe the wife, the soldier, and the military as a kind of (love) triangle:

During the separation, the military members tend to obtain emotional support from the military environment, resulting in a stronger emotional attachment to the military unit. Their spouses are more likely to feel excluded, adding to their feelings of loss. This dynamic is seen as a major contributor to the pattern of lower marital satisfaction among military couples immediately after and during separations. It appears that stress generated by the triangle of the military, the military member, and the spouse are transferred to the natural triangle of the family.

Mention of the triangle is the first tacit acknowledgment that there are opposing interests here, that there is a tug and tension of desire. As air force wife Danette Long said about her husband's family-free deployments: "I worry sometimes that he likes it too much."

MEANWHILE, back at Fort Drum, where three-quarters of the troops are deployed, overburdened wives are marching at double-time. As part of a two-day conference titled "Wives of Warriors Connected by Hope," they offer their own cadence:

I don't know what you've been told,
The Army Spouse is brave and bold.
We pay the bills and fix the car,
Then they go and raise the bar.

According to the Fort Drum *Blizzard,* the Christian Fellowship of wives running the conference invoked scripture in defense of good time management. "Be very careful of how you live—not as unwise, but as wise, making the best of every opportunity" one warrior wife said, quoting Ephesians 5:15–16. Attendees were given dozens of tips to help them move more efficiently through their busy days—and then de-stressing tips to help them recover. (Candle aromatherapy and music are apparently very effective.)

According to the army's own 2001 survey of families, 35 percent of spouses complained that the demands the army made on them were a problem. And that was in the days before deployments, and extended deployments, and repeated deployments to Afghanistan and Iraq. More current figures suggest things have gotten worse. Sixty-three percent of spouses thought army life was worse than civilian life, according to an independent March 2004 poll. Aside from on-the-job risks, 61 percent of wives said the stress of military life was greater. This takes its toll: 49 percent said their own morale was average or low.

In part the FRGs were designed to be an answer to the morale problem. But "morale building," as defined by the army, takes a lot of work—volunteer work, that is. The army's 2001 survey reported that 44 percent of spouses had trouble managing their regular volunteer hours and 53 percent had trouble with additional volunteer work they were asked to do.

FIFTY-TWO-YEAR-OLD JUDY HAGENBECK figures she volunteers twenty, thirty, or forty hours a week. Her husband, Gen. "Buster" Hagenbeck was commander of the U.S. forces in Afghanistan. For her part, Judy has been an army wife for thirty-one years and has volunteered on various posts across the country for all those years. She has had a few brief stints doing paid work. Once she was an office manager in a dental clinic when they were stationed in Washington, D.C. Once she worked in the public school her kids attended. Once she ran a book club for a publishing company. But volunteering has been a constant in her life.

"We used to 'task' volunteers," she says, explaining that they would tell wives that they needed to "volunteer" a certain amount of time. "For example, you used to say, 'All right, we need three volunteers from each unit to put on this fund-raiser or three volunteers from each unit per month to volunteer at the thrift shop. Because you can't pay people to keep the thrift shop open or you'd have no profit." But things have changed. "We don't do that anymore," she says, explaining that it is illegal. "Now it is strictly on a volunteer basis."

This required a change in thinking—as well as laws. "We had to get out of a mind-set of 'you owe us something' or something like that. Because it used to be that we just . . . there was such an obligation put on people, and now it's truly what it's supposed to be and what it should have been all along, which is you volunteer where you want to, not because you feel obligated."

Judy Hagenbeck puts this obligatory volunteerism in the distant past, but others are not so confident it's passé. "I found that the military has paid lip service to the idea that military spouses are independent beings who the military doesn't have any control over, but that actually the expectation for some spouses is even greater today," says Rand Corporation senior social scientist Margaret Harrell, who studies military families.

However, the fact that more wives do paid work outside the home has had an impact on the military's volunteering. "Sometimes you'll find it's the same pool of the same people and they volunteer all over the place," Judy says, describing Fort Drum's volunteer corps. "You know, they're the ones truly committed to the community." But things used to be different. "Thirty years ago we didn't have the conflict of work because truly it was a rarity that someone worked outside the home," she says. Hagenbeck describes how two separate camps evolved. "The ones that didn't work but volunteered had some resentment, wondering how come I'm the one making the community a good place to live and *they* don't feel any obligation to the community? So it became a little bit of a pittedness."

To downplay the "pittedness," a culture of volunteerism has evolved that is lighter on the old sanctions for nonparticipation and heavier on the accolades for service. Here the greater the self-sacrifice, the louder the applause—with women who gave up their own career aspirations to volunteer on behalf of their husbands' units (and therefore the truest patriots) garner the most encores.

EACH YEAR four military wives are selected to be honored at the American Veterans' Awards as Military Spouse of the Year. The women are nominated by their husbands, who pen paeans to their wives' virtues. Here are two 2003 winners—as seen through the eyes of their husbands.

Army Reserve Capt. Noel Palmer wrote that three weeks after joining the Reserves he was sent to Iraq. His wife, Leane, "was left responsible for everything else including doctor appointments, swimming lessons, soccer, potty training, Sunday school, trips to Grandma's, bills, car maintenance, cleaning, mowing the lawn, taking out the trash and everything else that goes with owning a home." When Leane found out that temperatures in the Middle East were over 120 degrees, she took action. "Being a good seamstress, Leane found a pattern for neck coolers. (They're like ties filled with crystals that, when soaked in water, swell up with moist gel that offers a bit of relief from the heat.)" Leane made 300 of them. Then she rallied people to help buy more materials. She sent 600 more. She also helped run the company FRG. Captain Palmer could not be happier. "The support she gives me through daily letters of encouragement, e-mails and expertly taking care of my children and issues at home allows me to focus on taking care of my soldiers," he writes from the Middle East. "I get one 10-minute phone call per week, most of that time is often consumed talking about FRG issues. Leane doesn't complain, she just tells me how happy she is to talk to me and that she supports me."

Marine Corps Col. Christopher Conlin assumed a command position in August 2003 and left for Iraq five months later. His wife assumed the role of key volunteer advisor, becoming point person for the families of 900 infantrymen. He applauds her. "[M]y wife Ava selflessly resigned her commission in the U.S. Navy Medical Corps to be a stay-at-home mom for our two daughters," the colonel wrote. "This was no small sacrifice, as she was a Lieutenant Commander with 8 years of service as a board certified preventive medicine physician. She did this without complaint because she felt it was her duty as a spouse, mother and American."

AS IN THE CIVILIAN WORLD, military wives volunteer for a number of reasons: they enjoy helping others; they want to give back to the community; they can't get a paying job; they have time on their hands; it makes them feel good; and that oft-cited explanation. "Well, somebody's got to!"

But volunteering is about more than simply getting the work done.

"[V]olunteerism serves two purposes," writes sociologist Laurie Weinstein in *Wives and Warriors,* a 1997 collection of research on women and the military. "It's cheap and it cements the wife's allegiance to the service by incorporating her into its mission." This way, the wife ceases to see herself as tugging futilely at her corner of the triangle ("What about my career?" "What about our family's needs?") and sees herself tugging *with* him to get the unit's mission accomplished.

Of course, military wives are not the only ones to engage in what sociologist Hanna Papanek dubbed in 1973 the "two-person career," the kind of job where only one person is paid for a job by a company—or the government—but both spouses keep the institution afloat with their labor. Laurie Weinstein and Helen Merderer, an associate professor of sociology at the University of Rhode Island, who have done extensive research on military wives, point out that ministers, diplomats, and politicians also engaged in two-for-the-price-of-one careers. The wife serves as an "adjunct" to her husband—and in the military that comes with a perception of power on the wife's part. Studying a group of navy wives over seven years, Weinstein and Merderer discovered that the system works because the wife becomes vested in her husband's career through a system of "vicarious achievement." His accomplishments are hers—a phenomenon that is even expressed linguistically. Wives say "we were promoted" or "we got orders" or "we're making a career move." For its part, the military does all it can to encourage this, with its own language of husband-and-wife "command teams."

Senior wives convey the system to new wives. "Wives also help reproduce the military culture," Weinstein and Merderer write. "Wives who perform their expected domestic and public duties are role models for other wives; indeed, some wives bluntly criticize those women who do not service their husbands' careers."

At the very least, these senior wives say today, participate. Take an army family team-building class. Or attend your FRG meetings. And just *why* you ought to go is explained in the same language of "bonding" and "cohesion" their husbands get. And the appeal is the same.

"For military members, combat bonding provides the 'highs' of affiliation, fellowship, and common purpose as antidotes to the military 'lows' of compulsory obedience, the rank system, and the absence of civic rights," write Deborah Harrison and Lucie LaLiberte in *Wives and Warriors.* "Wives often find the warmth and friendliness of this bonding irresistible. Wives are also drawn into military bonding by default, since they, too, have been posted every two years, they, too, have not put down meaningful civilian roots, and they, too, have been encouraged to depend on the military community for their identities (and often their paying jobs)."

According to Harrison and LaLiberte, U.S. military research on the family multiplied by ten between 1975 and 1985. Bearing in mind that "a particular event would not be experienced as stressful by people who had been conditioned to regard it as an 'adventure' or 'challenge' " this research was all designed to "pose the implicit or explicit question: How can the military encourage wives to develop a positive attitude toward military life?"

FRGs, or their differently named equivalents in the other branches of the service were seen as one way. "These structures function to secure wives' loyalty and sense of belonging to the military," Harrison and LaLiberte wrote.

> *They also provide wives with safe places to release their rage. These expressions of rage usually evoke sympathy from other wives, and have sometimes acted as catalysts for wives' resistance. At least as often, however, wives' collective realization that they bear the same burdens has paradoxically worked to trivialize the burdens and to deepen each wife's resolve to bear them in better spirit.*

It's the "adventure mythology," they say, and "according to this reasoning, a wife who can't get a good job should be almost as pleased to have a poor (or unpaid) job."

So, once again, more than a half-century after Nancy Shea's *Army Wife,* the women are being told to recast *hardship* as adventure. Senior wives school new wives on "good ways" to view the military experience. Formally, there are the family team-building class and Family Readiness Groups. Informally, there's good ole peer pressure.

"The most experienced military wives I know actually look forward to deployment in some ways," prompts Meredith Leyva in her 2003 advice book, *Married to the Military: A Survival Guide for Military Wives, Girlfriends, and Women in Uniform.* "Less successful military wives sit on the couch and mope. Which gal do you want to be?" Leyva's book is the sassier, slightly hipper younger sister to Nancy Shea's stodgy *Army Wife.* (If the pedantic *Army Wife* is *What to Expect When You're Expecting* then *Married to the Military* is *The Girlfriend's Guide to Pregnancy.*) But Leyva's book is "fem-lite," the kind of "low-cal" feminism that is chock-full of flavor but low on substance. With brassy attitude Leyva correctly nails the issues, but sidesteps solutions to systemic problems by offering personal coping strategies. Ultimately she joins Shea to nudge wives in the right direction. "I'm convinced that all women of every personality type are capable of succeeding in military life," Leyva writes as she ends her book. She admits it can be frustrating. "But in the end we can have the adventure of a lifetime. The question is: What kind of adventure will you have?"

In this way young military wives are taught to shape their narratives. Some buy it, some don't. But to make this work, the "sacrifices" must be recast as a "choice." The martyr mantle fits only if it is willingly donned. Today there must be a perception of free will. (Crystal chose to stay home with the kids. Danette chose to put off teaching until her kids were in high school.) "Wives said they made the decision to stay home and provide the continuity in the family to compensate for their husbands' absences," Weinstein and Merderer said of the submarine-officers' wives they studied. "By viewing their sacrifices as a choice, wives were able to rationalize their service." A little attitude adjustment works wonders. Wives said that the comings and goings of their husbands gave them 'independence,' and some measure of 'power.' "

The FRGs help them organize their thoughts.

The appeal is clear. It is the same as the military's supreme attraction: security. The security of being surrounded with people like you. Job security. The security of knowing exactly what is expected of you. The physical security of a fenced community. The security of a predictable world. Even with all the moving there are few surprises. Or the surprises you encounter are mitigated by the very sameness of every base you go to. (Here is the officers' club. Here is the commissary. Here is the package store. Here is the NCO housing area. Here is the flight line. Here is the shopette.) And maybe for military wives, it is just a little bit easier to surround yourself with others in the same boat, other wives who don't look at you like you're crazy for putting up with the things you do—the crazy hours your husband works, the long absences from family, the single-parenting, the personal career sacrifices. Here no one looks at you and asks why you don't get out. Leave the life. Leave him. Because all around you this is natural and normal. Here your sacrifices acquire meaning and cultural cachet. They are sacrifices wives freely make for their country.

Surrounded by like-minded folk, they are lauded as such.

As General Hagenbeck's wife, Judy, put it, "The army is family. It's not a profession or a job, it's a way of life. I think as soon as we accept that, as soon as we come to terms with that we're happier. Our quality of life goes up."

BACK IN WATERTOWN, Ulli tells me that part of the reason she is throwing herself into involvement with the FRGs is to help her prepare for her husband's imminent deployment. "I don't know what I would have done without the support of other wives," Ulli says referring to her husband's deployment when she first arrived at Fort Drum. "And it wasn't even really overwhelming support at first."

This sense of community can be lovely of course, or dangerous, depending on the level of conformity demanded. How does this manifest itself when it comes to politics? Ulli, who describes herself as a liberal and her husband as a "liberal incognito," says that the two of them love to talk politics. But she hesitates among her friends. "My husband knows I'm not the biggest Bush fan—and I never have been," says Ulli. "I'm a very liberal person, but sometimes it's better to not to advertise that." Politics is subject non grata. "There are certain things I simply don't talk about in certain groups."

As we speak, on this March 2003 day, the U.S. military is preparing to invade Iraq. Hoping to prevent the attack, thousands of U.S. peace protesters have been organizing marches across the country, and I wonder how military wives feel about this.

"I think a lot of military wives take the protests personally," says Ulli. "But I don't see these protests as being against the military, it's the administration they're protesting. That's my impression. Of course, that may be my European perspective." As Ulli has noted before, she is extremely skeptical about the presence of weapons of mass destruction in Iraq and her criticism of Bush and his policies echo those of most war protesters. But she draws her own line in the sand. "If some protester would come up to me and say something mean about the military and this war, I would fire right back in their face. If you actually attack my husband or his people, I would be very defensive."

How so?

"I'd say, they're doing their job. They go where they get sent. And they do what they have to do to do their job. And they'll do it again this time. And they'll do great—I hope. And they'll all come home as fast as possible." Ulli pauses for breath and changes course slightly. Can she reconcile a global wish for justice with a personal wish for soldier safety? "That's my biggest wish, I guess. That they go in, hit hard, come out—as fast as we can."

She is very nervous about this engagement. "I'm just scared that we'll have more casualties in this one than ever before. I just have a bad feeling. I don't know why."

I am drawn to Ulli because she is complicated. She's introspective, and articulate. And she is full of contradictions—which she is the first to acknowledge: She's a liberal who is down on Bush, but thrilled to meet him. She is fiercely independent, but speaks often of her loneliness. She has strong opinions and loves to talk politics, but says she avoids the topic among most other military wives. She is a gung-ho supporter of the army who volunteers with her Family Readiness Group but is quick to light into the "army bureaucracy" the instant she senses that she's getting the run-around.

And, of course, none of the above are *real* contradictions. Ulli just happens to be quicker than most to voice her full *range* of responses. Her two years at Fort Drum have brought about changes in Ulli who has moved from outsider—newly married, German, civilian—to insider—military wife, active in her FRG, wise to the ways of the army. Today, Ulli seems to be trying things on, finding what fits, what works, crafting her identity as an army wife.

THE NEXT AFTERNOON I catch up with Ulli at a local consignment shop. She is having lunch with the owner of the shop, her friend Nina Donnelly. Nina is an air force wife whose husband has been posted to Kuwait. Nina and Ulli sit around a coffee table and chairs in the front of the shop. I join them for a cup of coffee.

Nina has sold her shop, in anticipation of her husband's upcoming transfer to Pope Air Force Base at Fayetteville, North Carolina, and will be handing over the keys in a few weeks. She is already feeling a tiny bit nostalgic about Watertown as we sit, our chairs facing the storefront, looking out over the town square.

Still, we all agree it is drab. There are some new businesses like Nina's and a few persistent businesses hanging on waiting for downtown revitalization to take hold. There is the Crystal Restaurant, an old oak-paneled diner dating back to the turn-of-the-century with a menu and prices harkening back to mid-century. (Chipped beef on toast with green beans and ice tea will set you back $2.95.) There is its competition, Subway, across the street. There is Apex Army Navy where you can pick up state-of-the-art cold-weather survival gear for a song—as long as you don't mind that your balaclava, long johns, and ski goggles are a uniform camouflage. There is the local historical society, which has meticulously documented the 1941 disappearance of five 100-year-old hamlets, 24 one- and two-room schoolhouses, 6 churches, and 525 farms when the War Department annexed 70,000 acres for Fort Drum (then known as Pine Camp), displacing 500 families and 2,000 people—also for a song. There is the YMCA, two sad antique shops, a library up the street where the line for computer terminals with Internet access is always considerable (Internet cafes? "Fie!" says Watertown.), and a central fountain in an oddly shaped grass median—today a patch of mud and melting snow.

In the center of this commons, on this sleepy afternoon, six antiwar protesters stand holding signs.

"Can you believe these guys?" Nina says indignantly. "I can't believe they have the nerve to do this in Watertown, when half our husbands are over there!"

Ulli hesitates.

Then she nods. She agrees.

7
Heather

WALKING WOUNDED:
When the Battle-Scarred Come Home

Am I patriotic? Yes and no. I do believe in the military. I love the military.
I don't know why . . . well, my husband looks pretty good in a uniform,
maybe that's why. Sometimes now, I'm like, "Come on, honey, can't you
at least put the pants on, and that shirt on, for me?"

But seriously, now, I don't think we should be in Iraq and I don't like
Bush. I agree something needed to be done in Iraq because women had no
rights there, and from what I've seen on the news Saddam Hussein was
starving his own people. But why are we the ones that should do it? We
have lost 1,000 lives over there. Why are we the ones to do it? Look what
it's doing to our people. Look at the soldiers.

—HEATHER ATHERTON

ON A SATURDAY AFTERNOON IN JULY 2004, IN THE TINY TOWN OF
South Prairie, Washington, (population 382), a war hero is honored.

Twenty-five people gather on the front lawn of the fire station standing
before an American flag, the army flag, and two hand-stitched red-white-

and-blue quilts proclaiming "God Bless America." On a scraggly one-acre lot next to the fire station there are two picnic tables, two seesaws, two swings, and four yellow ribbons tied around the trees. This is Melrose Park, bordered by a muddy stream on one side and the fire station parking lot on the other, a railroad trestle and the road.

Today, Melrose Park is being re-christened Veterans Park in honor of Army Specialist Kris Atherton, a 24-year-old soldier and hometown boy who lost his left arm in Iraq a year earlier, in July 2003. When Kris came home for a short visit six months ago, an ad hoc group called South Prairie Cares gave him a hero's welcome with a four-block parade, a band, and a ride on an antique fire truck. At the time, he said that he hoped Americans wouldn't forget the soldiers still over there in Iraq and the vets from other wars who had made such big sacrifices. Now the community is honoring that wish with the newly renamed park and by breaking ground for a veterans' monument in front of the fire station.

There are no TV cameras today, no visible politicians, no highfalutin speeches—just a haphazard collection of ordinary, overweight Americans gussied up in the outfits they had pulled together two weeks earlier for their Fourth of July picnics: an Old Navy flag T-shirt here, star-spangled earrings there. Some kids chase a Frisbee on the edge of the parking lot, waiting for things to get started, and Kris, like a kid on the playground showing off his latest Pokemon cards, opens the back of his SUV, lifts the carpet over his spare tire, and shows some older Vietnam vets an array of daggers and weapons he scored in Iraq. Moments later, as the crowd is called to order, Kris's mom, forty-nine-year-old, Cynthia Hrinchak, a stocky woman in a T-shirt, blue-and-white-checked polyester shorts, and tennis shoes, moves proudly to the front row where she and Kris's brother, Kevin, take turns videotaping the event.

The ceremony is short and sweet. An older veteran with a trumpet plays "The National Anthem." Another vet makes a speech: "Kris Atherton is a hero," he says. He summarizes Kris's accomplishments, describing how Kris, a tank driver in the army, had volunteered for a dangerous mission, was severely wounded, and received a Purple Heart. He notes that last July, when Kris's two-Humvee convoy was blasted with an explosive that sent shrapnel everywhere, temporarily blinding one of his fellow soldiers and severing Kris's left arm, Kris refused to stop and put his fellow passengers in danger. Instead he calmly put his left forearm onto his lap, grasped the wheel with his right arm, and drove twenty minutes back to the medical facility at the army compound where he walked in carrying what remained of his arm; doctors promptly made a clean cut above the elbow.

When it is Kris's turn to speak, he walks to the mike while the trumpet player offers a few bars of "The Army Goes Rolling Along." Dressed in khaki shorts and a checked green shirt with the left sleeve lying flat, Kris is the kind of guy you'd pass in a mall and never notice. His military haircut, heavy frame, and lack of affect make him nondescript. But today he is center stage—and he is nervous and sincere. He pauses frequently to consult a crumpled piece of loose-leaf where he has scrawled some notes, and stumbles over his words. "Keep supporting veterans whenever possible because it's well worth the effort," he says in conclusion.

An official hands him a shovel and someone else urges his wife and daughter out of the crowd to join him. His wife, a skinny blond kid in a hot-pink miniskirt and white T-shirt is horrified to be in the spotlight. She blushes the color of her miniskirt. His thirteen-month-old daughter Mikia toddles around him as he tries to hoist the shovel by bracing the handle in his right armpit. Using this for leverage, he bends low and manages to move a bit of dirt onto the shovel and to the side, breaking ground for the new monument.

The crowd applauds.

Seventeen minutes after it begins, the ceremony ends when an ex-POW presents Kris with a folded flag and salutes him. It is an awkward moment. With the flag in his one hand, Kris cannot salute back. The vet waits for a moment, his hand held stiffly to his forehead. Kris knows what he wants but cannot deliver. He flushes, shifts the flag, and then makes a kind of bow.

●　　　●　　　●

KRIS IS ONE out of more than 9,700 soldiers wounded in Iraq or Afghanistan between the beginning of Operations Iraqi Freedom and Enduring Freedom and the end of 2004. Because of advances in protective gear, specifically some high-tech body armor, many more soldiers are surviving combat injuries than in any previous war. But that comes with a different cost. While the body armor protects a soldier's vital organs by surrounding his chest and back, it doesn't protect his limbs; amputees are a far more common casualty of this war than in earlier ones.

At Walter Reed Hospital in Washington, D.C., the army's largest medical facility, prosthetics is one of the busiest departments. There, soldiers who have lost an arm, a leg, both, or all four are fitted with state-of-the-art prosthetics ranging in cost from $2,000 to $50,000. But "state-of-the-art" should not be taken to mean perfection. In Kris's case, he was given three new "arms." One is merely decorative; it has a realistic-looking hand on the end that is mostly useless for any tasks. Another arm is a fancy, high-tech motorized model that can read the nerve endings at the tip of his amputation, bends at the elbow, has pincers on the end to grasp objects, and can rotate 360 degrees—but weighs thirty-five pounds. His third hand is a hook—standard issue as far back as . . . the Civil War?

Most of the soldiers who fill Walter Reed arrive with multiple injuries. In addition to lost limbs, many suffer from shrapnel wounds. The little chips of shattered metal that fly into a million pieces are one of the telltale products of an improvised explosive device (IED), which are hidden on or next to roads throughout Iraq and are a favorite device of Iraqi insurgents. One of the unanticipated problems that doctors here have struggled with is not just the shrapnel itself, which is typically scattered throughout the patient's body, but the bits of flesh—from the soldier who was sitting next to this guy in the Humvee—that penetrate along with the shrapnel, causing the kinds of serious infections associated with tissue rejection, as when a transplant patient rejects a new organ as foreign.

And then there are the psychological disorders that go along with combat. According to a 2004 *New England Journal of Medicine* study, 11 to 17 percent of soldiers returning from Afghanistan and Iraq are suffering from mental illness, ranging from major depression to anxiety to post-traumatic stress syndrome (PTSS), compared to 3 or 4 percent in the general adult population. When a soldier has been wounded, the likelihood that he will suffer from PTSS is even greater.

And for some soldiers' spouses, like Kris's wife Heather, these wounds are the hardest to deal with.

"HE'S CHANGED since he's been back," says twenty-four-year-old Heather Atherton. She knows that her husband suffers from Post-Traumatic Stress Syndrome because the doctors have told her so, but the knowledge doesn't make the change any easier to live with. "Before he went, he used to be very considerate of how I felt. Now he's not. He pulls away from me, doesn't really talk to me anymore, doesn't explain to me why he's getting mad at me." In the past, Heather says, there were times when she was so "pig-headed" she'd make him cry. "Now I'm the one crying."

To her mind, everything in their lives together has happened so fast that they've barely had time to look up and get their bearings before they're hit with another whammy.

Kris joined the army only four years ago in August 2000, when he was twenty. After fifteen weeks of basic training at Fort Knox, Kentucky, he was sent to Fort Riley, Kansas. He learned to drive tanks and was just adjusting to life in the army when the terrorist attacks of September 11, 2001, took place. Thirteen months later he married his wife, a Kansas local. Five months later on March 7, 2003, he shipped out to the Middle East and two weeks later joined the spearhead into Iraq, crossing the Euphrates River with the 3rd Infantry Division. Two months later his daughter was born prematurely. Two months after that his arm was blown off. Five months after that he was "medically discharged" and back exactly where he started, in a small town abutting South Prairie, Washington—minus one arm, plus one wife, one daughter, and some new nightmares.

That is the chronology of Kris's and Heather's story, the facts which fit a "hero's welcome." When looking closer, some messy realities intrude.

"We met in a bar called Happy's," Heather tells me as we sit at a picnic table in Veterans Park later that same hot summer afternoon. How did she initiate a conversation? Was it love at first sight? Heather rolls her eyes and gives a wry laugh. "I guess you could say that." She puts it differently. "I got pregnant two weeks after we met. Six weeks after that we got married," she says. "I said, 'I'm pregnant,' he said, 'Let's get married.' " Heather shrugs. "I have uniform syndrome." She says this as if she's at AA admitting she has a problem. "I'm not proud of it. I see a guy in uniform, though, and I think they look ten times better. They're clean-cut and they always have a job."

Heather, born and raised in Great Bend, Kansas, population 15,300, finds financial security sexy. Her parents separated when she was twelve. Heather recalls screaming fights, her dad hitting her mom, a bad situation. Her dad and her older brother left and were later arrested together for running a methamphetamine lab out of their house. They're both in prison now. "That was six years ago," Heather says. "I don't talk to my dad now. He screwed up my life enough."

Heather's mom, now in her late forties, had always worked hard to support herself and Heather; today she works full-time as a secretary for an accounting firm and part-time in the photo lab at Wal-Mart. "My mom wasn't the most wealthiest person in the world but she made sure we never did without," Heather says, explaining that her mother started teaching her about financial realities when she was thirteen and made sure she understood the value of a dollar.

To help out, Heather has been working herself since she was sixteen. In fact, she had three jobs then. Then she started having a little trouble finishing homework for school, and her mother had her drop one of the jobs. When she was a junior in high school she got a job in the kitchen of Central Kansas Medical Center, cooking, cleaning, and doing food prep. She loved it, and stayed at that same job until she moved away eight years later.

Today, like a kid at summer camp too long, she speaks of home yearningly. She loved those people she worked with at the hospital who had known her since she was seventeen and treated her like family. She missed

Kansas, where things were cheap. She thinks about the small town of Great Bend, where she felt safe and secure. And most of all, since she moved to Washington State two and a half months ago, she realizes how much she relied on familiar faces, family, and friends, who were her ballast in this stormy world.

She swings her skinny legs on this high picnic bench where they don't quite reach the ground, tucks a strand of blond hair behind her ear, and looks around her—our backdrop, the snowy peaks of Mount Rainier against an exquisite, bright blue sky—and scowls. Sad eyes and jutting jaw. "It's a nice area, I know," she says. "But it don't feel like home. Nothing feels like home. I don't even know the roads here." She sighs. "And I don't have my mommy." Then, for the ninth time in our interview, she buoys herself with the same hope, "Things are getting better, though."

"AS SOON AS I GOT BACK FROM IRAQ, boom! I'm instantly a father and a husband," says Kris when I drop by the Athertons' duplex one afternoon. When I arrive, Mikia, dressed in a blue sunsuit is stretched out on her belly, sound asleep on the couch; Heather is gone, working her first day as a cook at the local veterans' home. Kris, dressed in shorts and a blue T-shirt, is a large guy—tall, solid, and slow moving—and he offers up his feelings as though they belong to someone he knows but is not particularly intimate with. "I had to go from being around a bunch of guys in the desert to being a married husband and taking care of my daughter, and it's a struggle. Heather's changed a lot and I've changed a lot." He doesn't seem too comfortable talking about this.

We talk about the army instead.

"I always liked playing G.I. Joe as a kid and running around in the woods," he says, explaining why he was drawn to the army. That, and the fact that his father, his uncle, and both his grandfathers served in the military. But most of all, he says, he was attracted to the idea of imposed discipline. "I wanted some type of discipline because I never grew up with a father," he says, explaining that his parents separated before he was born. "I needed the stabilization of a job where I had no choice but to go and to do what they told me."

To Kris the army looked good. "I was the first one in my family to actually get the G.E.D.," he tells me, proudly pointing out that none of his five cousins had graduated from high school *or* taken the General Educational Development (G.E.D.) test. "So my grandmother was really encouraging me. Her and my mom wanted me to accomplish something in my life— and I wanted to do the same."

The army was better than most of his options. When he was in high school, Kris worked at Wal-Mart. The work was boring, the pay mediocre, and the hours terrible. Finally, when a supervisor insisted that he stay at work until 3 A.M., pointing out that Kris was eighteen and that no child-labor laws were being broken, Kris resisted: he had to go to school in the morning. The supervisor didn't care, so Kris quit and went to school—for a while.

He dropped out later that year, while a senior, and got a good job as a sheet counter at Commencement Bay Corrugated, a local cardboard-making company where he earned $17 an hour counting the bundles before they were shipped. But working four ten-hour shifts left him with too much time off for drinking and hanging out with buddies. Something had to change. "At first I was too scared to join the army and go out on my own, hop a bus all the way to a state I've never been to, not knowing anybody," he says. But he finally took the plunge on August 28, 2000, and after fifteen weeks of basic training, found himself stationed at Fort Riley, Kansas.

While we've been talking Mikia has woken up. She has that still-sleepy, near-weepy look about her and wants a wake-up cuddle, which Kris recognizes and somewhat awkwardly provides. He scoops her up in his arm and lets her sit in his lap for a few minutes. Occasionally he pats her back.

Then, when she starts to get wiggly, he sets her on the floor where she begins to toddle around on her spindly-thin, slightly bowed legs. He goes to the fridge and opens a Lunchable for her, sets it on the table, removes the high-chair tray, sets it down, picks her up and puts her in the high chair, puts the tray back, and hands her the food. He does this using only his right arm; once again, the left shirt sleeve hangs empty, with no prosthetic attached.

He tells me that the night the Iraq invasion began he sat at the border for three or four hours just looking out at the darkness, waiting. "All's you could see was the infrared blinky lights of soldiers moving across the desert," he says. "There were some shots fired, but all we were shooting at turned out to be some old tanks from the first Gulf War still sitting out there in the desert." He gives Mikia a slice of cheese from her Lunchable and watches her chew. "I kind of expected it to be worse than what it was at first," he says. "But then slowly it got worse."

He stands up to get a sippy cup from the cupboard, pours Mikia some milk, screws on the lid and gives it to her. He tells me that he witnessed his first casualty three weeks later. He had been told to give some soldiers a lift on his tank. "These seven infantry soldiers were on top of the turret," he says. "They didn't really have any cover at all. I was my company commander's driver. I told him, it's not really a good idea, but . . ." He shrugs, hands Mikia a slice of pepperoni. "Ten minutes later, one of the guys up there got hit from the side. It missed the plates of his body armor because it came from the side. It went right into his heart."

As Mikia finishes her lunch, he fast-forwards through some of the other casualties he witnessed. Slice of pepperoni, somebody shot up. Square of cheese, another death. There was the guy who had been their company's 1st sergeant who was following a kid to find some unexploded ordnance. The kid went for it and it blew him and the 1st sergeant up.

He holds the sippy cup to Mikia's mouth. "You want a drink?"

Two weeks later, at a checkpoint, his lieutenant had just checked out a car and was walking back when he got shot with a rocket-propelled grenade (RPG) in the back. "It didn't explode, but it hit him so hard it pretty much mushed up the inside of him."

He lifts Mikia out of the high chair and sets her on the floor. "That's when it really hit me because it was actually someone I talked to every day," he says. "And he'd just gotten married."

Then, out of the blue, Kris felt like calling home. A few days later he paid a local Iraqi to use his satellite cell phone, even though it cost him $2 a minute. Heather answered the phone: "Guess what? We've got a baby girl on our hands," she told him. "I know that," Kris said. Heather had already told him they were having a girl; the due date was three weeks away. "She said, 'No! I mean I'm lookin' at our baby girl! She's a week old.' "

Heather, who had gone into labor early, immediately notified the Red Cross, which is the standard procedure for getting emergency messages to soldiers.

"But I never did get any message—from them or anyone else," Kris says. He shakes his head, staring down at Mikia from where he stands near the fridge. Mikia is now eating and *wearing* a grape Freeze-it Pop. Purple goo dribbles down her chin onto her sunsuit. She puts a sticky hand out to touch his leg and he flinches. "That's how I found out I was a dad," he says.

"THERE'S TIMES when I want to be all lovey-dovey but he doesn't. He's just, like, 'Leave me alone!' " Heather tells me. He used to love it when she rubbed the back of his head; and she liked the bristly feel of his buzz cut. Now he gets freaked out, Heather complains. "It reminds him of the bugs and stuff over there." It doesn't really bother her, she tells me. "I'm like, 'Fine! Okay. I don't have to rub the back of your head or neck, less work for me.' " Then he gets mad. "He's got more of an anger problem now . . . but he's working on it."

For her part, she's trying to figure out how much is just who Kris is and how much is what the war has made him. But either way he irks her. "He's lazy to begin with," she says. "We won't even go there. He has this kind of woe-is-me thing going and I'll tell you, it's frustrating." She says he wouldn't help with the baby until she practically made him. The week before she got fed up. He'd never changed Mikia, claimed he couldn't. "I put my hand behind my back and said 'Look! Watch this. I'm changing a diaper with one hand and you can too!' "

It must be frustrating for him, I say.

Heather shrugs—and points out that it's frustrating for her, too. "At first I did everything for Mikia, he didn't really have any experience with babies and I'm very protective of her, but after a while, I'm like, 'You *can* feed her.' " She gives a sly smile. "He couldn't tie her bib, but I got Velcro ones."

She says he can do a lot more than he thinks with one arm. And he can do even more with the hook. "But that hook arm scares me," she says. "I'd rather look at his short nub, which I call his *third boob*. He even has this kind of strap he's supposed to wear over it. I call it his *bra*." She snickers. Lately though, he hasn't been able to wear his hook. He has gained too much weight—twenty or thirty pounds, she says—and it won't fit right. "Oh, boy, I've got myself a teddy bear, now!" she says, insisting that he looked like a "stuffed sausage" when he tried to squeeze into his uniform for the parade here six months ago. "And that's not healthy. I'm a health nut. I eat right, exercise. It just bugs me, the fact that he's gained so much weight." She sighs and shrugs it off. "But hey, it's his life." Then reconsiders: "It does bother me, though."

A few weeks ago, Kris and Heather went together to see a counselor at the local Veterans Administration hospital. "It was Kris's idea," Heather says. "Because all he hears is me nagging at him. I guess it's my own insecurities, but I don't communicate it in a very calm way," she says, explaining that they mostly fight about money. Heather is frugal, a fiscal conservative who is desperately worried that they have absolutely no financial cushion; Kris, she says, is a spendthrift who thinks nothing of dropping $25 on a new video game. They fight about money constantly. At the moment they are living on $2,540 a month that they get in Kris's veterans benefits ($180 a month less than what he was making at the cardboard factory when he quit to join the army four years earlier). Their rent is $875, and their monthly car payments are $530. That leaves $1,045 for heat, utilities, gas, car insurance, diapers, food and clothes for three. Living on the edge this way worries her. Sometimes she doesn't express it in the best way. "We need to communicate better," she admits. "But he needs to explain things to me when something's bothering him. Instead he sits there and tells me it's me."

Heather rolls her eyes. "Pleeeeze!" she says. "My mom says a lot of it's him. His own mother says a lot of it is him. And the counselor says the same thing." The counselor also warns about post-traumatic stress, and Heather is trying to understand how this is affecting their relationship. "The thing is with this, they pull away from those they love," she says. "He's so used to his life being threatened that he has to pull away to protect himself."

That makes it hard. Everything about their relationship is hard. "I'm more of a go-getter, organized, making sure I have all my ducks in a row. He's like the complete opposite," she says. At the end of the only couples session they attend, the counselor searched for the positive. "Okay, what *do* you like about each other?" she asked them.

Heather threw out the one answer she could think of: "I guess we like the fact that we're complete opposites?"

IF YOU ADD MORE DETAILS to the simple, abbreviated tale of heroics described at the Veterans Park dedication, the story shifts, distorts.

Forty-five days before he was slated to leave Iraq and get out of the army, Kris volunteered for a mission to retrieve a stolen gun, to cover for someone else's mistake.

The gun had been taken from the army's compound in Abu Ghraib. "There were always these kids coming in and out of the compound, selling guys pop and ice and cigarettes," Kris says. "One of the guys left his weapon on the table and was reading a magazine when this fourteen- or fifteen-year-old kid stole the gun."

Using an interpreter, some army investigators, and the local Iraqi police, the army learned that the teen had sold the 9mm semiautomatic pistol to somebody more than an hour's drive away in eastern Saddam City for $300. Police picked up the kid and held him at a police station in Baghdad. Volunteers were needed for a mission—go retrieve the kid and drive with him to eastern Saddam City, where he'd agreed to point out the arms buyer—and Kris's hand went up.

"Everybody told me not to go," Kris says. He discounted their warnings. He figured that most of the attacks that had taken place lately were be-tween 9 P.M. and 4 A.M., so they ought to be safe beginning their ride just before sunrise with two Humvees. The group picked up the teen from the police station and had just headed out of Abu Ghraib, when they passed an ice cream store. "That's when we felt a big blast," says Kris, explaining that they were hit with an IED. Kris's buddy, Spec. Mario Mancado, was man-ning the machine gun up top and fell down into the car screaming that his face was on fire and he couldn't see. (Indeed shrapnel had sliced him up badly, and he would later lose his eye.) "I was in shock and at first didn't even feel my arm," Kris recalls. He just knew that if they pulled over the at-tack would probably continue, so he spun around and kept driving, head-ing back toward the Abu Ghraib army compound. "That's when I looked over at my arm because it started hurting a little." Hanging by a few ten-dons, Kris grabbed it and placed it in his lap. "In five minutes the pain was unbearable," Kris says. "I had to put my sweat rag in my mouth to bite on, to keep from screaming."

Kris kept driving for twenty minutes until he reached the field hospital where—after some guards took their teenage prisoner and some medics took Mancado from the Humvee—Kris walked toward the operating room carrying his own forearm.

"The next thing I knew, I woke up as I was being put into a Black-hawk," Kris says. "I was getting sick and vomiting. This was my first heli-copter ride. At one point I just remember looking to my left—my arm was gone."

"HE CALLED ME at 10 o'clock our time," Heather says. "He said, 'Well, honey, I lost my arm.' And all I could think was, 'You son of a bitch! How are you going to help me with this baby?' " She didn't say this aloud. "I knew he'd been through hell and back," she says. "All I said was, 'Honey, we're married and we'll get through this together. You have me and I have you—so we're both kind of screwed.' " She smiles—a pretty mouth and a row of crooked teeth—explaining that sometimes sarcasm helps her through things.

In fact, Heather was taken by surprise when she found out he had lost his arm; the officer who first called to tell her Kris was hurt had said it wasn't serious, that he might lose a finger or two. She got this news when Mikia was three months old, the day after she'd returned to work following maternity leave. Kris's mom flew out to D.C. a few days later, shortly after Kris arrived at Walter Reed, but, Heather didn't go for over a month. She wasn't nervous about seeing him, she insists, but she was nervous about traveling. "I had never been on a plane before. And I had my newborn daughter; what was I going to do with her?"

Finally, in September Heather left the baby with her mother and flew to Washington. As she entered the army hospital, she called on her cell phone to tell Kris she was there. He took the elevator down to the lobby, as she rode it up to his room. Then, when he wasn't there, she went back down—as he was on his way back up. When the back-and-forth ended and she saw him at last, she scowled. "I'm gonna kill you!" Now, as she tells this reunion story, she sighs, so beyond star-crossed lovers are they. "That was the wrong thing to say," she says. "His life passed before his eyes."

KRIS, who had been flown from Abu Ghraib to Baghdad to Kuwait and then to Landstuhl, Germany, for a few days, had further surgery shortly after he arrived at Walter Reed. Called a "revision," the surgery shortened his arm even more by rounding out the sharp bone and removing some of the flesh. This would make fitting a prosthetic easier. "That surgery felt worse than the original injury," Kris says.

As he talks, Heather arrives home on her lunch break from the hospital. Dressed in khakis, a large T-shirt, and tennis shoes, she looks wiped. Pushing back some of the hair that has escaped her tight ponytail, she gives the baby a kiss and then falls onto the couch, exhausted. "Don't mind me," she says, waving at us to keep talking. She has a half-hour break and is just going to veg out and watch TV. Then she leans back toward Mikia and sniffs. "Did you change her diaper?"

Kris hasn't; he wonders if she will.

"Hey, you're on duty, not me," she says.

Kris sighs and picks up an empty milk jug that Mikia has dug out of the trash at least seven times in the last hour. Once again, patient as an ox, he takes the jug from her and puts it back in the trash. Once again, Mikia waddles over, lifts the lid of the trash, pulls out the jug, and starts chewing on the lid.

"Why don't you do something with it?" Heather says. She grabs the remote and flicks through the channels.

Kris takes the milk jug from Mikia, puts it in the trash, and finally moves the trash into the laundry room off the kitchen and shuts the door.

"Please," he says to Heather, referring to the diaper again.

"Hey, I've been on my feet all day." Heather gives a dramatic sigh and rolls her eyes. "Oh all right, get me a diaper, then, at least." He goes upstairs to get one and hands it to her. She diapers Mikia on the couch, one eye on the baby, one eye on the TV.

"When I arrived in Kuwait, that was the first time I could call home after my arm," Kris says.

"That's when I said, 'Oh damn, he's still alive!'" Heather interrupts from the couch.

He ignores her. "I called Heather and then I called my mom. I guess my mom already found out I was hurt somehow."

"That's because I called her," Heather says. "I'm your first contact. Remember, I'm your wife. Till death do us part."

A beat: They both look at each other and I can't tell if the look is love or hate. She goes back to the TV, he goes back to our conversation.

Kris tells me that the care he got at Walter Reed Hospital was good, but being an outpatient was not. He tried to make it to the group counseling sessions that were scheduled, but the times often conflicted with his appointments with the overworked prosthetics lab and occupational therapists. He was lucky if he could make it every other Tuesday. Then he was moved into guest quarters near the hospital, and when things started getting crowded, as the wounded poured in that fall, they started doubling soldiers up with roommates there. "I got a guy who was suffering from flea bites," Kris says with disgust. "Here he is complaining about his bug bites, and me with an amputated arm!" Eventually hospital policy changed so that amputees bunked with amputees. Happily, Kris got a new roommate. "He was an above-the-knee," Kris says, explaining that they could joke around and commiserate with each other. Still, being there five months left him very depressed. "It's like another deployment altogether because you're still away from your family and your home," he says. They would have let Heather and Mikia come, but the room was the size of a small hotel room. Both agreed it wasn't the best arrangement, with the baby waking up all night, the three of them crammed in a room, and Heather having to quit her job.

As our conversation wends on, Heather finishes the can of pop that was her lunch and jumps up. "See you later," she says, switching off the remote and heading back out the door to work.

Some day Heather would like to go back to college and take classes to be a pharmacist's assistant. She had attended a community college for over a year just out of high school, but dropped out. Kris too has decided he'd like to go back to school and will use his G.I. benefits to pay for it. The Veterans Administration set him up with a career consultant and a career advisor. He told them he liked science and math and that he liked being outdoors. They have decided he should enroll in civil engineering—and that sounds good to him. "Here in Washington State they make four thousand dollars to six thousand dollars a month," he says. "And to me, that's really good to support a family on."

Mikia is scooting around the living room on a Play-and-Learn plastic truck. She pounds the horn and he jumps. Then looks sheepish. "She's tired," he says, but he is the one who looks tired.

He tells me that he feels anxious a lot and jumpy, that he freaks out over weird things, that going over railroad tracks sounds like machine gun fire to him. Sometimes he can't make himself care, sometimes he cares too much. "I tend to hold things in and let them out at the wrong time," he says. "And emotionally, being a husband is really hard because my emotions are just not there anymore. It's almost like the caring has just gone away."

"SOMETIMES I DON'T FEEL LIKE we have any emotional connection at all," Heather says. "I feel like he's just a friggin' roommate." She looks at me, baby-blue eye shadow over baby-blue eyes that are wide with surprise, as if she didn't expect to be here, for this to be her life.

I wonder how she pictured herself, how she sees herself in the years to come.

"I didn't know what to expect when I married him," she says. "Now, I don't even try to set a plan out in my mind for the future." She is resigned. "It'll just get screwed up, so why bother?"

"We didn't really know each other to begin with, so we're just trying to get along in a married atmosphere," she explains. Besides fighting about money and what he can and cannot do with one arm, they fight about time. He hates it when she goes out and leaves him too long with the baby. She hates it when he wants to spend all his time hanging out with his high school buddies, when he says he will be home at 6 P.M. but shows up at 10 instead. "Seems like since we've got married we've just had a lot to deal with—go, go, go from one thing to another. Everybody tells me I've handled our situation pretty well, especially because I've had a kind of difficult past with my dad and all."

The only time I have seen Heather cry is when her father comes up like this in the conversation. She brushes her tears away with the heel of her hand. We are standing in a parking lot, and she is not embarrassed to be crying, just impatient. She doesn't know why she is crying about her dad now, when she has other more important things to cry about but for some reason Kris and her fighting, their marriage, reflecting on raising a kid with Kris, what they're doing right, what their parents did right—and wrong—with them, get all whirled together and mixed up with her feelings about her dad. And she cries. "Whatever," she says with a shrug.

.　　　.　　　.

KRIS AND HEATHER'S STORY reads one way in the press, and quite another behind the scenes. It is messy and untidy with no clean narrative arc, no easy protagonists. The story of this unlikely hero and his family, randomly handed to me by an army public affairs official, is so flimsy in construction that it begins to unravel the moment one of its many loose threads snags on a reporter's question. What do we do with this story, so antithetical to our familiar tropes? Discard it?

The problem is, Kris's real life and Heather's real life—though perhaps different in minor aspects from their contemporaries—truly are the story.

Most of the returning wounded are amputees; most of them are under twenty-five; most of them earn less than $30,000 a year; most of them suffer from multiple problems—including post-traumatic stress syndrome; most of them jump when they go over railroad tracks (or hear a car backfire or a balloon pop); and most of them find their marriages are a new battleground.

KRIS TELLS ME that he was already seeing a counselor for depression before he was shipped out to Iraq; that he has been on medication for his anxiety and on the antidepressant Zoloft since his injury but stopped taking them both two months ago because they didn't seem to be doing any good; that he woke up one night to Heather's yells and realized that he had his hand around her throat, choking her. He sees a counselor at the local VA hospital.

Heather, like most vets' wives, doesn't.

"You just deal with change the best way you can," she says. "Getting married is just the hardest thing. Period."

Heidi

PEACE ON POST:

Against the War, but Married to It

I don't want to see anybody going through a war like this unless it's ab-solutely necessary—and I don't see that in this war with Iraq. I feel that a preemptive war is insane because that gives other countries the justifi-cation for doing the same. If anybody now stands up and says, "Hey, I'm going to knock you out first before you get me," what can we say? That idea—I'm going to knock you out first before you get me—that's just not civilized in my eyes.

—HEIDI KLAUS-SMITH

I T IS MORNING ON MARCH 20, 2003, THE FIRST DAY OF THE WAR against Iraq. And up at Fort Drum it is raining. Hard.

As Defense Secretary Donald Rumsfeld's early-morning radio address reminds waking Americans that there is sacrifice involved in patriotism, two dozen soldiers with forty-pound rucks on their backs practice urban warfare techniques in a march across Fort Drum's main road. Machine guns in hand, the soldiers approach an intersection and scan the horizon.

Two of them dart into the center of the street to stop traffic. Then, one by one, the mostly very young soldiers file past, their camouflaged uniforms caked with mud, their grim and grimy faces fractured by rivulets of rain.

Three minivans with moms on their way to the commissary or the office or to drop the kids at school pause on one side of the intersection. Opposite, two soldiers in a Humvee wait. As traffic backs up, no one honks in irritation, as they might in New York City. The drivers sit patiently, respectfully, sadly at the intersection, as if waiting for the passage of a funeral procession. They have seen this a hundred times.

Later that same afternoon, Frederick Calladine, chief of Casualty and Mortuary Affairs at Fort Drum, whom we first met in Chapter 1, will brief his new casualty officers, reminding the notifiers to "give them the news, then get the hell out of Dodge."

And even later that same afternoon, outside the post's gates, on a small grass median in the center of Watertown, the gaggle of six peace activists, also mentioned earlier, will stand in the dusk, in the pouring rain, trying desperately to keep the requisite candles lit in this candlelight peace vigil. These are the same protesters that Ulli and Nina watched from Nina's shop on the square, the ones with such "nerve," protesting while half of Fort Drum was deployed.

As this day wanes, the protesters huddle together on a scrap of dry sidewalk beneath umbrellas quickly saturated by the cold spring rain. Two cardboard posters, the Magic Marker beginning to run, are taped to sticks that have been jabbed into the soft ground. Writ large: "We support our troops." Writ small: "Bring them home!"

Standing among the protesters is Heidi Klaus-Smith, a forty-two-year-old army wife who feels compelled to voice her objection to the war. She is against this war and worries about what will happen to her husband, her friends' husbands, this country.

She is not alone in her worries.

All people in this military town have freeze-framed their lives to watch the war unfold today. It is a day where everyone is somber. Where families new to Fort Drum sit in waiting rooms to register cars, dogs, preschoolers and shush their toddlers mercilessly as they huddle around the TV decoding events. Where other office workers in this same administration building add half-hour detours to their trips to the drinking fountain, standing in front of these same TVs—CNN being more forthcoming than the DOD announcements, which trickle in over their computers. Where everyone wonders if everyone else knows something, heard something, saw something that will shed more light. Where the numbers of casualties being calculated won't rest in peace but provoke a scramble for details— battalions, units, names, posts-of-origin—that will offer small comforts to each news-gatherer: The deceased is a stranger.

On this day in which the war with Iraq begins, the confluence of events, lives, symbols gather steam. There is a sense that we are charging forward—but toward what?

HEIDI, STANDING AMONG THE ANTIWAR ACTIVISTS, is very emotional. (Is it tears or rain that have smudged her eyeliner?) Her soldier husband has not been deployed—yet—but she knows the possibility exists. She also knows she is on dangerous ground. For Heidi, coming out against the war in this very conservative military community has meant wrestling with her conscience. Will it jeopardize her husband's career if she speaks out? Will she jeopardize her own values if she doesn't? Does silence equal complicity?

She struggles with these questions—yet she stands in the square.

Clearly Heidi Klaus-Smith is not your typical military wife. But neither is she utterly atypical. As a German who married an American soldier while he was stationed overseas, she is a member of a large group of foreign military wives who include South Koreans, Japanese, Vietnamese, Europeans, Panamanians—basically women from anywhere the U.S. military has had bases and therefore a cadre of young dating soldiers. What these women bring to the military is the same challenge—or asset—that immigrants have always brought to this nation: different cultures, different ways of being, different points of view.

Like most of these wives, Heidi met her husband while he was stationed at an army post near her hometown. She was working in the housing office at Downs Barracks in Fulda, Germany. For thirteen years, she helped American families find housing and negotiate with their German landlords. She met and married her husband, and in 1995 the couple moved to Oklahoma for a brief half-year as her husband underwent some training. Heidi, interested in Native American cultures, nature, and hiking was in heaven there; moving to Fort Drum slammed her back down to earth. "It was a big wake-up call. I had my culture shock then. We arrived in the middle of January 1996," she says—and anybody who knows the North Country knows that January there is a special kind of cold, white hell. (In 2003 the low temperature for January was –31 degrees Fahrenheit, and seven feet of snow fell.) "I didn't know anybody. We bought a house [off-post] in the country. My husband left immediately for six weeks in Panama. My pipes froze. My garage door crashed down stuck while my car was inside. My husband was gone for barely a week when I slid off the road into a ditch. And I'm sitting there in the ditch thinking, 'Oh my God, what am I going to do before I freeze to death? I don't know anyone. Not one person in this entire state.' "

As Heidi goes on to describe that first harsh transition to life as a military wife at Fort Drum, the fact that she doesn't know a soul surfaces as a refrain no fewer than six times in as many minutes. "Luckily, moments after I slid into the ditch someone stopped. They pulled me out with their pickup. They invited me to breakfast—which in Germany would never have happened. And I've been in touch with that family ever since. I've gotten to know the whole family—brothers, sisters, aunts, and uncles. These are some of my best friends now. Turns out driving into that ditch was the best thing that happened to me."

Eventually Heidi's circle of acquaintances widened. "I met some other wives through the coffee groups," she says. "And shortly thereafter, I became involved in volunteer work with a Family Readiness Group."

Later, Heidi confides to me that her "volunteer" work was actually not so voluntary. "In fact, we had major . . . almost marital problems over that because I didn't feel obligated to do this and he totally expected me to," she says, explaining that because she was a commander's wife, he insisted it was necessary. "He wanted me to do this because if I didn't, people would say I wasn't supportive of the military. That really upset me. We had quite a struggle with that." In the end, Heidi went ahead and volunteered, but she resented it. "If I didn't write some friggin' newsletter that meant I wasn't supportive of the military?" she asks. Although she admits she didn't really mind the newsletter per se, she resented the assumption that it was her job. "And all that fund-raising! I hated fund-raising. I hated doing it—bake sales, hot dog sales, pie-throwing contests, silly stuff, on and on."

For Heidi it was the element of coercion that made her feel "phony" and "untrue" to herself. "There are a lot of things in the military that are expected automatically. They *say* if you don't do it, it's no problem, but my husband thought it would be a problem for his career. And a lot of wives *think* it will affect their husbands' careers if they don't do this kind of stuff," she says. Heidi had done a little volunteer work before in Germany for her local equivalent of a humane society, but she had mixed feelings about the whole idea of wives' shouldering volunteer work on-post. "On the one hand, I think it's a good thing, but on the other I think it's taking pay away from other people," she says. "These are jobs that are not formally being created because they're relying on volunteers."

Heidi, who married her husband when she was in her late thirties, is less malleable than some of the younger wives. This, combined with her German background, has made her an outsider in the military community. She has resisted its lure. In the beginning, she tugged a little; as time goes on she will pull hard—nearly extricating herself.

Her first public act is the peace protest in Watertown's square. Talking to a reporter, she is even more brazen. "Are you sure you're okay with me using your real name?" I ask her the day we meet, when she tells me about her trepidations going public with her antiwar views. She feels very strongly, she tells me. She will speak for attribution.

Growing up as a child in Germany, Heidi was weaned on horror stories about World War II. "I grew up with knowledge about the Holocaust, and the message that I took away from that was, we have a responsibility to speak up when we see the government doing wrong," she says. She is sympathetic with her friends, the many military wives who she says are against the war in Iraq but are afraid to voice their opinions. Still, she has made a conscious decision to do otherwise. "I remember when I was in school seeing a film about a young Jewish girl named Rachael who was sent to a concentration camp. Many good people in her town knew what was happening to the Jews but stayed quiet," Heidi says, her face lit intermittently by headlights as cars swing through the square. "So I stand here today for Rachael."

FAST FORWARD six months into the war, and Heidi Klaus-Smith has a bit of company. The murmurs of discontent among military families has grown louder: Deployments are stretching out past the originally anticipated six months, with more than 50 percent of the army's combat brigades stationed overseas (and the remaining 50 percent in a holding pattern, waiting to replace them), more than 1,600 U.S. soldiers have been injured at this point and "peacekeeping" deaths reach the 200 mark—for the first time exceeding the number sustained during the active combat stage of the war. In a survey of soldiers deployed to Iraq conducted by the *Stars and Stripes,* half the respondents say that their unit's morale is low and their training inadequate, and they don't plan to reenlist. Struggling to hold onto an overworked force, the Pentagon has been forced to institute "stop loss," which forbids soldiers in select jobs from getting out—even if they have served their time. (The marines ordered a corps-wide stop loss.) The rush to serve predicted in the aftermath of September 11 has not materialized, and some recruiting requirements were lowered so that the services could meet their quotas. Meanwhile, interviews with military families in the Fort Drum area and beyond show a growing unease with Bush's Iraq policy. Some is direct. "This is just not a war I believe in," says Tammy Schmitt, wife of an air force officer stationed at Fort Drum. And some is oblique. "You have to support the troops; what are you going to do?" Ulli

Robinson tells me at this point, then goes on to voice indignation at Bush's after-the-fact plea for UN support and the troubling fact that no weapons of mass destruction (WMD) have surfaced in Iraq. "I'm surprised the CIA hasn't planted some [WMD]. I'm like, please, just plant something and let me believe."

But will these conversations in kitchens and commissaries ever translate into organized opposition? And what happens when they do? Six months into the war peace activists are cautiously optimistic.

For now military wives' presence in the peace movement is symbolic. The number of those willing to go public with their views is small (compared to the significant numbers who privately say they oppose the war), but the visuals are powerful.

After all, military families bring an insider's perspective to the antiwar effort. Many parade firsthand knowledge of the waste of manpower, the unnecessarily harsh conditions soldiers endure, and the inadequate compensation families receive. And they're an irresistible photo op—typically patriotic in get-up with fatherless kids (temporarily, hopefully) in tow. Candance Robison, a twenty-seven-year-old Texan who organized an early protest in Crawford, Texas, where Bush was spending his vacation, says she was angry enough to sit on the side of the road holding a poster with her soldier husband's picture on it and to bring along her one-year-old son and her six-year-old daughter to sit beside her. Even though she had "zero experience" as a political activist, Robison learned fast. Since her husband, an engineer in the Army Reserve was deployed to Iraq in February 2003, she has written letters to the president, organized protests, and traveled to Washington, D.C., to testify at a congressional briefing. She tells me she addressed her remarks, there to the secretary of defense: "Donald Rumsfeld, get the spare room ready because me and the kids are coming to stay," Robison said, in her cocky Texas drawl. She explained that army pay was far less than what her husband had been making as a sales manager for a steel company. Although the company had been making up the difference since her husband's February deployment, that wasn't expected to continue with the deployment having been extended a year. She didn't know how she was going to keep up the mortgage payments. " 'Hope you and the missus can put us up!' I told them."

From the beginning, Robison questioned the necessity of this war—"I needed more evidence that there were weapons of mass destruction before I was ready to accept my husband might come home in a body bag"—but her husband, an ex-naval officer and currently an officer in the Army Reserves corps of engineers, was excited and eager to go. "He believed in what we were going over there to do," she says. "He felt that there were weapons of mass destruction and was very anxious to try and do what he had been training to do for twenty years." But now she says that has changed: " 'I would be here and be proud to do my job, but I'm not even sure what my mission is,' he says now." While Robison's husband supports what she's doing, many in his stateside military community don't. "One of the wives who heads up the family support group read me this supposedly official memo over the phone," Robison said. "She said I am essentially aiding terrorism by speaking out. 'Well,' I said. 'That wouldn't be me, that would be our president—the one who is leaving our soldiers there as sitting ducks.' Then she said that I am never to speak out on behalf of the family support group or the U.S. military. Well I never have. Because I'm not a member of either one!"

Robison is unusual among military wives in that she, like Heidi, didn't grow up a military brat. Also she has never lived on an army post, and she currently lives an hour from the nearest military facility. But most wives live their lives deeply immersed in the military community on a daily basis. For them, the gap between holding certain political beliefs and speaking out publicly about these beliefs looms like a canyon. Crossing it carries tremendous risk.

"The wives are afraid. In fact everybody told me, 'Do not come here and talk to a journalist,' " Heidi says, explaining that she had intended to bring along other antiwar wives to speak with me when we met for our second interview at Watertown's Salmon Run Mall. "I thought I would find some to talk to you because we are all of the same opinion about the war—

and most of them I would consider quite outspoken . . . but they are too nervous." Heidi says they had almost convinced *her* to cancel the interview. "Several told me stories about their husbands getting in trouble because of their wives being outspoken. 'If you find your name in the paper, your husband's career is ruined,' they said."

Whether this is true or not is *almost* irrelevant. As long as the fear of repercussions exists, vocal opposition will be stifled. Indeed, the rules regarding a soldier's political activism on any issue are so filled with legalistic minutiae—ranging from straight-out forbidding any activism in partisan politics or the use of "contemptuous words against officeholders" to specifying that "large" political signs may not be displayed on soldiers' cars but standard bumper stickers may—as to make most soldiers afraid to exercise any of their free-speech rights. Soldiers are beyond nervous when it comes to political activism—and that extends to their families. Does an outspoken wife implicate her husband? Guilt by association? As with bake sales and volunteer work, no one can say definitively that a wife's behavior affects her husband's career, but most are confident this is so.

In any case, outspoken wives get tarred with the "unpatriotic" brush. "One wife told me to stop my craziness and let these guys be proud of what they're doing. I *am* proud of my husband," says Robison. "I'm disappointed in my government and the military."

Others disagree. "I take these antiwar protesters personally," twenty-eight-year-old Amy Wortham, a Fort Drum army officer's wife, told me as her husband was fighting in Afghanistan. She sees them as unpatriotic and antimilitary. "By definition I support my husband, therefore I support the military and the war." Referring to Operation Anaconda, a March 2002 incident in Afghanistan where soldiers from Fort Drum were pinned down and two helicopters came under fire during an eighteen-hour battle resulting in eight American casualties, Wortham chides the protesters. "My husband puts his life in jeopardy so they could have the freedom to protest."

That they've chosen to exercise that right is not consolation, but ingratitude.

Clearly, a soldier's wife who questions the necessity of U.S. intervention in Iraq steps into a hornet's nest of military values. When husbands spend all day doing what they're told, even when they might think it's stupid, there is a way in which blind faith becomes virtuous. Doubt is for the lazy and faint of heart; it's for those who can't hack it the way it is. Questioning equals complaining. Within that culture, military wives typically preface any criticism—or political analysis, for that matter—by pointing out that the president of the United States is their husbands' boss. What they mean by this, is that it's not nice to call their husbands' boss a jackass. But what they also mean is that it's hard to accept the sacrifices the military requires of them without believing that it is for some greater good, that their husband missed the birth of their daughter because national security was at stake. Unlike most civilian wives—plenty of who think their husband's boss is a jackass—military wives have to bring their thinking around to encompass the notion that their husband might *die* because his boss is. Sometimes they have to believe this boss knows something they don't know—*there really must have been weapons of mass destruction in Iraq, right?*—because, otherwise, how do you live with the knowledge that your husband's life is on the line in Afghanistan or Iraq?

So they believe.

Sort of.

But doubt creeps in around the edges. While their husbands signed on the dotted line when they joined up, wives are conscripts. With a smidgen less institutional loyalty, they are a tiny bit more outspoken. And yet, tremendous loyalty to their husbands and a daily life steeped in the vocal patriotism of a military post makes them uneasy critics. The way every mother feels compelled to begin criticism of her children with, "I love her to death, but . . ." so the army wife qualifies with a verbal tic, "I love my husband/the army/this country but . . ." Implicit in the I-love-my-country-but qualifier is the notion that love ought to be blind, meaning without criticism. In this version of democracy, those who chide and criticize the government into doing things differently—presumably better— are somehow less patriotic than those who "blindly" follow our leaders.

So they fret.

"I understand the wives, and especially the soldiers, that feel they have no choice but to support the war because otherwise you go insane because you can't live with it, with that contradiction," says Heidi. "You can't go into a war and say, I'm totally against it but I'm going to shoot somebody anyway. That doesn't work. And the wives are in the same shoes. In your mind . . ." Heidi struggles to find the right words. "It is possible to train your mind to support something that maybe in your true heart, that's not what you believe in. I see that in this community."

UNDER THESE CIRCUMSTANCES, seeing any organized war opposition evolve from within the military community might be unrealistic. But perhaps being a peace activist, by definition, requires some determined optimism. Nancy Lessin and Charley Richardson, co-founders of the antiwar group Military Families Speak Out (MFSO), became so persuaded that there were thousands of military families privately fuming about Iraq that they created an organization to represent them in November 2002.

Richardson and Lessin, veterans of the '60s peace movement and parents of a soldier-son who's been deployed to Iraq, were quick to recognize the unique power military families could bring to the larger antiwar effort. "We were very concerned about media coverage that tried to characterize the antiwar movement as those who supported the troops and those that didn't," says Lessin. With that in mind, she and Richardson, who were invited to speak at rallies, demonstrations, and even at congressional briefings—tried to erase that distinction. For example: "We're glad to be here at the biggest *pro-troop* rally in the country," Lessin told half a million New Yorkers when she spoke at the February 15, 2002, antiwar rally in Manhattan. Similarly, their campaign slogan "Bring Them Home Now" is a calculated nod toward soldier safety. Even the most Republican of military families might feel comfortable standing under that banner.

While MFSO's membership hovered at only about 600 in November 2003, Richardson said the group's configuration and numbers were rapidly changing. (And indeed, by August 2004, it had 1,600 families involved.)

"When President Bush made his reckless 'Bring Them On' comment from the safety of his briefing room, surrounded by armed guards, military families were incensed," Richardson says. Banding together with Veterans for Peace, MFSO began a "Bring Them Home Now" campaign and was immediately flooded with 5,000 to 6,000 e-mails from military families and veterans. Although some of the e-mails simply expressed agreement, many letter writers wanted to know how they could participate.

According to Lessin and Richardson, the vocal presence of military wives like Robison, who organized the Texas protest at Bush's ranch, mark a welcome shift in the makeup of their membership. While parents of soldiers have a long tradition of speaking out to protect their kids, they are largely immune from the repercussions. (Uncle Sam isn't likely to blame G.I. Joe for the sins of his father—or his ex-hippie mom.) But military wives have always been more reticent than parents. "In the beginning our organization had more parents of soldiers with many, though not all, coming out of the Vietnam antiwar movement," says Lessin. "Recently, though, we have had an influx of military spouses, mostly wives."

What makes spouses a potentially more powerful ally for peace activists is that they hold more sway over their husband's reenlistment decisions—and that can be a mighty tool. For example, in its 2003 annual statement to Congress, a worried Air Force pointed out that 77 percent of its enlisted force is eligible to reenlist—or not—in the following two years.

But teasing out the impact of military antiwar sentiment can be tricky. If military wives base their opposition to the war on the grounds that the troops have been there too long, and are overworked and constantly deployed, it can backfire—witness the ongoing debate about whether *more* troops will solve the Iraqi crisis and whether we ought to reinstate the draft.

But, if there isn't a formal analytical framework, or any effort to develop one beyond a simple "Bring Them Home Now" slogan, trouble could ensue. Suggesting that the United States ought to simply drop everything and get out may put these activists at odds with the larger antiwar movement, which wants a smaller military presence but would like to see the country clean up its mess first, before it "gets the hell out of Dodge." So far, it's not clear how opposition to the current deployment breaks down between wives who object broadly to U.S. unilateralism and those who object because they worry that the personal price—potential death of a loved one—is just too high.

Heidi, who protested week after week on the Watertown square, exemplifies how intertwined all these ideas can be among military families. "We think that our husbands, when they signed up for the service, and also us, when we co-signed by marrying them, were well aware that the ultimate sacrifice might be their lives," she says. "But we want to be sure, as wives, that there is absolutely no doubt whatsoever that this sacrifice was necessary." When asked whether that means she is against this particular engagement or whether she identifies herself as a pacifist, Heidi laughs. "I identify myself as a hypocrite," she says. "I'm a pacifist who married a soldier."

BY MARCH 2004, a year after the war in Iraq began, 33 percent of military spouses are telling pollsters things are going badly in Iraq, and 27 percent of them disapprove of the way Bush is doing his job. This is less than the general public, 48 percent of whom disliked the way the president was doing his job in the spring of 2004, but still a significant statement for the Republican-stacked military community (55 percent of which is registered Republican—with probably more voting that way).

Occasionally, even soldiers voice their discontent with the war. Heidi's husband, who had evolved into a Democrat after thirty-nine years as a Republican, began to talk tentatively about his opposition to the war among army colleagues—and met with a lot of disapproval. Some soldiers went even further.

On January 2, 2004, Specialist Jeremy Hinzman, twenty-five, went AWOL rather than participate in the war in Iraq. Slated to ship out for Iraq with Fort Bragg's 82nd Airborne within the next few weeks, Hinzman and his wife Nga Nguyen instead loaded their car with whatever possessions they could fit, tucked their pajamaed baby into his car seat, and took off for Canada at midnight—hoping their baby would sleep through the long drive they had in front of them. (He didn't.)

Eighteen long hours later, as they crossed the border into Ontario at Niagara Falls, Hinzman became the first official "war deserter" from Operation Iraqi Freedom as he formally applied for political asylum in Canada.

When I talk to Nga six months later, we sit in her basement apartment in Toronto. For $750 a month it is small—one bedroom plus one room that functions as the kitchen/living room/dining room. Sparsely furnished with a kitchen table, a few chairs, a TV, it has that college-student-traveling-light look except for the tidy pile of toddler toys in one corner. Nga, who was born in Vietnam, but moved to the U.S. when she was three, has dark hair that she wears back in a ponytail and speaks with a Midwestern accent. With her round glasses, a sweater, jeans, she also *looks* the part of a college student. She is not used to talking to reporters, she apologizes—most of them want to speak with Jeremy—but she tells the family's story concisely.

The couple met in Grand Rapids, South Dakota, where they both grew up. Nga had graduated from college with a degree in biology and psychology; she was working as a social worker for Head Start, the federal preschool program for low-income children. Jeremy worked various jobs, trying to decide what he wanted to do.

Eventually they decided they wanted to try life in a big city and moved to Boston. There they both got jobs at a health food store. Still not sure what he *really* wanted to do with his life, Jeremy decided to join the army in January 2001. Nga says he liked the idea of working for some larger purpose—and that he also liked the idea of getting money toward college.

Nga did not like the idea.

And indeed, could we personify the army, the feeling would probably be mutual: Nga Nguyen is likely the army's worst nightmare. She is college educated, politically informed, antiwar, and has a quiet determination. Worse, when Jeremy decided to join anyway and the pair moved to Fort

Bragg, she practiced a little passive resistance. She never went to the army family team-building classes. She didn't join the spouses' club. She attended a few FRG meetings, but quickly stopped. "I felt really out of place there. I pretty much isolated myself," she says. Understanding what was being asked of her, she says, "I just could not picture *myself* in the military."

Instead of FRG meetings, Nga started going to Quaker meetings with Jeremy. Then, along with some of these same Quakers, they started going to a few peace protests. Jeremy started reading about Buddhism. Meanwhile, the more Jeremy thought about and talked about his beliefs, the more he realized he wanted no part of killing. Part of what surprised him about the army was not that soldiers were expected to kill—he realized this would be the case when he joined—but that the training required him to be enthusiastic about it.

Both Nga and Jeremy were changing, their beliefs evolving. They decided to act on their convictions. Nga, who says she had hung around lefty types all her life and had always been sympathetic to these causes, had still never actually participated in a protest march herself. After the wars in Afghanistan and Iraq broke out, she began joining protesters. "This wasn't something where I could say it's about those people over there so that's fine. In this case, my husband was right there in the middle of it. He's a part of it," she says. "I couldn't keep my head stuck in the sand anymore." Neither could Jeremy. In August 2002, exactly a year after he moved to Fort Bragg, he filed for conscientious objector (C.O.) status with the army.

The army lost his form, and four months after filing he was sent to Afghanistan. (The forms were finally found nearly a year after Hinzman filed them; when he heard they were lost, he refiled.) Because his conscientious objector hearing was still pending, the army allowed him to work in a noncombatant position while in Afghanistan: he washed dishes for six months. While there, his superiors heard his claim for C.O. status but denied it when he admitted that he would fight back to defend himself if his camp or home were attacked. A few weeks after that, in July 2003, Jeremy and his unit left Kandahar and returned to Fort Bragg.

But in December they got word that they were shipping out again—this time to Iraq—and this time the army would not let him serve as a non-combatant.

Jeremy mapped out two options for Nga. "One was that he'd refuse orders and do jail time, the other was that he—or we—would leave the country." Nga's response—to either—was relief. "My number-one reasons were selfish, I didn't want to lose him. Every day the Fayetteville papers were full of casualties, pictures and names and memorial services," she says. "And I wanted our son to have a father." Nga told Jeremy she didn't have a preference either way, that it was his decision and she would back him. "In the end, he didn't feel like he was wrong to oppose the war. He didn't believe he should be punished and sent to jail for doing something he thought was morally right." To his mind, what he was doing was legal: The U.S. invasion of Iraq was a "criminal enterprise," not sanctioned by the United Nations and therefore his *participation* was illegal.

SEEN IN AN ISOLATED CONTEXT, Jeremy Hinzman and Nga Nguyen are mavericks—no more bother to the army than a few pesky flies it can easily brush away. (In 2003, only 60 soldiers in the entire armed forces applied for C.O. status, with 31 applications approved; in 2002, 23 soldiers filed, with 18 approved.) In fact, one even wonders why the military bothers to turn down half the C.O. applications, the total numbers are so insignificant to a force of 2 million. Indeed, the services lost more people to suicide last year (53 in the army alone, in 2003) and driving accidents (95 in off-duty driving accidents in just the army in 2003) than it lost from pacifism. But the army may worry about that trickle turning into a flood.

In an historical context Jeremy and Nga's story assumes a different meaning. Of course their pacifism comes from a traditional pacifist church. As long ago as the seventeenth century, when the Quakers were first settling Pennsylvania colony, religious exemption from the militia existed. As military sociologists Charles Moskos and John Whiteclay Chambers II have noted in their book *The New Conscientious Objection,* throughout American history three traditional pacifist sects have consistently resisted military service in every war the country fought: the Quakers, the Mennonites, and the Brethren. The U.S. military has responded to these conscientious objectors in various ways—from allowing them to buy replacements, to brutalizing them into compliance with orders, to offering them noncombat jobs or alternative civilian service, to court-martialing and jailing them (as the marines did with 50 young men during the Gulf War). We don't read much about it in our history books, but the numbers of conscientious objectors in *all* our wars are surprisingly high. For example, during World War I, 65,000 drafted soldiers applied for C.O. status over the course of a single year, from 1917 through 1918. Of course that number is far higher than the number of exemptions *granted,* which is because the criteria to determine legitimate objectors were very specific. Exemptions were typically granted only to members of the historic peace churches.

This was the basic rule for most of our history until the Vietnam War. In 1965 and 1970, the Supreme Court heard two cases and tweaked the definition of conscientious objection slightly. In the first case, the Court said a pacifist could be exempt from service on religious grounds even if he didn't believe in God, so long as his pacifist beliefs occupied a central, religious-*like* place in his mind. In the second case, the Supreme Court agreed that the pacifist could be exempted even if he was an atheist, as long as his pacifism was an essential part of his ethics and morals. But what the court did not recognize—and what the military continues to reject—is the notion that someone could have a principled objection to a particular, unjust war. It also declines to differentiate, in this context, between fighting back in self-defense, like if a mugger holds a knife to your throat, and calculated acts of aggression like, say, a war against Iraq (not entirely surprising since most wars are actually framed as "self-defense").

Thus claims like Jeremy Hinzman's continue to be rejected, and so the military continues to hew to the letter of the law when it comes to granting

C.O. status. For those in the higher echelons of the military, many of them Vietnam-era vets or at least well versed in the era's lore, the lessons of that period hit hard. Even with many Vietnam-era soldiers simply fleeing the country rather than formally filing for C.O. status, local draft boards of yore struggled mightily with resisters. In 1973, when the U.S. death toll in Vietnam reached 58,000, 73 percent of those who were drafted filed for C.O. status.

In Jeremy's case, he and Nga immediately sought out the Quakers in Toronto asking them for shelter—they knew no one in the city—and for a recommendation as to how they ought to proceed. The Quakers, who had some rooms upstairs in the meetinghouse, put the Hinzmans up for nearly two months until they could move into their basement apartment. They also recommended an attorney, Jeffry House, who during the Vietnam War, had made Canada his home and such causes a passion. House filed a petition with the Canadian immigration authorities requesting political asylum for Hinzman—which put the authorities in a bit of a bind. On the one hand, Canada did not support U.S. intervention in Iraq without UN approval, and so might be sympathetic. On the other hand, as Canadian immigration officials have said, political asylum was designed to protect folks from persecution, not to save them from jail when they have broken a law.

As this book went to press, the case was still pending—and the media were all over it: there were stories everywhere, from Fox News to the *Air Force Times* to the *Village Voice*. Photographs of Jeremy, Nga, and their baby, Liam, were plastered all over U.S. newspapers. In one widely published picture the couple sits cuddled on their couch. Jeremy wears a tuque and holds his pink-cheeked baby on his lap. He has his arm around Nga, who leans in close, and both of them smile—like they're posing for their Christmas card photo.

Nga confesses she was surprised at the vehemence of some of the reactions they got. When Bill O'Reilly ranted about Jeremy and the Canadians who were sheltering him on his weekly "O'Reilly Factor" talk show and warned that Americans might boycott Canadian products unless the "deserters" were turned over to U.S. authorities, Jeremy got a lot of hate mail at the web site supporters had set up. That and some of the negative print coverage have thrown Nga. "I just never pictured us in this situation before," she says, a guileless, deer-in-the-headlights look on her face, "where people would send us hate mail and dislike us so much for something."

BACK AT FORT DRUM Heidi struggles with problems of her own. In November 2003, her husband was transferred to Fort Knox, Kentucky. She decided not to go with him.

Their marriage is drifting, she tells me. She is in flux. She doesn't know what she wants to do with her life.

"The first three years I was married, I volunteered to do all this stuff with the military," she says. "I still had this gung-ho feeling at the time. But it wasn't too long before I started to burn out." Being the point person for her FRG group, which she co-chaired with a friend, became exhausting over time. Her enthusiasm waned. "Yes, volunteering keeps people busy and it's a tremendous asset to any organization to have all those volunteers, but it's also a way of keeping people content and feeling worthy," she says. "You could easily spend a whole day volunteering—which plenty of wives do—and you get a volunteer-of-the-year parking spot and a pat on the back at a ceremony once a year, but that doesn't help your career." Heidi worries that this has compromised her independence. "You go, you're busy, it's a nice life, you're doing good things, but . . ." She pauses. Reflects. "Right now it's scaring me a bit. If something happened, I'd be on my own, I'd be—excuse the language—screwed."

It's not clear if that "something" Heidi worries about is that her husband will end up a casualty of this war or if their marriage will. In fact, it's a little of both. Fear of deployment is omnipresent. "As wives, we used to be distraught when our husbands had to go to Bosnia," she says. "Then we said, better Bosnia than Kosovo, then better Kosovo than Afghanistan, then better Afghanistan than Iraq. Hopefully we won't find ourselves saying soon, better Iraq than Korea." For now her husband is safe, stationed in

Kentucky. She seems less certain about her marriage. "If we were to go our separate ways, or if something were to happen to him, what would I do?" she wonders.

Heidi, who had worked since she was nineteen, in Germany, hasn't been employed since her marriage and move to the U.S. more than nine years ago. "I am so 100 percent relying on my husband right now. And if I think of him not being here, that's really, really scary," she says. She wonders how other women sit comfortably with this fear. Or do they worry as well? "They have housing paid for, and a paycheck, and this protected family feeling for years in the military community, but what if something happens? What if people separate? How many of these women have their own retirement plans? I don't know anybody that does."

Heidi used to look for work when she first moved to Fort Drum. But the depressed economy and all the other military wives looking for work made good jobs hard to find. "There are minimum-wage jobs, working for McDonald's and such, but not much beyond that," she says.

Heidi is not alone here. According to the army's own 2001 survey, 37 percent of wives are dissatisfied with their job opportunities—and it's no wonder. Military families, even with two wage earners, earn $10,200 less on average than civilian families. And while civilian wives average $15,800 a year, military wives average only $10,200 a year—with the biggest difference occurring among college-educated military wives, who made $116 less per week than their civilian counterparts. Military wives were also less likely to work, with only 49 percent of military wives who were high school graduates working, compared with 62 percent of civilian wives. Among military wives with a college degree 56 percent worked outside the home, while 70 percent of civilian wives do. And, at any given time one out of every 10 army wives is actively looking for a job. (That is excluding those wives, like Heidi, who gave up long ago.)

"It took me one-and-a-half years to find a job in Watertown," says military wife Vivian Shiffer, who finally landed a temporary job at Fort Drum doing administrative work. "You can imagine what that does to a family financially." Shiffer, who had a secure job she enjoyed while the family was stationed at Fort Bragg, gave it all up when her husband was transferred. "It makes it hard to be supportive," she says.

Julia Pfaff, who runs the National Military Family Association, an independent nonprofit, says that aside from the frequency and duration of deployments, lack of work is the number one problem for military wives. "DOD realizes this and works on a lot of initiatives," she says. "But most of them haven't really worked out." For example, it negotiated with a major hotel firm to give military spouses career progression and let them transfer, as their soldiers were transferred. It did the same with some defense contractors, basically saying that we send business your way, you hire our spouses. It turned out to be a problem, Pfaff tells me. As she explains it, the military is not allowed to do anything that amounts to endorsing a private industry.

Most recently the army held a job summit in 2002, where it tried to persuade various corporations to hire military spouses. They are well educated, culturally diverse, and already have health insurance, the army coaxed. Thirteen Fortune 500 companies, headquartered in towns where there are military bases, like Home Depot, Bell South, and CVS entered "job partnerships" with the military in 2003—but how they'll play out is still unclear.

In the mostly rural areas, where army posts are located, the available work tends to be service jobs. Not only do these jobs pay poorly, but many require employees—especially entry-level employees, as most of these military wives are and remain, since they move on average every two years— to work unusual hours. Waitresses, store clerks, cashiers can't count on 9-to-5 work. This quickly proves problematic.

For example, Fort Drum wife Julie Shropshire got a job delivering Chinese food for a local restaurant. She worked from noon until 11 P.M. three days a week. "On a good day I could come home with between one hundred and twenty dollars and one hundred and thirty dollars," Julie says. "And I didn't mind the work." But the logistics were complicated. Her seven-year-old daughter was in school until 3 P.M., when a downstairs neighbor would pick her up; Julie reciprocated for the neighbor's daughter three days a week, while that neighbor delivered food for the same restaurant. Meanwhile, Julie's infant and toddler went to a woman who ran a licensed home-daycare out of her home, charging $30 a day. That was fine until the deployments started happening. Suddenly Julie's husband was in danger of shipping out any day. Then, he wouldn't be available to pick the kids up from daycare after work, to take them home, give them dinner, and put them to bed. Plus, with all the soldiers' being deployed, the demand for take-out Chinese plummeted (single soldiers' taking a break from the mess hall were the restaurant's bread and butter—or egg roll and dumplings). Julie's tips dropped to $70 a day. When she was working 11 hours for $40 ($70 minus $30 in daycare fees) and faced a childcare crisis, the job ceased to be viable.

What this means for Julie, and Heidi, and thousands of other military wives is that their jobs are sporadic, their work history abbreviated, their retirement funds nonexistent. Military wives not only earn less but are rarely promoted because they are so frequently transferred before they acquire seniority. Professionals face similar problems. For example, teachers and nurses usually have to be recredentialed each time they move because of licensing requirements that vary from state to state. Between finding a new job and securing the new license, they lose months of work each time they move—if they get a job at all. Air force wife Tammy Schmitt spent more than a year trying to get a full-time, permanent teaching job in Watertown, but insists her applications all landed in the "circular file"; an insular Old Girls' network meant jobs went to local friends and relatives, she says, and a military wife who obviously couldn't commit to the school district for life just was not considered a serious job applicant.

"I always believed in being independent," Heidi says, "and yet I give it up . . . for love." She laughs. "I let myself be lulled into leading this halfway comfortable life when work was so important to me before." Her self-criticism is harsh. "I'm not independent anymore and that is something I despise."

She wrestles with this. And it is not until later, when I am studying the transcripts of our interview that I notice how the conversation about work and volunteer work bleeds into a conversation about peer pressure, how peer pressure and the army's unspoken expectations quietly direct wives. Going against these expectations makes Heidi a little nervous.

Later, when I have used notes from our conversation to quote Heidi in an article I'm writing about military peace activists, she will talk to a fact-checker at the publication about just using her maiden name in the piece. She is struggling to decide how comfortable she is speaking her mind. When we speak, she comes at the issue sideways. She describes a wife she knew who never brought stuff for the bake sales or volunteered to help with events, then one day when she called the wives' group for help, no one would help her out.

This comes across as a mini-morality tale and serves the same purpose. It's best to roll with the punches, shoulder your share, do your part so others will do unto you. The message is everywhere, *but*, Heidi insists, the volume has been jacked up here in the military community and the price for nonparticipation is high. Heidi describes the way things work, beginning in the more distant second person and ending in first person. "It's difficult to judge because on the one hand, the family support groups are a good thing, especially for the very young wives who have no clue, but at the same time, you become so integrated it's hard to go against the stream," she says. "It becomes easy not to be true to yourself anymore. I found myself doing things I didn't want to do. I was like, hey, I don't feel like doing this, but I felt this friendly force that said, 'Do it anyway.' And this is not just bake sales, but political opinions. What if people really knew what I was thinking? Would they still like me? Would I still be a part of the group?"

ON A FRIDAY EVENING in August 2004, Heidi and I sit beside a hotel pool some fifteen minutes from Fort Drum. My seven-year-old son plays in the water, Heidi's visiting twelve-year-old nephew slouches in a chair beside us, engrossed in his brand-new Game Boy. In halting English, the German boy tells me that he is playing "zero zero seven," which I take to be a riveting James Bond adventure more powerful than the lure of a pool on a summer night. Confident that these international spies have him in their grasp—and that his limited English leaves him oblivious to our conversation—Heidi confesses that things are not going well with her marriage.

"I feel like we're drifting apart, further than we already were," she says. Since her husband moved to Fort Knox ten months earlier, she has gone to visit him once and he has come here once, but their lives have taken different paths. "We've always been a little separate," she says. "But this is putting even more of a wedge between us."

Do they talk about this wedge?

Heidi shrugs. "I try to, but he doesn't like to," she says. She pushes a few strands of her dark black hair off her face. A gentle breeze has tugged them loose from her ponytail and they flutter around, dark bats swooping toward her dark eyes. She sighs—the hair? the relationship?—and I notice for the first time a few strands of gray creeping in. "He is a master of denial and doesn't want to hear that I'm not happy. I don't think he realizes things aren't going well because he's a lot busier than I am. I don't think he thinks about our relationship as much as I do. To him it's not so bad." Heidi glances at her nephew—still perfectly oblivious—and goes on, picking her words carefully as though articulating them for the first time. "But I'm not ready to throw in the towel yet."

She tells me that he, too, struggles with loneliness but that he works all day and then takes classes at night because he is working toward his master's degree. He doesn't have as much time to think as she does. "He doesn't see that I get frustrated with things here," she says, explaining that she sometimes feels like a "modern pioneer woman" living way out in the country in a farmhouse where something is always going wrong—pipes freezing, window breaking in the barn, garage door blocked by massive snowdrifts—and where the isolation is intense. "I really struggle with loneliness," she says. "And I feel changes in myself when I am alone so much. I feel like I am turning into a hermit. It's very contradictory in a way, but I am desperate to socialize and talk to people sometimes but then I find myself not wanting to see people, like it seems like too much trouble to get dressed and drive twenty miles in the snow to go out and see someone. It's difficult to explain. I feel like I want to, but . . ." Her voice trails off. And it is not hard to envision her, indeed, as one of the pioneer women in O. E. Rolvaag's *Giants in the Earth,* another immigrant in America battling severe winters and depression in a world where both prove seductive—and dangerous.

She tries to talk to her husband about her feelings, but she doesn't think he understands. As for *his* feelings, she's not so sure. "Like so many men, he's not so good about talking about his desires or personal matters in general," she says. Then, perhaps realizing that he might encounter her assessment of their relationship in a book someday, she changes the subject. She reminds herself—and me—that her husband's physical absence, this random assignment to a nondeployable unit that tests new transportation technology, may save his life. If he were back at Fort Drum, he could easily be sent to Afghanistan or Iraq.

Right now Heidi and her husband are weighing whether or not he'll stay in the army. He has four more years until he can retire with twenty years under his belt. This would give him half his salary and free health care for the rest of his life. But Heidi says he's not sure if he can stick it out. He has been passed over for promotion from captain to major once; he gets only one more chance. Worse, he's dissatisfied with the petty office politics where he works and with national politics in general. It's hard to work day in and day out for a cause you no longer believe in. He used to be a Republican—everyone in his family is Republican (except Heidi, of course)—but this year he became a Democrat. ("I used to always tease him that I was going to get my American citizenship just to neutralize his vote." She laughs.) Now he, too, thinks the war in Iraq is wrong but feels trapped where he is, Heidi says.

Meanwhile, even though her own opposition to the war hasn't changed, Heidi has stopped going to protests. First of all, the local peace activists seem to have disbanded and the regular protests in Watertown's square have petered out. Second, the central slogan of the activists—"Support our troops. Bring them home now"—seems misguided at the moment. After all, the country has made a mess of Iraq and we have some responsibility to stabilize the situation, Heidi believes.

All of which makes her situation very complicated and discouraging. "It's not that I really expect I'll convince anyone of my opinions," she says. "But I never even see a glimpse of understanding." She cites the 9/11 commission report, points out that the link between Al Qaeda and Iraq has never materialized, wonders what happened to the weapons of mass destruction, but faces friends and neighbors who say, "Well, we freed the Iraqi people." She is shocked that the lies by our own leaders don't matter. One typical response comes from a friend whose husband is currently deployed. "She always says, 'I can't say anything because he is a soldier by heart and soul and wants to be there.' It's as if she won't allow herself an opinion because it might not be the same as her husband's!" Heidi shakes her head dismissively. "Out of some misguided loyalty, because he is supporting this war she thinks she must too."

This presumption of loyalty runs so deep it still catches Heidi by surprise sometimes.

She tells me about a woman she met at one of her craft shows, another vendor who struck up a conversation. "She wanted to know all about my military husband and if he was deployed and what the army was like and we exchanged e-mails," she says, explaining that the woman sent her dozens of e-mails over the next few weeks with different tidbits about home remedies and such. "Then an e-mail comes saying she read an article on an Internet site about a military wife with my name who was opposed to the war . . . and was that me?" Heidi realized the woman had "Googled" her and found a site that had reprinted one of the articles I had written, in which Heidi was quoted. "I outed myself and wrote that yes, it's me," Heidi says. "Yes, I strongly believe that you can support the military while not supporting the war," Heidi wrote. The woman zapped Heidi from her e-mail list. Not a peep for weeks. Then, because it nagged at her, Heidi finally sent a follow-up e-mail, a little Native American poem she once received on a birthday card: "Let me not judge anyone till I have walked in his moccasins for two moons." The woman replied with a diatribe: " 'How dare you! Your husband could get into a lot of trouble for your opinions! How selfish of you!' On and on. . . ."

As she tells me this anecdote some months after it happened, Heidi waves her hand dismissively, as if the incident is so trivial she can shoo it away. But clearly the criticism hits home. She had not been thrashing around in the recesses of her mind to dredge up the details of this story. The incident stays with her, resonates, throws her off balance. She lists.

The same way that an acquaintance in crisis—a marriage falling apart, a child in the hospital, a death in the family—can be a bundle of raw emotion, spilling out into intimacy hitherto absent, Heidi exudes sorrow. She is troubled, brooding, at odds with her world. And she is smart and introspective enough to know it. And to struggle.

"My husband could be down at Fort Knox for two more years," she says. "He's trying to get back here, but if he does, he might be deployed." Two years is a long time. "I don't think he realizes there is a problem with our relationship. I'm waiting to see what happens." It is hard for her to move one way or the other. She glances over at the top of her nephew's head, and lowers her voice, though the nephew is still so deeply engrossed in the trials of "zero zero seven" that he doesn't hear us. "I'm just not ready to make any major decisions now."

In the end, as we stand in the parking lot saying good-bye after a year of talking about love, war, and politics, Heidi gets nervous. She is spooked—by the craft fair acquaintance? Fear for her husband's job? A year as a pacifist among warriors?—and worries about her name being out there in public, in a book.

Does she want to use a pseudonym, I ask her, as I asked her in our very first interview.

"Would you mind?"

"That's fine," I say. I don't want to nail anyone. And after all, I walk across the parking lot and out of this world.

Heidi stays.

For now.

CONCLUSION

OCCASIONALLY, WHILE I WAS WRITING THIS BOOK, FRIENDS WOULD ask me what I was finding out, had I discovered anything that really surprised me? I had two answers. The first one always disappointed them; there was nothing racy about it. "I'm surprised that the military has been *so* helpful to me," I tell them. "I think the military's public affairs officers are the most efficient and helpful I've ever dealt with." I gush: "They *always* return my calls, they call me ma'am, they set up interviews for me, and the people they line up to speak with me always show." Probably they liked me, I figured. And why not? While the rest of the press was all over them with "hard" questions about various "mishaps"—the friendly-fire deaths of some Canadian troops, the Iraqi civilian wedding party U.S. forces attacked, the mounting suicide rate among deployed U.S. soldiers, ex-special forces/private security contractors kidnapped in Iraq—I would call with "soft" questions like, "Can you tell me what kind of support groups you have for wives whose husbands are deployed?"

These were easy questions for them to answer. They were sure the army had all its ducks in order here. They trusted these would evolve into feel-good fluff pieces for women readers. And frankly, they probably considered my questions irrelevant, given the rest of the hot potatoes they were juggling.

These public affairs officers, or PAOs, simply trusted that their family-friendly programs were good ones and that the wives they referred me to would have nothing but good things to say about the army. This, perhaps more than anything, illustrates the vast disconnect between what the army *believes* about wives' experience and the *reality* of that experience.

Similarly, the military seems oblivious to the level of opposition among wives to the U.S. war in Iraq. This was the second big surprise of my research. I found far more opposition to the war among wives than I ever thought. These women, who straddle the military world—one foot on post, one foot in the civilian sector—were getting their news from civilian sources and they were weighing the "inevitability" of this war with the potential personal costs. They may have voted for George Bush in November 2004, but scratch the surface and many confessed serious reservations about his Iraq policy.

The army believed I would hear good things from wives who were proud of what their husbands were doing—and I *did,* though many separated their husbands' service from the president's call for war. The army also assumed I would hear good things about its family programs—and I *did,* but those were laced with a serious dose of disenchantment. I am guessing, but I suspect the army's PAOs simply assumed I'd hear good things about the "Army family." That's because the army, master manipulator, has worked hard to craft a proper narrative of wives' experience . . . for them.

But here a little reality has jammed the cogs in the propaganda machine. Turns out the military's efforts to systematize human relations, to socially engineer supportive wives, to manufacture cohesion and bonding among women falls short. It is as if the military heard wives' complaints about poor housing, too many deployments that last too long and pay too little for their husbands, inferior schools for their children, lack of job opportunity for themselves, and responded with some "inspirational" programs like the army family team-building classes or the Family Readiness Groups not to improve wives' actual circumstances but to improve their attitudes.

These methods may have been effective for a while, but in 2005 it is harder to remain a true believer—a simple, flag-waving patriot who doesn't question authority when basic democratic, egalitarian values are given short shrift not only inside the military establishment but inside our government. Americans have grown cynical. Soldiers and their families are not immune to this. Talk about war for oil, exposés of Halliburton, the ever-elusive weapons of mass destruction, our history with Afghanistan and Iraq as documented in big-sellers like *Ghost Wars, House of Bush, House of Saud,* and *Fahrenheit 9/11* make blind patriotism harder to come by.

While military brass mourns these new "skeptics," lamenting the loss of idealism and the rise of a crass pragmatism, I see a different trajectory. The kind of "institutional loyalty" military brass yearns for today may be failing because the values it tries to promote have grown less relevant—maybe even antithetical to contemporary military families. Does the idea that women ought to be paid for the work they do, rather than volunteer for the good of their husband and their husbands' units really mark a decline in "idealism?" Or is a different kind of idealism ascendant, the idealism that sees a world where individuals are valued regardless of gender for the work they do and the contributions they make?

But the military is a conservative organization. Change comes hard.

Picture the military bureaucracy as a great, lumbering beast traveling through the world at 5 mph, while the rest of the civilian world zips past at

55 mph. Suddenly it looks around, dazed and confused, to find itself standing in the twenty-first century where the rules of the game have shifted. A savvy, cynical military community looks at this beast in askance, wondering whether it has noticed things are not what they were. Not only can it stop stocking Breck and Prell at the PX, but it can ease up on efforts to win families' hearts and minds and develop genuinely useful programs and opportunities for wives instead. Otherwise, insisting that soldiers' families become "mission multipliers" may be driving many of those couples with higher aspirations—perhaps the best and the brightest—from their ranks.

Wives, who are not in the Army, need to be released from their Army tasks; wives need real improvements in their circumstances, not attitude adjustments. While women's sacrifices on behalf of their husbands' career continues to be glorified in the army, many wives today believe they have an equal right to an income and jobs of their own. (Again, a different kind of "idealism.") How many of the soldiers who've walked, getting out of the service when their time was up, have done so because their wives wanted a better life? The military needs to act decisively to stem a brain drain, to change its way of thinking about "social engineering" so that the smart, ethical, and innovative rise to the top.

That's not happening now, and a myriad of problems have ensued. The center isn't holding: Military police ordered to guard prisoners abuse them. Bad orders cause a small mutiny among Army Reserves in Iraq. Everyone decries the lack of good leadership. Morale is plummeting, says the *Stars and Stripes,* and more than half the deployed soldiers say they won't reenlist.

Meanwhile, sexual harassment complaints, rape complaints, and domestic-violence complaints appear to have blindsided a complacent military. (Here again, the military functions about twenty years behind the rest of the country—only now facing issues that rocked the rest of America in the '80s and '90s.) Military wives, who are struggling to reconcile personal career aspirations, with love for their soldier husbands and their country, are no longer persuaded of the validity of that central tenet of military training—hardship builds character—nor are they persuaded that military leadership is acting in their best interest—or so quick to accept that our nation's leadership is acting in America's best interest.

These are not disconnected issues. Nor are they "soft" issues. The problems the military faces, from abuses at Abu Ghraib to rapes at the Air Force Academy to its response to domestic violence, conscientious objectors, politically opinionated soldiers and spouses, widows, waiting wives and its persistent efforts to manipulate wives into silent, supportive compliance with the Army's agenda, show a military out of step with American values.

Meanwhile, wives are urged to stop straddling two worlds—the military and the civilian—and to consider themselves part of the army family, to allow their individual identities to merge with the group's, the army's goals to become their goals. In this way, women will come to accept the sacrifices of military life as inevitable.

But suppose the sacrifices are not inevitable? Just take one example: the frequency of moves. An Army family moves, on average, every two years, but Air Force families move, on average, every three or four years. What is the Air Force doing differently? And why can't the Army try it? Significantly, the Army has begun to experiment with a new program called "force stabilization." Under this initiative, certain units will train and deploy together and redeploy and remain together. What this means for families is that they can remain in one place for as long as seven years, instead of the typical two years. Introduced in February 2004, the agenda sounds promising but the details—how swiftly and widely implemented it will be—remain unclear.

In fighting to win hearts and minds—here and in Iraq—the military is losing on two fronts. What the military's outdated "institutional" model demands is blind loyalty: accept our foreign policy and military methodology without question. Don't sweat the details, it says to soldiers in Iraq and families on the homefront. Focus on the fact that we are part of something larger than ourselves. Because being a part of something larger than ourselves can be a powerful motivator—for everyone from the Christian

Evangelist embarking on a mission to the pro-lifer in front of an abortion clinic to the Greenpeace activist chaining herself to the fence of a chemical plant. We will make tremendous personal sacrifices for things we believe in. The trick is, we must believe that the sacrifices are inevitable and we must believe we are doing this for some achievable greater good.

For today's military family, neither is a given.

NOTES

For the most part, I have tried to identify sources in the body of the text. When there is enough information there for an interested reader to easily locate a study or document, I have not cited it here. When I have drawn from other sources more fleetingly referenced, I've provided detailed documentation here so curious readers can pursue the topic.

Introduction
XV **Indeed, one survey by the Kaiser Family**   "Survey of Military Families," (Kaiser Family Foundation, *The Washington Post*, Harvard University, March 2004), p. 18.

XVI **"Don't fool yourself . . ."**   LTC Keith E. Bonn, USA (Ret.), *Army Officer's Guide* (Mechanicsburg, PA, Stackpole Books, 1999), p. 422.

XVII **Department of Defense is the largest "company"**   "America's Largest Company" DOD website: www.defenselink.mil/pubs/dod101/index.html

Chapter 1
6   **Eleven thousand, one-hundred thirty-four**   These figures come from the Department of Defense website: www.defenselink.mil, as of November 29, 2004. But the numbers are not ever presented by DOD as a total of 11,134 war casualties. The Defense Department always breaks the figures down, in this case, listing total deaths for Operation Iraqi Freedom as

1,251; total OIF nonmortal wounded, 9,326; total deaths for Operation Enduring Freedom (Afghanistan, etc.) 148; total nonmortal wounded in OEF, 409.

17 **DOD issued a report to Congress** Department of Defense, "Report to Congress on Military Funeral Honors for Veterans" (DOD, 1999).

19 **"During World War Two, more than"** Dr. Steven E. Anders, "With All Due Honors: A History of the Quartermaster Graves Registration Mission," *Quartermaster Professional Bulletin* (September 1988).

19 **These specialists tout a record of progress** CPT Arnd Frie, CPT Thomas Moody, CPT Garth Yarnall, CPT Jamie Kiessling, CPT Benett Sunds, CPT Gerald L. McCool, CPT Robert Uppena, "Fallen Comrades: Mortuary Affairs in the U.S." *Quartermaster Professional Bulletin* (Winter 1998).

Chapter 2

33 **21 percent of army wives** U.S. Army Community and Family Support Center, "Survey of Army Families IV" (U.S. Army, Spring 2001).

38 **Fort Drum's *Guide for Newcomers*** (San Diego: MARCOA Publishing, Inc., 2002). This is an "authorized publication" written under contract with Fort Drum. However, "contents are not necessarily the official views of, or endorsed by, the U.S. government, Department of Defense or Department of the Army."

41 **Ranging from $429 to $1,205** *2002 Handbook for Military Life* (Springfield, VA: Military Times Media Group, May 2002), p. 48

Chapter 3

57 **"The destructive, the inconsiderate"** Nancy Shea, *The Army Wife* (New York: Harper & Brothers, 1942), p.147

57 **Where once she crowed** Shea, *The Army Wife* (1948), p. 1

57 **"represent the cream"** Nancy Shea, *The Air Force Wife* (New York: Harper & Brothers, 1951), p. xvii

57 **"appreciate your cheerful"** Shea, *The Army Wife* (1948), p. 13

58 **"The German youth of today"** Shea, *The Army Wife* (1948), p. 285

58 **"one of the most photogenic"** Shea, *The Army Wife* (1966), p. 237

58 **"Army More Democratic"** Shea, *The Army Wife* (1954), p. ix

58   "Every successful business"   Shea, *The Army Wife* (1948), p. 113

59   "If you stop to finish"   Shea, *The Army Wife* (1948), p. 115

59   "Learn to enjoy"   Shea, *The Army Wife* (1954), p. 147

59   "Your living room paints"   Shea, *The Army Wife* (1948), p. 89

60   "His mind cannot"   Shea, *The Army Wife* (1966), p. 4

60   the professionalization of housework   Barbara Ehrenreich and Deirdre English, *For Her Own Good: 150 Years of Experts' Advice to Women* (New York: Anchor Books-Doubleday, 1978) pp. 141–181

61   "The home was an ideal 'container' "   Ehrenreich and English, *For Her Own Good,* p. 149

61   "Domestic scientists set up 'Housekeeping Experiment Stations' "   Ehrenreich and English, *For Her Own Good,* p. 163

62   "Homemaking is a full-time job"   Shea, *The Army Wife* (1954), p. 146

63   "I feel it is important early"   Shea, *The Army Wife* (1954), p. xi

63   relatively unchanged in contemporary "wife" books   Ann Crossley and Carol A. Keller, *The Army Wife Handbook: A Complete Social Guide* (Sarasota, FL: ABI Press, 1993), p. 368

This book, reprinted in 1996, with a foreword by Alma Powell, Secretary of State Colin Powell's wife, continues the lengthy tradition of "clarifying" for new wives how their husband's rank affects them. Crossley and Keller write: "Soldiers know that the Army is not a democracy, but some Army wives have difficulty realizing that this truth has application in their lives as well. If you have a disagreement with the commander or his wife and you can't with reasoned logic, convince him or her of your point of view, then give up."

63   "Regardless of her husband's grade"   Shea, *The Army Wife* (1954), p. 9

63   "Army life is like a three-ringed circus"   Shea, *The Army Wife* (1948), p. 374

64   "If you are unhappy"   Shea, *The Army Wife* (1954), p. 6

64   An army wife "should be interested"   Shea, *The Army Wife* (1954), p. 7

64   "You share equally"   Florence Ridgely Johnson, *Welcome Aboard: A Service Manual for the Naval Officer's Wife* (Annapolis, MD: The United States Naval Institute, 1954), p. 251

65   "An army wife never complains"   Shea, *The Army Wife* (1948), p. 112

67   **"gallantly take off our peacetime party dresses"**   Shea, *The Air Force Wife* (1951), p. xiii

69   **"It is a hard task for American Army"**   Shea, *The Army Wife* (1948), p. 284

69   **"The Army's mission overseas"**   Shea, *The Army Wife* (1954), p. 294

70   **"The prerequisites for a successful"**   Shea, *The Army Wife* (1954), p. 356

70   **"It is important that Army wives today"**   Shea, *The Army Wife* (1954), p. 13

70   **"Wives may lose sight"**   Clella R. Collins, *Army Woman's Handbook* (New York: McGraw-Hill Company, Inc.: 1942), p. 149

70   **"He pointed out"**   Shea, *The Army Wife* (1948), p. xv

72   **"There has been a change"**   Morris Janowitz, *The Professional Soldier: A Social and Political Portrait* (New York: The Free Press, 1960), p. 9

73   **"First sergeants in today's Army"**   unidentified author, Army Sergeant Majors' handout, 2003

73   **"Basic Training for Army Families"**   unidentified author, "AFTB: Empowering Families for the 21st Century" (brochure), back cover

73   **"The basic philosophy of AFTB"**   unidentified author, "AFTB Program Army Regulation 608–48" (Washington, D.C.: Headquarters, Department of the Army, October 2003), p. 12

73   **"The Army of the future"**   unidentified author, "U.S. Army Sergeant Major Academy (FSC-TATS L668)" handout, 2003

Chapter 4

84   **"The change is forever"**   U.S. Marine Corps, "Marines, the Few, the Proud" (Washington, D.C.: U.S. Marine Corps, 2004), Marines.com website, under heading "Those who are warriors," then heading "Transformations"

84   **"To belong. This is family."**   U.S. Marine Corps, "Marines, the Few, the Proud" (Washington, D.C.: U.S. Marine Corps, 2004), Marines.com website, under heading "Those who belong," then heading "To belong"

85   **"What keeps soldiers in their foxholes"**   Testimony of Gen. Norman Schwarzkopf before the Senate Armed Services Committee on May 11, 1993

86   **"create soldier perceptions that you care"**   Mady Wechsler Segal and Jesse J. Harris, "What We Know About Army Families" (Arlington, VA: The Army Research Institute for the Behavioral and Social Sciences," 1993), p. xiv

87   **Institutional versus occupational**   Charles C. Moskos and Frank R. Wood, "Introduction," *The Military: More Than Just a Job?* Edited by Charles C. Moskos and Frank R. Wood (McLean, VA: Pergamon-Brassey's International Defense Publishers, 1988), p. 4

88   **According to a 2002 Rand Corporation**   Richard Buddin and Phuong Do, "Assessing the Personal Financial Problems of Junior Enlisted Personnel" (Santa Monica, CA: Rand Corporation, 2002), p. 11

92   **That the force is a microcosm**   unidentified author, "Population Representation in the Military" (Washington, D.C.: Department of Defense, 2000) *The statistics on the makeup of the armed forces in this chapter were drawn from this document, unless otherwise indicated.*

93   **The reasons for this are twofold.**   Charles C. Moskos and John Sibley Butler, *All That We Can Be: Black Leadership and Racial Integration the Army Way* (New York: A Twentieth Century Book published by Basic Books, 1996), p. 38

94   **A mere 8 percent**   unidentified author, "Military Personnel: Active Duty Benefits Reflect Changing Demographics, But Opportunities Exist to Improve" (Washington, D.C.: GAO Report, November 2000)

95   **Military sociologists also note**   Moskos and Sibley Butler, *All That We Can Be*, p. xiii

97   **"Military members are still twice as likely"**   Buddin and Do, "Assessing the Personal Financial" (Rand Corporation), p. 27

97   **"[t]his finding suggests"**   Buddin and Do, "Assessing the Personal Financial" (Rand Corporation), p. 55

98   **That morning, while Richard**   Tim McGirk, "Battle in 'the Evilest Place,' " (*Time* magazine, November 2, 2003), p. 42

Chapter 5

118   **According to DOD figures**   "Domestic Violence and the Military Community: Facts and Findings and a Historical Perspective" (Newtown, CT: Miles Foundation, undated), p. 1

118   **The army consistently shows**   "Domestic Violence and the Military Community, p. 1

118   **In the 1990s, the military**   Fox Butterfield, "Wife Killings at Fort Reflect Growing Problem in Military," *New York Times,* July 29, 2002, p. A-9

119   **Although a current breakdown of lesser**   "Domestic Violence and the Military Community," p. 5

119   **Also, fear of adverse effects**   Linda D. Kozaryn, "Task Force Calls for Crackdown on Domestic Violence," *American Forces Press Service,* March 9, 2001

120   **There is a quote**   Christine Hansen, "A Considerable Service: An Advocate's Introduction to Domestic Violence and the Military," (Newtown, CT: Miles Foundation newsletter, April/May 2001,) p. 5

120   **An exhaustively reported 2003 *Denver Post* article**   Miles Moffeit and Amy Herdy, "Home Front: While civilian prosecutors crack down on domestic abuse, the military emphasizes counseling and tells commanders to consider the accused's career," *The Denver Post,* November 17, 2003, p. A-01

121   **Or that Nelson's first wife**   Miles Moffeit, "Ex-Sergeant Arrested in Revived Murder Case Investigation in North Carolina," *The Denver Post,* March 26, 2004, p. A-01

122   **It is by far the largest**   *Guide to Military Installations Worldwide* (Springfield, VA: Military Times Media Group, 2003), p. 14

123   **There were 19 murders in Fayetteville**   "Crime in North Carolina— 2002" (Annual Summary Report of Uniform Crime Reporting Data, 2002)

125   **Andrea's family contends**   Per various press accounts, including: Maureen Orth, "Fort Bragg's Deadly Summer," *Vanity Fair,* December 2002, pp. 222–240

125   **At the time, Fort Bragg garrison commander**   Estes Thompson, "Army Grapples with Domestic Violence," *AP,* July 28, 2002

131   **"Study Links Combat, Domestic Violence"**   Pamela Hess, "Study Links Combat, Domestic Violence," *UPI,* July 29, 2002

131   **"Four Soldiers' Wives Slain"**   Dennis O'Brien, "Four Soldiers' Wives Slain in Recent Weeks, and Authorities Say the Husbands Are the Killers. At Fort Bragg, Some Wonder if It's a Cost of War," *The Virginian-Pilot,* July 27, 2002, A1

131   **For example, Sean Hannity**   Hannity & Colmes, Fox, July 31, 2002

131   **For example, an Associated Press**   Estes Thompson, "Army Fights New Enemy at Fort Bragg: Domestic Violence in Soldiers' Homes," *AP,* July 27, 2002

131   **"Our most important resource is the soldier"**   Barbra Bateman, "How Will Fort Bragg Face the Murders?" *New York Post,* August 1, 2002, p. 27

131   **"Reassure your spouse"**   Unidentified author, "Coming Home: A Guide for Spouses of Service Members Returning from Mobilization/Deployment," 2004 brochure. *Though this brochure prominently bears the Department of Defense seal on the cover—and the four separate Army, Navy, Marine Corps and Air Force seals on the middle fold—a small disclaimer on the back states that the points of view "do not necessarily represent the official position of the U.S. Department of Defense."*

134   **Noting in understated jargon**   Defense Task Force on Domestic Violence "2002 Second Annual Report," pp. xiv–3.

135   **In a heated, back-and-forth**   Defense Task Force "2002 Second Annual Report," pp. xi–xii

138   **"But chaplains are not always clear"**   Defense Task Force "2002 Second Annual Report," p. xx

Chapter 6

146   **According to a *New York Times* reporter**   Monica Davey, "For Soldiers Back From Iraq," *New York Times,* May 31, 2004, p. 1

155   **According to a 2002 army survey**   Dennis K. Orthner, Ph.D. "Survey Report: Family Readiness Support and Adjustment Among Army Civilian Spouses" (U.S. Army, January 2002), p. 1

156   **Fewer than half rated the programs**   Orthner, "Survey Report: Family Readiness Support," p. 3

156   **Less than a third**   Dennis K. Orthner, Ph.D., "Army Leadership Support for Families and Adjustment of Army Non-military Spouses," (U.S. Army, June 2002), p. 1

156   **Only 57 percent of spouses**   "Survey of Army Families IV." Slide presentation by Dr. Richard Fafara, U.S. Army Community and Family Support Center, slide number 25, p. Q96

156 **Twenty-two percent said** "Survey of Army Families IV." Slide presen- tation by Dr. Richard Fafara, U.S. Army Community and Family Support Center, slide number 26, p. Q63

156 **The answer is alluded to in the 2000 leaders' handbook** Walter R. Shumm, Mady W. Segal, D. Bruce Bell and Lynn M. Milan, "The Family Support Group (FSG) Leaders' Handbook" (Arlington, VA: U.S. Army Re- search Institute for the Behavioral and Social Sciences, April 2000), p. 1

163 **An air force chaplains' guide** "Link: Staying Together While Apart" (Maxwell AFB, Montgomery, AL: USAF Chaplain Service Institute, Re- source Division, January 1997), pp. 13–15

163 **"Over there, I was in charge of people"** Donna Miles, "Fort Campbell Families Adjusting to Newfound Togetherness," *American Forces Press Ser- vice,* March 25, 2004

164 **"During the separation"** "Link: Staying Together," p. 17

165 **More current figures suggest** "Survey of Military Families," (Kaiser Family Foundation, *The Washington Post,* Harvard University, March 2004), pp. 10–12

168 **"Volunteerism serves two purposes"** Laurie Weinstein, "Introduc- tion," *Wives and Warriors,* ed. by Laurie Weinstein and Christie C. White (Westport, CT: Greenwood Publishing Group, Inc., 1997), p. xvii

169 **Weinstein and Helen Merderer** Laurie Weinstein and Helen Merderer, "Blue Navy Blues: Submarine Officers and the Two-Person Ca- reer," *Wives and Warriors,* pp. 7–16.

169 **"For military members, combat bonding"** Deborah Harrison and Lucie LaLiberte, "Gender, the Military, and Military Family Support," *Wives and Warriors,* pp. 35–51

171 **"The most experienced military wives"** Meredith Leyva, *Married to the Military: A Survival Guide for Military Wives, Girlfriends, and Women in Uniform* (New York City: Fireside, Simon & Schuster, 2003), pp. 178–179

171 **"I'm convinced that all women"** Leyva, *Married to the Military,* p. 179

171 **"Wives said they made the decision"** Weinstein and Mederer, "Blue Navy," *Wives and Warriors,* p. 15

Chapter 7

180 **According to a 2004 *New England Journal*** Charles W. Hoge, M.D., Carl A. Castro, Ph.D., Stephen C. Messer, Ph.D., Dennis McGurk, Ph.D.,

Dave I. Cotting, Ph.D., and Robert L. Koffman, M.D., M.P.H., "Combat Duty in Iraq and Afghanistan, Mental Health Problems, and Barriers to Care," *New England Journal of Medicine,* July 1, 2004, vol. 351, pp. 13–22

Chapter 8

206   **For example, in its 2003 annual statement**   "Air Force Handbook to 108th Congress," p. 31

207   **33 percent of military spouses**   "Survey of Military Families" (Kaiser Family Foundation, *The Washington Post,* Harvard University, March 2004), p. 13

207   **This is less than the general**   Pew Research Center for the People and the Press poll, May 2004

210   **As military sociologists**   Charles C. Moskos and John Whiteclay Chambers II, *The New Conscientious Objection: From Sacred to Secular Resistance* (New York: Oxford University Press, 1993), pp. 3–63

214   **According to the army's own 2001 survey**   U.S. Army Community and Family Support Center, "Survey of Army Families IV" (U.S. Army, Spring 2001); Information briefing, 12 December 2002, slide 22, Q64

214   **Military families, even with two wage earners**   James Hosek, Beth Asch, C. Christine Fair, Craig Martin, Michael Mattock, *Married to the Military: The Employment and Earnings of Military Wives Compared with Those of Civilian Wives* (Santa Monica, CA: Rand Corporation, 2002), pp. 1–7

214   **Military wives were also less likely**   James Hosek, Beth Asch, C. Christine Fair, Craig Martin, Michael Mattock, *Married to the Military: The Employment and Earnings of Military Wives Compared with Those of Civilian Wives* (Santa Monica, CA: Rand Corporation, 2002), p. 35

ACKNOWLEDGMENTS

Who said writing was a solitary endeavor? In my case, it took a village. I'd like to thank Hazel Brys, my grandmother, for the seed money to craft a book proposal, the MacDowell Colony for a crucial residency, and Norman and Doris Baker for being an oasis in the North Country. For tending to my son so I could write, I thank Anita Nunns, Heather and Duncan Sampson, Judy and Bryan Ogden, Susan Breton, Jennifer Gilman, Gail Ruhkamp, and Patricia Houppert (who also supported this project with faith and frequent "artists grants"). Thanks to my son Zack, who sacrificed many a game of Parcheesi so I could report and write. Thanks to my agent Sandy Dijkstra and her staff for both enthusiasm and suggestions, to Susanna Porter, Signe Pike, and Johanna Bowman for their work on behalf of the book, and to Rachel Tolliver, my Army public affairs escort, who went above and beyond the call of duty. For reading and commenting on various chapters, I thank Joe Cummins, Dede Kinerk, Celia Wren, Alex Viets, and Geoff Coll. Thanks also to Betsy Reed, who edited parts of the final chapter and Wendy Williams, whose sharp read of the entire manuscript was indispensable. Without my savvy and persistent editor, Elisabeth Kallick Dyssegaard, who can make a kick in the pants feel like a nudge of encouragement, none of this would have seen the light of day, so I thank her for that and for her incisive comments throughout this project. Finally, I'd like to thank my husband, Steve Nunns, who has read and edited and reread this manuscript many times—at the expense of his own—helping me to pare and clarify with his usual unsparing red pen. Most of all, I'd like to thank the many "waiting wives" who shared their thoughts, feelings, and daily lives with me.

INDEX

ABOUT THE AUTHOR

KAREN HOUPPERT was a staff writer for *The Village Voice* for many years where she wrote features on politics, in particular, women's issues. She grew up as a military brat and today lives in Brooklyn, where she works as a freelance journalist.

ABOUT THE TYPE

This book was set in Minion, a 1990 Adobe Originals typeface by Robert Slimbach. Minion is inspired by classical, old-style typefaces of the late Renaissance, a period of elegant, beautiful, and highly readable type designs. Created primarily for text setting, Minion combines the aesthetic and functional qualities that make text type highly readable with the versatility of digital technology.